Privacy:
The Right
To Be
Let Alone

Privacy

The Right To Be Let Alone

by Morris L. Ernst and Alan U. Schwartz

GREENWOOD PRESS, PUBLISHERS
WESTPORT, CONNECTICUT

Library of Congress Cataloging in Publication Data

Ernst, Morris Leopold, 1888-
    Privacy--the right to be let alone.

    Reprint of the ed. published by Macmillan, New York,
which was issued in: Milestones of law series.
    Includes index.
    1. Privacy, Right of--United States. 2. Privacy,
Right of--Great Britain. I. Schwartz, Alan U., joint
author. II. Title. III. Title: The right to be let
alone.
[KF1262.E7 1977]   342'.73'085   77-10983
ISBN 0-8371-9805-4

Originally published in 1962 by the Macmillan Company,
New York

Reprinted with the permission of Macmillan Publishing Co., Inc.

Reprinted in 1977 by Greenwood Press, Inc.

Library of Congress Catalog Card Number 77-10983

ISBN 0-8371-9805-4

Printed in the United States of America

For Russell Leffingwell—

wise lawyer, important public citizen

and, above all, supreme exponent of

the private life

Introduction

Morris Ernst and Alan Schwartz are to be editors of a series of statements of the law in book form. This is the first one, on the Right of Privacy, or the Right to Be Let Alone.

This book is not aimed at lawyers, law libraries, or law schools, but at laymen. Of all the millions of words for which the legal profession is annually responsible, most of them wear uniform, and few mufti. They are tantalizingly close to pure English, and when a layman wants to see for himself what the court has done to him he can get most of it by hard labor; but it has an indigenous and deceptive compactness, since lawmen are truly busy and try to save time, and now and then there is a terrible phrase compounded of French and Latin that has become smeared and worn from use in a medium other than its own. The layman may miss the point and call the law names.

Anything as arguable as the law is hard to render acceptable to the loser. It is hard to make it satisfy more than half of its customers, and the layman is apt to suspect that all judges do what only the greatest can do, like John Marshall, who it is said used to tell his law clerk: "This is my decision. Now find me the precedents to support it." It is important that someone help make the growth of a legal rule articulate so that people who must pay toll to travel the road can look about on it and see whence they have come and whither they are likely to be going.

To do so, it isn't necessary to sacrifice the process of thought that has made a rule, but only to keep it faithful to the language of the street. The Right of Privacy is a good one to start with. Its origins do not lurk in the gloom of the far past, for if we go to England, the source of common and

American law, we shall not find it. It is odd that the British, who really fasten themselves in behind walls and gates and hedges and live quite impregnably, have no rubric privacy, but so it is. Its growth is a good sample of American common law, of taking the mother country's means and applying them to our ends.

Our law on the subject is an offshoot from others—from libel and from the right of property in a written letter and the consequent right to publish it. In the early days of the Republic the transmission of news depended on letters and on simple newspapers of limited circulation. It was not until the development of the camera that the modern assault on privacy really began, and its Plymouth Rock was the publication of an article in the *Harvard Law Review's* issue of December 15, 1890, by Professor Samuel D. Warren and a young lawyer named Louis D. Brandeis, to which almost every case on the subject since then has referred. For a time it might be said that the protection afforded by the rule of privacy kept pace with the national development, but with the recent outburst of electronic devices the rule has become almost paralyzed, while gadgetry fleeth ever before. Radio, television, and a host of detectional apparatus now threaten even the privacy of the bedroom and the closet, for what is whispered there can be amplified from the housetop.

There is a very real and very difficult line of distinction to be drawn and maintained between the individual's right to seclusion and the right of the public to be informed. On the one hand is the accepted rule of privacy: "A person who unreasonably and seriously interferes with another's interest in not having his affairs known to others or his likeness exhibited to the public is liable to the other." On the other hand is the First Amendment to the Constitution of the United States and its analogue in the constitutions of the states, that there shall be "no law abridging the freedom of

speech, or of the press." The fascination of the subject, as
of all legal subjects, is in the location of the demarcation between these conflicting ideas from case to case. It is time for
the law to move ahead again, because electronics are not
static. A decision against the admission of evidence illegally
obtained or against evidence from wiretapping is not the end
of the story. The field, once inert, is becoming ever more
sensitive and acute.

Our authors show this clearly, and enable their readers to
take part in deciding actual cases whose opinions have been
left intact save for obtrusive technicalities. Now the layman
can think with the lawyer and see what he is up against, and
until one is told, the answers to the cases are not always
obvious. How would one judge them, left to oneself with the
facts, and why?

So, Messrs. Ernst and Schwartz are addressing themselves
in this book not only to a fascinating field of law; in the
series they are also trying to make the process of the law
more intelligible to laymen. It is a useful and a welcome
effort.

CURTIS BOK
Supreme Court of Pennsylvania
Philadelphia
April, 1962

NOTE: Judge Bok died on May 22, 1962.

Editorial Note

SINCE this volume is intended primarily for nonlawyers, we have attempted to delete esoteric legalisms wherever possible and to reduce both opinions and articles to terms that are comprehensible to the layman. Judicial language is therefore often paraphrased, references to other decided cases have been deleted, and much of the collateral phrases of the opinions, which lawyers call "dicta," has been removed. For the sake of clarity, all judicial opinions and legal articles have been set in different type, and are set off from the text by the symbol ▶. The headings, where they appear, are inventions of our own.

M. L. E.
A. U. S.

Foreword

THE adjustment of conflicting desires between people, or people and their rulers, has only recently in the long march of man from cave to housing development resulted in the creation of a science called Jurisprudence. And, as with all other science, it is probably only in its adolescent phase.

The delicate machinery of democracy requires full understanding by a literate and critical citizenry. Political campaigns for mayors, governors, presidents, and innumerable minor offices supply to some extent the knowledge needed for political processes. This is peculiarly true in our small towns that still, happily, enjoy the town meeting and caucus for political debate and decisions and the needed adjustments of differences of opinion. Democracy's serious problem is not to represent the majority but always to protect the minorities. To this end law is a great aid.

In the field of law, artificial barricades have been erected to interfere with a citizen's understanding of the beautiful processes of the law. Newspapers report in the main from the courtrooms as if lawyers, judges, and jurors were primarily concerned with murder and divorce. Our people, having been fed this distorted diet, think of law as a twin of sex and sadism. Much of our press and TV seems to be dedicated to this distorted picture of law.

Lawyers themselves often stand in the way of public comprehension of the intriguing search for truth in the courts. Just as clerics used Latin long ago and doctors write prescriptions unintelligible to patients, so do lawyers sometimes maintain their power over clients by the use of outworn legalistic gobbledygook.

Books reinforce the idea that law is static, and most of the novels that deal with law are not really lawbooks but murder mysteries, such as *Anatomy of a Murder;* they entertain but they provide no real insight into the truly exciting process of the law.

Unless we soon create a bridge of communication between lawyer and public, the gap of ignorance will increase, and lawyers will lean even more heavily on mumbo jumbo, while laymen will become resigned to the notion that law is a mystery beyond their comprehension. This is far from true.

Law is subtle, mercurial, and fascinating, but certainly in no sense a mystery. It may not be sound; it may have to be changed from time to time; but it is the result of forces understandable to anyone with a real concern for justice.

The editors engaged in this series of volumes entitled "Milestones of the Law" hope to convoy the public behind the screen of mysticism created by most pronouncements of the Bench and Bar. For behind that screen lies the key to an understanding of the delicate (and all too human) balance that provides the standards by which we *all* are judged.

We plan, at the outset, three volumes, of which this is the first. In some ways they are designed to be casebooks, but casebooks for laymen, free, we hope, from the arbitrary jargon of the trade. As far as possible we want to help you interpret these cases for yourselves, to help personalize the supposed impersonality of judicial pronouncements.

The next two volumes will concentrate on the censorship of obscenity and the right to a fair trial, both subjects of current and paramount importance in the protection of our civil rights. Volumes on other vital aspects of the law will follow with regularity thereafter.

For the first volume in our series we have chosen a subject uniquely personal in nature and one that affects every one of us: the Right of Privacy, or, as we like to call it, the Right to Be Let Alone. We are not here concerned with problems of search and seizure and wiretapping, which are more properly reserved for a later volume. Rather we are talking about a right that is a relatively new legal invention in our Republic—indeed, it is less than seventy years old. But as we shall see, it has developed rapidly during this short time, and must go on maturing in an attempt to keep pace with our electronic age of communications. In 1776, even in our biggest city (Philadelphia—population 30,000), the struggle to be let alone was not much of a chore; but we now have to work hard to protect our privacy against the omnipresent eyes and ears of radio, television, motion pictures, the press, and the subtle wiles of the ad man and public relations impresario.

There are, as might be imagined, hundreds of privacy cases from which to choose our examples. Naturally, no book of this kind could, or should, include them all. We have selected for this volume what we think are pivotal and absorbing cases in this most personal and most sophisticated area of legal protection. We hope to give the nonlawyer reader a feeling and a flavor of the birth and development of a vital legal right.

MORRIS L. ERNST
ALAN U. SCHWARTZ

January, 1962

Table of Contents

INTRODUCTION BY JUDGE CURTIS BOK   vii
EDITORIAL NOTE   x
FOREWORD   xi

1   A POET, a VETERINARIAN, and a PRINCE   1

2   DEAR SIR—THE PERILS of PERSONAL CORRESPONDENCE   24

3   PRIVACY COMES of AGE   44

4   A PICTURE, a STATUE, a GRAVESTONE, and a FIVE-CENT CIGAR   71

5   THE SAD PLIGHT of ABIGAIL   108

6   NEW YORK and GEORGIA DISAGREE   127

7   THE ACID TEST: PRIVACY IS CONSTITUTIONAL   149

8   SHOW BIZ and the WORLD of LETTERS   157

9   THE CHILD PRODIGY, the MAESTRO, and the PRO   180

10   ADVERTISING—ON PURPOSE and by ACCIDENT   203

11   FINAL REMARKS—VINTAGE 1962   227

INDEX   233

1

A Poet,
a Veterinarian,
and a Prince

PRIVACY—or the Right to Be Let Alone—is perhaps the most personal of all legal principles. It is also one of the newest, since only the more sophisticated of societies have the interest and the ability to nurture that subtle and most personal possession of man, his dignity. Privacy, like most of our important legal landmarks, is a minority concept. The very word connotes a necessary alienation between the individual and his society, an alienation or distance that is at the core of all our civil liberties.

The word "privacy" has different meanings for all of us. Recently it has been used in connection with unwarranted searches of one's property and with wiretapping. However, the privacy with which we are here concerned has a much broader application. It is violated whenever something unique about an individual—his face, his name, or even his dog's likeness—is taken by another without his consent and revealed to public gaze in order to enrich the misappropriator. Every violation of privacy, in this sense, is an indignity to the individual.

1

Of course, there are some among us who actively relish the idea of having a picture or name used publicly, even in the advertisement of some particularly unsavory product. To these people privacy has a very different meaning. They are not so much concerned with the Right to Be Let Alone as with the right to make money from *not* being let alone. In other words, they are interested in how much they can get because their picture is used, either in terms of money or publicity, or both.

There are two ways of looking at the Right of Privacy. As will be developed later, an invasion of the right might be thought of in terms of a misappropriation of one's private property. On the other hand, and perhaps more subtly, the injury done to a person when he wakes up one morning and finds his picture advertising flea powder may very well be something more than a simple misappropriation of something that belongs to him. In fact, a public image of him has been created without his consent and often without veracity. The indignity one feels about an invasion of the thing that he protects against the state above all others, namely, his own privacy, constitutes the core of a person's very self-respect. As such, its violation is an evil of the most personal and intimate sort, and requires a unique legal remedy.

Each of us, in the incredibly nosy world we have created, runs the risk of being thrust into the public eye without his consent. If you have a picture taken and the photographer comes up with an exceptionally fine likeness and decides to display this picture in his shop window in order to advertise his work, you might take offense. It has happened. If you have a favorite dog or a cat, and the photographer uses your pet's picture without your permission, you might also take offense. This too has happened. If you had in your youth a certain notoriety you wanted to forget, and wanted others to forget, and you then found your picture and your story splashed, many years later, before a large reading public you might well feel hurt and indignant. If you are an important public person whose name and picture have been often in the news, you might nevertheless feel upset and damaged to see your name endorsing a soap or a beer. You may even be a respectable person and, much to your chagrin, see yourself on a movie screen in the middle of a story about the white-slavery racket simply because you happened to be walking down a street at the time the picture was being shot. Or perhaps you don't care very much for your own personal reputation, but you care for the reputation of those near and dear to you. How then would you react if someone used a picture of your recently deceased parent on a cigar wrapper?

All these things have happened, and people have been hurt by them, hurt not often in a monetary sense but rather in the more devastating and upsetting sense of loss of stature and respect.

It requires a conscientious and sophisticated society to recognize such subtle injuries. More than that, it requires a society dedicated to concern for the individual in the face of the mesmerizing depersonalization that operates so insidiously in our modern world. There is no privacy in a totalitarian state except for the privacy of the dictator. The aim of a democratic society is to maintain the self-respect of the individual as best it can. In this connection, the protection by the state of complaints that may seem trivial, but are nevertheless uniquely personal, is, in some way, a measure of the success and value of that society.

In view of the foregoing it is not surprising that the Right of Privacy is only a recently established principle of law. In fact as late as 1902 the highest court of the State of New York reported that, prior to 1890, the word "privacy" did not appear ever to have been used either in legal literature or in literature about the law. However, privacy as a legal concept did have its ancestors: legal principles that contained the seed of a brand-new branch or jurisprudence. In the early days of our Republic, and earlier still in England, these principles were nurtured by lawyer, judge, and scholar, each in a separate garden without relation to the other. Centuries of experience and enlightenment and the brilliant imaginations of a very few were necessary to sift from ancient concepts of law, such as property rights, trespass, defamation, and personal injury, those elements which, when put together, would provide modern man with a cloak of protection for his self-respect.

The early history of personal grievance is fraught with bitter individual frustration. Although the Right of Privacy is new to our history, the injuries suffered by individuals as a result of the invasion of their privacy are old and bitterly familiar. As you read the early cases in this volume, you may well suffer with those sensitive souls who cried out for justice but found that the law simply did not have a convenient legal pigeonhole in which to file their claims. They had been injured without recourse, and there was nothing that they could do, nothing their lawyers could do, and indeed nothing the judges could do, for the actions causing their injuries were in no way illegal. To make things even worse, as communications improved, publicity became big business and very often indecency became profitable.

By the turn of the last century it was clear to many lawyers and nonlawyers alike that a legal principle was needed to protect individuals from these previously unredressable wrongs. It was at this point that ingenuity fathered the invention of privacy as a legal principle. But ingenuity alone was not enough. For the ingenuity to work, it had to rest on a bedrock of communal need. Because this need was there, however, ingenuity triumphed over what had previously seemed unanswerable legal hairsplitting.

The birth of the Right of Privacy, although accomplished, as we shall see, by two incredibly brilliant men, is not a unique process in the law. Indeed, many of the wrongs this new legal principle now prevents were earlier redressed by means of processes and legal principles that had other names. But the Right of Privacy has given us a legal principle at once more personal and more universal than all its legal ancestors combined.

The evolution of the Right of Privacy is just one of many illustrations of the vitality of our legal process, a process that subjects itself continually to regroupings and reshufflings and, indeed, to groping exploration in its unending search for ways in which to help individuals live with one another.

The seeds of what we now call privacy were sown first in England early in the eighteenth century and then transplanted to our shores. We begin with three English cases. Their dates are 1741, 1820, and 1849. They were instituted respectively by a poet, a veterinarian, and a prince. Although the veterinarian remains unknown, the poet and the prince are celebrities in their own right. But in the history of jurisprudence it is not the actor who counts, but the cases in which he is involved, and these three cases are classics.

The English attempt to circumscribe what we now call the Right of Privacy began with personal correspondence. Although in 1741 there was no such thing as a Right to Be Let Alone, the English law had, even at that date, a long series of judicial precedents, dating back almost to the time of the Norman Conquest, relating to the sanctity of individual property rights. It was therefore natural that the courts should, in that age of the sanctity of property, protect a man's letters from unauthorized use by others, not on the ground that his privacy had been invaded, but rather on the theory that his property had been stolen.

Some time before 1741 an enterprising bookseller named Curl managed to get hold of certain personal letters to and from various literary figures, two of whom were Jonathan Swift and Alexander Pope. He published these letters without the consent of their authors and found himself slapped with a lawsuit by the indignant Mr. Pope. Pope, naturally, wanted the book taken off the market, and insisted that Mr. Curl be prohibited from similar action in the future. The case was finally decided by England's highest court, the House of Lords, and the opinion was written by England's highest judge, the Lord Chancellor. We have here reproduced a copy of the Lord Chancellor's judgment as it was printed in the current records of his court. To the reader of today it is of interest not only for the quaintness of its type and format but also for its terseness and commonsensical phraseology:

---

342   C A S E S Argued and Determined

Cafe 235.   *Pope* verſus *Curl,* *June* 17, 1741.

The defendant, A Motion was made on behalf of *Curl* the bookſeller, upon
on his anſwer his having put in his anſwer to diſſolve an injunction, which
being put in, Mr. *Pope* had obtained, againſt his vending a book intitled,
moved to diſ-
ſolve an injunc- *Letters from Swift, Pope, and others.*
tion againſt his
vending a book of letters from *Swift, Pope,* and others.

LORD CHANCELLOR:

The firſt queſtion is, whether letters are within the grounds
and intention of the ſtatute made in the 8th year of Queen *Anne,*
c. 19. intitled, An act for the encouragement of learning, by
veſting the copies of printed books in the authors or purchaſers
of ſuch copies.

I think it would be extremely mifchievous, to make a dif-
tinction between a book of letters, which comes out into the
world, either by the permiffion of the writer, or the receiver of
them, and any other learned work.

A collection of letters, as well as other books, is within the intention of the 8th of Queen Ann, the act for the encouragement of learning.

The fame objection would hold againft fermons, which the
author may never intend fhould be publifhed, but are collected from loofe papers, and brought out after his death.

Another objection has been made by the defendant's council, that where a man writes a letter, it is in the nature of a
gift to the receiver.

The receiver of a letter has at moft a joint property with the writer, and the pof-feffion does not give him a li-cence to pub-lifh.

But I am of opinion that it is only a fpecial property in the
receiver, poffibly the property of the paper may belong to him;
but this does not give a licence to any perfon whatfoever to
publifh them to the world, for at moft the receiver has only
a joint property with the writer.

The fecond queftion is, whether a book originally printed
in *Ireland*, is lawful prize to the bookfellers here.

Reprinting a book in Eng-land, which originally was pirated and printed in Ireland, will not be fuffered, being a mere evafion of the act

If I fhould be of that opinion, it would have very pernicious
confequences, for then a bookfeller who has got a printed copy
of a book, has nothing elfe to do but fend it over to *Ireland*
to be printed, and then by pretending to reprint it only in
England, will by this means intirely evade the act of parliament.

It has been infifted on by the defendant's council, that this
is a fort of work which does not come within the meaning of
the act of Parliament, becaufe it contains only letters on fami-

liar fubjects, and inquiries after the health of friends, and cannot properly be called a learned work.

It is certain that no works have done more fervice to man-
kind, than thofe which have appeared in this fhape, upon familiar fubjects, and which perhaps were never intended to be
publifhed; and it is this makes them fo valuable; for I muft
confefs for my own part, that letters which are very elaborately written, and originally intended for the prefs, are generally
the moft infignificant, and very little worth any perfon's
reading.

No works have done more fer-vice to man-kind than thofe upon familiar fubjects, and which never were intended to be publifhed.

The injunction was continued by *Lord Chancellor* only as
to thofe letters, which are under Mr. *Pope*'s name in the book,
and which are written *by him*, and not as to thofe which are
written *to him*.

The injunction continued as to letters written by Mr. Pope, not as to thofe written to him.

Pope v. Curl (1741)

Lord Chancellor,

▶ The first question is, whether letters are within the grounds
and intention of the statute made in the 8th year [1710]
of Queen Anne, c. 19. entitled, An act for the encouragement
of learning, by vesting the copies of printed books in the
authors or purchasers of such copies.

I think it would be extremely mischievous, to make a distinction between a book of letters, which comes out into the
world, either by the permission of the writer, or the receiver
of them, and any other learned work.

The same objection would hold against sermons, which the
author may never intend should be published, but are collected from loose papers, and brought out after his death.

But I am of the opinion that it is only a special property
in the receiver, possibly the property of the paper may belong to him; but this does not give a licence to any person
whatsoever to publish them to the world, for at most the
receiver has only a joint property with the writer.

The second question is, whether a book originally printed
in Ireland, is lawful prize to the booksellers here.

If I should be of that opinion, it would have very pernicious consequences, for then a bookseller who has got a
printed copy of a book, has nothing else to do but send it
over to Ireland to be printed, and then by pretending to
reprint it only in England, will by this means entirely evade
the act of Parliament.

It has been insisted on by the defendant Curl that this is
a sort of work which does not come within the meaning of
the act of Parliament, because it contains only letters on
familiar subjects, and inquiries after the health of friends,
and cannot properly be called a learned work.

It is certain that no works have done more service to man-
kind, than those which have appeared in this shape, upon
familiar subjects, and which perhaps were never intended to
be published; and it is this which makes them so valuable;

for I must confess for my own part, that letters which are very elaborately written, and originally intended for the press, are generally the most insignificant, and very little worth any person's reading.

The injunction [prohibition on publication or sale] was continued by Lord Chancellor only as to those letters, which are under Mr. Pope's name in the book, and which are written by him, and not as to those which are written to him. ◀

So the privacy of Pope's letters (and also, by implication, Swift's and everyone else's) was upheld because the court felt that the writer of a letter has a *property* right in his words. Note in the last paragraph that the court does not give Mr. Pope any right in the letters written *to* him. Note also, though, that the Lord Chancellor suggests that the sender of a letter relinquishes "a special" kind of "property" to the receiver, "possibly" he says, "the paper," thereby implying that the receiver has no property rights in what is *on* the paper. "At most," he adds, "the receiver has only a joint property with the writer." In other words, the right of publication remains in the sender of the letter, not the recipient. This decision still applies today, both in England and in the United States, but it raises some important questions. Ask yourself this: If today unpublished letters of Swift or Pope fell into your hands, would you feel it your duty to seek out their heirs, to gain permission to publish them, or would you feel free to sell or give the letters to a public library for exhibition? Or for publication? Does exhibition equal publication? We are still, in 1962, pondering this sort of question, still trying to strike an equitable balance between the individual's right to the sanctity of his letters and society's right—and need—for the unfettered flow of legitimate historical information.

The year is 1820, and the British courts, still using the

principle enunciated in *Pope* v. *Curl*, turn from the letters
of famous men to the medical recipes of the veterinarian
named Yovatt.

The case, called in the lawbooks *Yovatt* v. *Winyard*, iden-
tifies the plaintiff and defendant for our second case, Yovatt
being the veterinarian and complaining party, and Winyard,
his former journeyman assistant, the defendant. In due
course, Winyard had quit Yovatt's employ and set himself
up as a veterinarian, using Yovatt's own secret medicines
that Winyard could only have obtained "surreptitiously" and
"clandestinely." So Yovatt went to court, and another strand
in what was to become the cable of privacy was spun.

Yovatt had been circumspect about his medical formulas.
He kept them in a book—which, without his knowledge or
consent, was read by his employee, Winyard. Winyard set
up in business for himself and used not only the recipes but,
what was even more intangible, copied Yovatt's techniques
of administration, and of controlling the animals while being
doctored. Yovatt wanted to put an end to such competition,
for fear, no doubt, of loss to his own trade.

Here is the essence of the decision of the court rendered
on May 15, 1820:

▶ Mr. Yovatt, who was the proprietor of medicines, had employed Winyard for some time as an assistant or journeyman,
under an agreement, by which he was to have a salary, and
to be instructed in the general knowledge of the business, but
was not to be taught the mode of composing medicines; he,
some time since, left his employer Yovatt and entered into
business for himself, and Yovatt had lately discovered that
he had, while in his service, surreptitiously got access to his
books of recipes, and copied them, and was now selling the
medicines, with printed papers for administering them, which
were almost literal copies of those composed by his employer.
Winyard, the former employee, afterwards offered, for a
small salary, to agree not to divulge the recipes.

Yovatt, the employer, contended that though the Court might not protect a secret from disclosure by one to whom the proprietor had himself communicated it, yet it would, when the person had clandestinely possessed himself of it. There had been other cases where trade secrets had been communicated for a particular purpose, and it was then attempted to prevent the party from using them for any other; but here said Yovatt the first discovery was obtained by a breach of duty, and in violation of a positive agreement.

The Lord Chancellor ordered the ex-employee to stop, upon the ground of there having been a breach of trust and confidence; but he did not prevent the former employee from administering the medicines to any animals under a course of treatment, because he feared that a sudden discontinuance would be prejudicial to the animal. ◀

There are several implications of great importance tucked away in this historic and early case. The theft was of *ideas,* not *things*. It had taken centuries before the ideas of man were looked on, as in this case, as property worthy of court protection. If only the medicines had been stolen by the ex-employee, all would agree that the bottles should be returned. But what does society do with the illegal acquisition of an idea? It may be and probably is worth much more in pounds and shillings than any quantity of bottles. But here the turning point seems to be that the employee broke a confidence, and violated a positive agreement. In the present framework of law this case smacks more of "unfair competition" than of privacy. But the line is not always easy to define. The important thing is that it was decided that personal secrets are inviolable, or, at least, that if they have been put in writing, they may not be pilfered with impunity. They may not be property in the tangible sense of the word, but they may enjoy the legal protection afforded tangible property.

In 1820 man was just beginning to try to define "private

possessions": your reputation, your name, your *ideas*. As our law has developed, different areas of legal specialization have developed to contend with each of these possessions. But what we now call "unfair competition" and "plagiarism" and "privacy" were all wrapped together, in Yovatt's time, under the principle of "property."

The time is 1849, about a century after *Pope* v. *Curl.* We ask you to consider now another important English case, one which, because of the eminence of the parties involved, epitomizes the strong cravings for privacy of even our most public figures in the face of the pressures of an inquisitive society. Aside from the import of its decision (still cited today), this case represents a fine example of the extent to which our Anglo-Saxon system of constitutional law turns a blind eye to the previously uncontested privileges of rank and power. For here is royalty itself forced to plead for its privacy—or property, if you like—in the courts of law . . . a far cry from the days of divine rule and a far cry from Mr. Khrushchev's Russia.

The principals involved were no less personages than Queen Victoria and her Royal Consort, Prince Albert. It seems that this royal and engaging couple were given to the harmless pleasure of amateur art, much as Sir Winston Churchill and Dwight D. Eisenhower, in a later age, were dedicated Sunday painters. In the case of Victoria and Albert, the craft practiced was that of etching. The finished products, rendered strictly for their own amusement, were reserved for the eyes of their friends and intimate circle only. The plates were kept by Her Majesty under lock and key. Certain etchings, it developed, were hung in the private apartments of Her Majesty at Windsor Castle.

Now it so happened, according to the record, that some of these privately printed impressions fell into the hands of one William Strange, printer and publisher, of 21 Paternoster

Row. It was Strange's not incomprehensible intention to profit from his windfall, and with this in mind he printed up a sort of catalogue such as we use at auction rooms today. The title page read:

▶ A Descriptive Catalogue of the Royal Victoria and Albert Gallery of Etchings ◀

and this notice followed:

▶ London— . . . Every purchaser of this Catalogue will be presented (by permission) with a fac-simile of the autograph of either Her Majesty or of the Prince Consort, engraved from the original, the selection being left to the purchaser.
    Price Sixpence. ◀

The preface contained the following passage:

▶ This Royal and most interesting collection is now submitted to the inspection of the public, under the firm persuasion and in the full confidence that Her Majesty's loyal and affectionate subjects will highly admire and duly appreciate the eminent artistic talent and acquirements of both Her Majesty and her illustrious Consort His Royal Highness Prince Albert.

"You must not be the grave of your deserving: England must know the value of her own. 'Twere a concealment Worse than a theft, no less than a traducement, To hide your doings."

SHAKESPEARE. ◀

Victoria did not start a suit. This would have been unseemly. So her spouse takes the headline in the lawbooks of

England: *Prince Albert* v. *Strange and Others.* Unquestionably both Albert and Victoria were indignant that this aspect of their personal and private lives should be bared to the public view for the gain of an unauthorized exploiter. In any case, Albert took his case to court, even as any poet or veterinarian, on the grounds, perhaps, that a cat might with impunity look at a king but not invade his privacy. He asked the court to order the return of all the impressions and copies of the several etchings involved, and in addition demanded that Strange be prevented from making any additional copies or from printing further copies of the descriptive catalogue. Finally, so that Albert and Victoria might fully control what they thought to be *private* material Albert prayed the court also to order Strange to turn over all previously printed copies of the catalogue, so that they might be destroyed. The etchings were in fact original portraits of members of the royal family and personal friends, including some "favorite dogs," as well as etchings made from old and rare engravings owned by the queen.

And then a crack occurred in the walls of complete privacy. The royal couple did confess that copies had been given from time to time—one to one friend and one to another. Albert said, though, that he knew of no collection such as Strange was advertising for sale, and thought that no such collection could have been assembled other than surreptitiously.

Then another odd item appears in the pleadings of Albert. He admits he had seen the Strange collection, for a set had been left by Strange at the palace, directed to the queen's attention, with a note indicating Strange's intention to exhibit.

At this point it must cross the mind of the reader that Strange did not feel guilty about his venture, for he did not hesitate to let Albert and Victoria know what he was up to. Or perhaps, knowing he could not keep the sale a secret, he adopted a front of honorable notice of sale. At this point the reader is probably curious about the manner in which Strange acquired these prints without any word getting back to the royal couple. Would Albert's suit run into difficulty if some of those who had been given prints had sold or loaned or given their copies to Strange and it developed that Strange had come by his collection in good faith, and innocently? Surely the court might view the case with more concern if Strange had bought copies in good faith than if he procured them through the aid of a printer who worked at Windsor and who ran off some extra copies for himself without permission of the owners.

As the court developed the facts, various persons at the palace or close thereto became involved. It seems that Mr. Strange had been approached by a man named Judge who had purchased the prints from a man named Middleton. Judge in turn had approached Strange and suggested an exhibition at the Egyptian Hall or some other respectable public place. Strange had no reason not to believe that the etchings had come into Judge's possession "fairly, honestly and regularly." Argued Strange's lawyer:

▶ It can scarcely be supposed that he had any evil intention when he took the course of, in the first place, bringing his intended publication under the eyes of the very parties whom he was charged with intending to offend. There may be a want of delicacy in his conduct and a want of comprehension of the feelings of persons in an elevated position, but there has been no infringement of any legal right. No one has a legal right to complain of the publication of a catalogue describing articles in his possession, letting the world know what they were. Another, who has seen the articles and acquired a knowledge of their nature, may embody in a publication the result of the exercise of his own faculties. It is not suggested that the property in the etchings has been interfered with. He, Strange, does not seek to publish *even a likeness* of them. An owner of a print is not the owner of a description which a stranger has made of it, nor can he hinder a stranger from describing it. There is no authority affording the least ground for such a proposition. ◀

Strange's lawyer goes on to ask the court:

▶ Suppose one of the pictures had been given to the Emperor of Russia and a traveller had seen it in the Emperor's Palace. Might he not in writing about his travels describe this as well as any other work of art? Why then suppress the catalogue? On what theory is freedom of press to be thus curtailed? A decision adverse to this principle would interfere with one of the most valued rights of the people of this country—the freedom of the press. No tribunal of the country has laid down the doctrine for two hundred years [that is, up to 1849] that a person may not look upon the property of another, and state his impressions and opinions, provided, in so doing he does not offend against the law. May he not tell another his impressions? And, if so, why not write and print them, subject to rational limitations? ◀

Since Strange had no reason to believe that his coadventurer Judge had obtained the property by dishonorable means, the question is one of legal right. So a line of questions are put to the court: May a banker's clerk divulge the accounts of the customers? May a workman hanging pictures in a gallery claim the right to catalogue that gallery? Is there a statute that protects against copying an uncopyrighted painting? This is not a simple case of pirating the etchings of the queen. If Strange were to sell anything, he would sell a fraudulent, inaccurate copy.

But let us continue with Mr. Strange's argument as put forward by his lawyer:

▶ It has been argued that privacy is the essence of property, and that the deprivation of privacy would make it, in fact, cease to be property. But the question here is not of that kind; the question is not, what is right and fitting to be done, but what is the law of the land. The notion of privacy is a notion altogether distinct from that of property. That a thing belongs to a man constitutes property; that another man should or should not see it is not property. There is no such property as the exclusive rights of seeing and talking about property. The right of the Prince in the etchings may prevent anyone from printing and publishing copies of them; but Mr. Judge had this collection of them, and, so having them, had he not the right to look at them? or could an order of the Court have been obtained to prevent him showing them to other persons, or imparting information to them?

That doctrine, it is true, might be pushed to an inconvenient extent and it might be well if a rule could be laid down by which the invasion of that which is strictly private could be prevented; but that is not now the law and never can be. Some of the conditions on which the happiness of life and well-being of society most depend are not and cannot be the subjects of positive law, or be enforced by any human tribunal. ◀

At this point it is well to note how Strange's lawyer attempts to create a distinction between *privacy* and *property rights*. We have seen that this distinction was not formerly attempted. Although the able lawyer is perhaps far ahead of his time in presenting this argument, he does so not for theoretical reasons but because there was no separate privacy right at the time. If he could convince the court that Albert's claim did not involve property, the claim would fail and Mr. Strange would win the case. If the lawyer were alive today, though, he would feel pretty silly about that last statement. Later we shall see just how far our courts have given the lie to the statement that privacy rights "are not

and cannot be the subjects of positive law, or be enforced
by any human tribunal."

The lawyer then concluded:

▶ If there were any circumstances which attracted public
attention to a particular individual, anyone might record
his sayings and doings if he had the opportunity, unless in
violation of the law or public morals. Suppose, for example,
His Royal Highness, Prince Albert wrote verses. A person
knowing this and reading the verses might inform the world
of the fact and express his opinion of the merits and demerits
of those verses. So in the present case. His Royal Highness
has devoted a few of his hours to a most praiseworthy pursuit, which he seems to have cultivated with great success.
The catalogue gives a list of the subjects of some sixty of his
etchings, and also the order in which they have been executed,
and the marks upon them. What by such an account was said,
but that the Prince had done such and such things, in such
and such years, and in such and such a manner? It is said
that the dates and figures in the catalogue must have been
taken from the etchings themselves. But, Mr. Judge having
the etchings, he had a right to look at them, and if he got a
fact or a date he had a right to publish it. ◀

The Vice Chancellor wrote a lengthy and learned opinion.
He was, as you will see, troubled because the case raised
novel claims dealing with manners and feelings and emotions. Though he had no fear of losing his head should he
come to a conclusion incurring royal displeasure, still it
seems that he bent over backward to render an enduring
judgment and to do so with full appreciation for the high
station of the plaintiff:

▶ Mr. Strange contends in substance, that, so far, the Royal
Couple complains of an offence not against law, but against
manners; with reference to which Mr. Strange's lawyer re-

marked in effect and I agree with him, that the order and
well-being of life depend greatly on things not within the
cognisance of laws, and can in very many instances not be
protected or vindicated by them. It was asserted, indeed,
by a great orator and writer of the last generation, and
perhaps truly, that manners are of more importance than
laws, as giving their whole form and colour to our lives, still,
however, some breaches of good manners are breaches of law
also. There is no difficulty here about the former. The question, I agree, is of the latter.

Mr. Strange's counsel say that a man acquiring a knowledge of another's property without his consent is not by any
rule or principle which a Court of Justice can apply (however secretly he may have kept or endeavoured to keep it)
forbidden without his consent to communicate and publish
that knowledge to the world, to inform the world what the
property is, or to describe it publicly, whether orally, or in
print or writing.

I claim, however, leave to doubt whether as to property
of a private nature, which the owner, without infringing on
the right of any other may and does retain in a state of
privacy, it is certain that a person who, without the owner's
consent, express or implied, acquires a knowledge of it, can
lawfully avail himself of the knowledge so acquired to publish without his consent a description of the property.

It was suggested that, to publish a catalogue of a collector's gems, coins, antiquities or other such curiosities, for
instance, without his consent, would be to make use of his
property without his consent; and it is true, certainly, that
a proceeding of that kind may not only as much embitter
one collector's life as it would flatter another—maybe not
only an ideal calamity—but may do the owner damage in
the most vulgar sense. Such catalogues, even when not descriptive, are often sought after and sometimes obtain very
substantial prices. These, therefore, and the like instances
are not necessarily examples merely of pain inflicted in point
of sentiment or imagination: they may be that and something
else beside. ◄

Note how the Vice Chancellor is here laying the ground-work for his decision by intimating that there are many un-mannerly acts that are also made illegal by a broad applica-tion of collaterally applicable legal principles. Eloquently and elegantly the judge finally closes in on his quarry:

▶ Most certainly the sole owner of any copy may determine whether he will print it or not. If any person takes it to the press without his consent, he is certainly a trespasser, though he came by it by legal means, as by loan or by devolution; for he transgresses the bounds of his trust, and therefore is a trespasser. And again, "Every man has a right to keep his own sentiments, if he pleases. He has certainly a right to judge whether he will make them public or commit them only to the sight of his friends. In that state the manuscript is, in every sense, his peculiar property; and no man can take it from him, or make any use of it which he has not authorized, without being guilty of a violation of his prop-erty."

Now, this protection, by the law, of literary compositions that have never been, with the consent of the author, the owner, generally published, cannot, I apprehend, be evaded by a translation, by abridgement, a summary, or even a review; for a review professes to treat of the general char-acter of the work reviewed to analyse or dissect it, and to show from the contents some reason for the praise or dis-praise which it may be the particular critic's task to dis-seminate.

A work lawfully published, in the popular sense of the term, stands in this respect, I conceive, differently from a work which has never been in that situation. The former may be liable to be translated, abridged, analysed, exhibited in morsels, complimented, and otherwise treated in a manner that the latter is not.

Suppose, however—instead of a translation, an abridge-ment or a review—the case of a catalogue—suppose a man to have composed a variety of literary works which he has never printed or published, or lost the right to prohibit from being published—suppose a knowledge of them unduly obtained by some unscrupulous person, who prints with a view to circulating a description catalogue, or even a mere list of the manuscripts, without authority or consent, does the law allow this? I hope and believe not. The same principles that prevent more candid piracy must, I conceive, govern such a case also.

By publishing of a man that he has written to a particular person, or on particular subjects, he may be exposed not merely to sarcasm, he may be ruined. There may be in his possession returned letters that he had written to former correspondents, with whom to have had relations, however harmlessly, may not in after life be a recommendation, or his writings may be otherwise of a kind squaring in no sort with his outward habits and worldly position.

Again, the manuscripts may be those of a man on account of whose name alone a mere list would be a matter of general curiosity. Now many persons could be mentioned, a catalogue of whose unpublished writings would, during their lives or afterwards, command a ready sale.

The question, however, does not turn upon the form or amount of mischief or advantage, loss or gain. The author of manuscripts, whether he is famous or obscure, low or high, has a right to say of them, if innocent, that whether interesting or dull, light or heavy, saleable or unsaleable, they shall not, without his consent, be published; and I think, as I have said, that to use a dishonest knowledge of them for the purpose of composing and publishing, and so to compose and publish a catalogue of them, amounts to a publication of them within the principle of the rule.

Assuming the law to be so, what is its foundation in this respect? It is not, I conceive, referable to any consideration peculiarly literary. Those with whom our common law orig inated had not probably among their many merits that oı being patrons of letters; but they knew the duty and necessity of protecting property, and with that general object laid down rules providently expansive—rules capable of adapting themselves to the various form and modes of property which peace and cultivation might discover and introduce. ◀

The conclusion was clean-cut. Mr. Strange lost the case. The significance of the decision lay in the fact that not only was the unauthorized reproduction of the etchings prevented, but the mere listing in a descriptive catalogue was also prohibited. What is most significant is that the philosophy underlying the decision rested on an expanded and still expanding Right of Privacy. Privacy had become *a kind* of property right. It rested on a still older case (1820) where the judge declared that if the doctor attending the king kept a diary of an illness recording what he heard and saw, the court would not in the king's lifetime permit its publication.

Prince Albert's plea was sustained. Some authorities, such as Judge Samuel H. Hofstadter of the New York Supreme Court, doubt if similar legal reasoning could be applied today. But as we develop this Right to Be Let Alone, this case is significant not only because of the expansion of the definition of personal property but also because courts had not yet considered how long the privacy of Albert and Victoria should be preserved. Could this catalogue be legally published in 1962?

When evaluating the result in this case, remember that there are among us today certain artistic dabblers who are famous in other fields. Leaving aside matters of taste, should the recipient of an Eisenhower painting now possess the right to sell it at auction, to give it away, or to have copies made by one of our effective techniques of reproduction? Or what about the privacy of Sir Winston's oil paintings before they were exhibited in a London gallery? Or after that display? These are questions you may ponder along with the most thoughtful of today's lawyers and judges. The answers have yet to be written.

When you consider the next example of privacy's impact on our culture and law, we trust you will give a gracious bow of indebtedness to the British controversies of long ago. These early cases are significant because England, even up to 1962, has never gone very far in establishing a Right of Privacy as distinct from property. The House of Lords has not yet recognized "offensive invasion of privacy." But a step was taken in what many think to be the right direction. In 1960 a professional photographer had to pay £1,000 for what was technically a breach of copyright but was, intrinsically, what we call invasion of privacy. Two newspapers printed pictures of the Williamses' wedding, which took place after the murder of Mr. Williams's father-in-law. A man named Settle had been hired to take the photographs, and without Williams's consent sold them to the *Express* and the *Daily Mail*. There was no claim by the Williams family that it had suffered financial loss, so the £1,000 (or $2,800) was truly a punishment for "unscrupulous invasion" of privacy.

How explain England remaining less perturbed than we in the area of privacy? Perhaps the strictness of British libel law has deterred invasions such as we experience. Or perhaps privacy is maintained by a habit of reserve, a societal taste that respects the individuality of personality, while some Americans relish publicity even when deployed in its most tawdry—but nonlibelous—aspects.

Thus England, having given us the earliest outlines of what has now come to be a distinct Right of Privacy, did not develop it significantly. It remained for the American courts, after a slow start, to forge ahead where their characteristically polite cousins perhaps had little need to tread. They now watch us nurture the seed they had previously exported.

2

Dear Sir— The Perils of Personal Correspondence

I<small>N</small> 1787 ours was an aristocratic Republic of the literati. As in Europe, only a small proportion of the total population could read and write, and literacy went hand in hand with the ownership of land, which was the basic requisite of the right to vote. In fact, the 250,000 people who voted on the adoption of the Constitution in 1787 just about represented the number of people who could read and write. Of the other 4,250,000 inhabitants of the young country, some 600,000 were Negro slaves who were kept ignorant on purpose, and about 2,000,000 were women, whose higher education was pretty much limited to playing the spinet and plying the needle.

At that time the written word was at a premium. Sermons would often find their way into print, but in general much of the reading matter of the day was dependent on personal correspondence. Our forefathers, if they were literate, wrote

24

voluminously, and the letters to and from one another were treasured and preserved, fortunately for posterity; out of today's attics have been assembled the great collections of papers of Madison, Jefferson, and Adams, all holographic. Letter writing was taken seriously; it was, indeed, almost an art form. Franklin's letters, for instance, were, in effect, monographs.

Certain legal questions concerning correspondence were raised early: Who was the rightful owner of the letter—the sender or the recipient? Was the recipient under an obligation to safeguard the letter? Or keep it confidential? Or in some cases destroy it? Could the sender later reclaim it? Soon it became a part of the law that the recipient actually owned that piece of paper, parchment, or vellum that had been sent to him by its author. He could, if he wished, exhibit it, leave it to his children, or sell it—though that practice came much later. Today personal letters and autographs of the great dead are sold at auction or donated to libraries, in which case the assessed value of the documents are tax deductible. A Button Gwinnett (a signer of the Declaration of Independence) autograph is worth about $45,000 now, so rare is his signature.

It is impossible to cite the first instance, however, of a case of injured or outraged feelings in the breast of a living man whose correspondence has been trafficked in without his consent or approval. Private or even public exhibition of a personal letter was one thing, but the sale of a letter to a newspaper and its subsequent publication in the public prints was quite another. For one thing, such publication for commercial purposes put a value on the document in question. Who was entitled to the money derived from its sale? The original author, or the "owner" of the piece of paper in question? Who, in fact, had the right to negotiate such sale, and on what conditions? What if the letter had been clearly marked "for your eyes only," as was sometimes the case?

Did this admonishment provide the writer with any real protection?

As the mail service improved, the hazards of letter writing increased. One could be fairly certain of the discretion of a friend or relative who lived in one's own locality, but what about people in another city or colony whom one did not know well? Might not the sense of obligation decrease in proportion to the geographical distance separating sender and recipient? Such often proved to be so, and more and more often personal correspondence was turned over to commercial publications for purposes of profit or propaganda.

The law of "privacy" in letters in this country had its beginnings in what was, from the point of view of English law, a narrow and somewhat shortsighted approach to the subject. Disregarding English precedents, the highest court of the State of New York decided in 1848 that the right to prevent the publication of private letters would only be granted when it appeared that the letters possessed a certain value as literary compositions. By so doing the court relied perhaps even more heavily than had the English courts upon the characterization of the right involved as one of "property" rather than of "privacy." In fact, as you will see, the court even limited the Right of Property in letters solely to those letters that were "literary" compositions.

HOYT v. MacKENZIE AND OTHERS (1848)

It seems that one MacKenzie and his associates got hold of some letters belonging to a Mr. Hoyt by breaking open a chest in the customhouse where Mr. Hoyt had put them for safekeeping. MacKenzie and his group published the letters, and a bookseller in New York—a Mr. Taylor—sold several copies as agent for MacKenzie. Hoyt protested that he alone had the right to publish the letters he had written and that the right to publish letters he had received still belonged to the writers of those letters and that in any event, he did not want his own letters to be published by anyone. The lower court agreed with him and stopped the publication and sale by the issue of an order of injunction. This is a powerful order, for if it is violated the violator can be fined or jailed by the judge for contempt of court. Moreover, the guilty party is tried without a jury by the very judge who issues the order to stop printing.

The case was appealed, and the chief judge of the New York Court of Appeals, then called the Chancellor, cancelled the injunction and allowed the publication to continue. Here is his opinion:

▶ I have no doubt that by the principles of the common law the author of a book or other literary production, whether in the shape of letters or otherwise, has a right of property therein; at least until it has been published with his assent. In 1741, in England Curl was restrained by injunction from publishing Pope's letters to Dean Swift. Again in England in 1758, the court restrained the printing of an unpublished manuscript history of the reign of Charles the Second, by Lord Clarendon; a copy of the manuscript had been taken with the permission of a personal representative of the author, and the person who thus received the document sold it to a publisher for publication but without authority.

The decisions to which I have referred settle the law on the subject in England. And as they were all made before the separation of the colonies from the mother country, I consider them as binding upon this court. I should therefore affirm the decision of the lower court, so far as relates to the three letters written by Hoyt himself, if those letters were in fact of any value to him as literary productions, or if his right to multiply copies thereof was worth anything to him. In relation to the letters written to him by other persons, however, if those letters were of any value to the authors, as literary productions, or for publication, the right belonged to them, and not to Mr. Hoyt who received their letters without any authority express or implied to publish them.

It is evident, however, in relation to all of these letters, that Hoyt never could have considered them as of any value whatever as literary productions. For a letter cannot be considered of value to the author, for the purpose of publication, which he never would consent to have published; either with or without the privilege of copy right. It would therefore be a perversion of a correct legal principle, to attempt to restrain the publication of these letters, upon the ground that the writers thereof had an interest in them as literary property. No one, it is true, whose moral sense is not depraved, can justify the purloining of private letters, and publishing them for the purpose of wounding the feelings of individuals, or of gratifying a perverted public taste. And it is hardly possible that any one who has been connected with the publication and sale of the pamphlet in this case, could for a moment have supposed that these letters were honestly obtained for publication; or that they were published with the approbation of the writers thereof, or of Mr. Hoyt to whom most of them were directed.

But this court cannot restrain and punish crimes, or enforce the performance of moral duties, except so far as they are connected with the rights of property. In another case, very correctly decided, it was held that a court could not properly exercise a power to restrain the publication of private letters on the ground of protecting literary property, where they possessed no attribute of literary composition. And upon that principle the injunction must be reversed. ◀

So, in the Hoyt case, the court refused to do what earlier English courts had done: namely, extend the doctrine of "property" so as to include the Right of Privacy of one's personal communications. Note also the rather specious argument of the court that the letters obviously did not have any literary value, otherwise their authors would have published them. Compare this reasoning with the more intelligent approach of the English court in the much earlier case of *Pope* v. *Curl*.

Obviously America still had quite a way to go. *Hoyt* v. *MacKenzie* represented no advance whatsoever either in privacy or, for that matter, in a definition of literature; it was, in fact, a step backward. This, however, was not an unmitigated misfortune, for it pushed a vexing legal problem back far enough so that a better perspective could be obtained—far enough back so that forest and trees could be distinguished from one another and seen in their true relationship. If this case actually paved the way for the next case, it would not be the last time that the principle of privacy was to gain through defeat, as we shall see later on.

Anyway, in 1855 the seven judges of New York's highest court decided it was time to review thoroughly the law of private letters. Or rather, the case of *Woolsey* v. *Judd* gave them this opportunity, and they accepted it.

The case arose in this way. Woolsey claimed that by some unlawful means the New York *Chronicle*, a weekly journal (Judd being the responsible person), had "possessed" itself of a copy of "a certain letter—wholly private in character," which Woolsey had written and forwarded to a man named William Crowell in St. Louis.

The newspaper declared its intention to print the letter. The editor of the *Chronicle* denied that he had come upon the letter by unlawful means, and was emphatic in arguing that the letter was not "wholly" private in character. He had received it from a gentleman of the "highest respectability," with authority to make such use of it as the paper thought proper. We are told that the letter related to a religious society, the American Bible Union. It was agreed that the letter had no value as a "literary production." Neither Woolsey, the writer, nor Crowell, the recipient, told the court that his reputation would be injured by the publication of the letter concerned. Therefore the court declared that a "naked question" was raised: Should the court prevent publication of a letter without the consent of the writer and contrary to his wishes?

We suggest that as the opinion is read one question be kept in mind against the sober, thoughtful reasoning of the court: If the *Chronicle* is not allowed to publish the letter, is it also denied the right to give or sell the letter—to a library, an autograph collector, the Bible Society that may be interested in it? And if the *Chronicle* may not so dispose of the letter for general public view, do you think the receiver of the letter, Mr. Crowell, should have the right so to do? In other words, what distinction should society make between publication in print and exhibition under a glass cover to a possibly large audience in a library?

JAMES WOOLSEY v. OWEN B. JUDD (1855)

▶ The court said:

The question is one of more than ordinary interest, and we have felt that it deserved to be examined with more than ordinary care.

We believe that few, who reflect upon the mischievous consequences which would certainly result from the unrestrained and frequent publication of private and confidential letters, will dissent from the opinion that it is highly desirable, looking to the best interests of society, that courts should possess and firmly exercise the jurisdiction which is questioned. Our own views and feelings, we do not hesitate to declare, correspond entirely with those which Mr. Justice Story, in the most elaborate and useful of his works, has very forcibly expressed. We agree with him, that the authorized publication of such letters, "unless in cases where it is necessary to the vindication of the rights or conduct of the party against unjust claims or imputations, is, perhaps, one of the most odious breaches of private confidence, of social duty, and of honorable feelings which can well be imagined. It strikes at the root of that free interchange of advice, opinions and sentiments, which seems essential to the well-being of society, and may involve whole families in great distress from the public display of facts and circumstances which were reposed in the bosom of others, in the fullest and most affecting confidence that they should remain forever inviolable secrets."

But, although, with Mr. Justice Story, we cannot do otherwise than condemn a practice which springs from the motives, and leads to the consequences which he has depicted, and which, from the feelings of resentment it is calculated to provoke, is dangerous to the peace as well as the morals of the community, we must not be understood to assert, that these considerations are alone sufficient to justify the interposition of a court. A court is not the general guardian of the morals of society. It has not an unlimited authority to enforce the performance, or prevent the violation, of every moral duty.

We must be satisfied, that the publication of private letters, without the consent of the writer, is an invasion of an exclusive right of property which remains in the writer, even when the letters have been sent to, and are still in the possession of his correspondent. If this legal right can be shown to exist—it seems evident that it is only by an injunction that it can be protected from an invasion.

We commence the inquiry into the existence of the legal right of property, observing that there is probably no doctrine which is more fully sustained, and, indeed, established by authority, than that the author of an unpublished manuscript has an exclusive right of property therein—a right which entitles him to determine for himself, whether the manuscript shall be published at all; and in all cases to forbid its publication by another; and it is equally certain, that whenever this exclusive right is in danger of being violated, a court is bound, upon the application of the author, to prevent the wrong by a perpetual injunction. So far, there is no controversy.

What then is the foundation of this exclusive right? Does

it exist only when the manuscript is intended to be published? Or does it depend upon its pecuniary value or intrinsic merits as a literary composition? To each question, we think, the reply may be confidently given, certainly not.

We, therefore, agree that the exclusive right of an author in a manuscript yet unpublished, rests upon the same foundation as that which sustains every other species or description of property. Its sole function is "the right which every man has to the exclusive possession and control of the products of his own labor." We can perceive no reason for doubting that the exclusive property of an author rests exactly upon the same ground as that of a manufacturer or artist—a painting may be a wretched daub—a statue, a lamentable abortion; yet, should either be purloined by an enemy with the view to secure profits to himself, or to disgrace the artist by its public exhibition, a court would renounce its principles should it refuse to protect the owner.

Such being the true foundation of the exclusive right of an author before publication, the next inquiry is, into the nature and extent of his right. And it is assuredly a great mistake to suppose that it is confined to the material on which his manuscript is written; and that it is only because he is the owner of the paper, that a court interferes for his protection. The exclusive right, which alone a court is bound to protect, and which, from its nature, can only be protected by an injunction, is his right of property in the words, thoughts and sentiments, which his manuscript embodies and preserves. This composition—whether, as such, it has any value or not, is immaterial—is his work, the product of his own labor, of his hand and his mind; and it is this fact which gives him the right to say that, without his consent, it shall not be published, and makes it the duty of a court to protect him in the assertion of that right, by a permanent injunction. Of this, it is a conclusive proof, that the right to control the publication of a manuscript remains in the author and his representatives, even when the material property has, with his own consent, been vested in another. The gift of a manuscript it is settled, unless by an express agreement, carries

with it no license to publish. The author has an absolute
right to suppress as well as to publish; and he is as fully
entitled to the protection and aid of the court, when suppres-
sion is his sole and avowed object, as when he intends to
publish.

The general doctrine, as to the right of an author in an
unpublished manuscript, being such as we have not endeav-
ored to explain, it is evident that it casts the burden of the
argument upon those who contend that private letters must
be excepted from its application. If the doctrine is just as
applicable to them as to all other manuscripts, it is clear
that the writer of the letter, Mr. Woolsey, is entitled to the
relief which he claims. It must be shown, therefore, that there
are valid reasons for admitting an exception of private letters, or that the exception, whether reasonable or not, is
established by decisions that we are not at liberty to disregard.

There are only two grounds upon which it has been insisted that private letters are an exception from the general
doctrine. The first is, that the transmission of the letters vests
the whole property in the receiver, and operates as an absolute gift. The second, that if the writer retains any property
at all, it is only in such letters as are stamped with the character and possess the attributes of literary compositions. ◀

The court then proceeds to reevaluate the decision of the
Chancellor in *Hoyt* v. *Mackenzie*, which, you will remember,
held that there was no property right (and therefore no
privacy right) in letters that were not "literary compositions," and decides the other way:

▶ But we deny that a recent and solitary decision of any
Judge, however eminent, ought to be regarded by us as conclusive evidence of the existing law; and we deny that we are
bound by the decisions of the Chancellor, in the same sense
in which we are bound by those of the court of ultimate resort.

It is known to us all that the cases are numerous in which judges have felt it their duty to reconsider and reverse their own decisions and those of their predecessors; and deplorable, indeed, would be the actual state of the law, had not these powers of revision and correction been frequently and firmly exercised. We must all remember that the judgment in *Hoyt* v. *MacKenzie*, from the sanction which it apparently gave to a very dishonorable proceeding, excited general surprise and regret, so that even those who admitted its legality, were anxious to relieve the law from the reproach which it occasioned. We are convinced that this reproach, that of giving a sanction to immorality, is one to which the law was never justly liable, and from the continuance of which it ought, therefore, to be freed.

The proposition which we hold to have been settled as law, for more than a century before the judgment in *Hoyt* v. *MacKenzie* was pronounced, is that which was laid down by Sir Samuel Romilly, and affirmed by the decision of Lord Eldon, in *Gee* v. *Pritchard*. It is that "the writer of letters, though written without any purpose of publication or profit, or any idea of literary property, possesses such a right of property in them, that they can never be published without his consent, unless the purposes of justice, civil or criminal, require the publication." If this proposition be true, it follows that the distinction which has been supposed to exist between letters possessing a value as literary compositions, and ordinary letters of friendship or business, is wholly groundless. The right of property is the same in all, and in all is entitled to the same protection. ◀

Since judges are only human, and times do change, it is neither surprising nor rare to see a court, as here, flatly disagreeing with the decision of an earlier court in the same state. In doing so, however, a court must be sure to marshal its dissent with care and comprehensiveness. As we read on in the *Woolsey* case, we shall see that the court makes a good job of it and, in the process, gives us a magnificent summary of prior English cases, beginning with our old friend *Pope* v. *Curl*:

▶ What, then, are the propositions which Lord Hardwicke, by his decision in *Pope* v. *Curl*, established by law? It seems to us, that, by the plain and necessary interpretation of his language, they are these:—First, that the receiver of letters has only a special or qualified property, confined to the material on which they are written, and not extended to the letters as expressive of the mind of the writer. Second, that neither the receiver thereof nor any other person has any right to publish the letters without the consent of the writer. And, lastly, that the property, which the writer retains, gives him an exclusive right to determine whether the letters shall be published or not; and, when he forbids their publication, makes it the duty of a court to aid and protect him by an injunction. It appears to us equally certain that these rules are laid down, and were meant to be laid down, as universal in their application, as embracing all letters, whether intended to be published or not, and whatever may be the subjects to which they relate. Not only was there no intimation that there is any distinction between different kinds or classes of letters, limiting the protection of the court to a particular class; but the distinctions that were admitted to be made, and which seem to be all that the subject admits, were expressly rejected as groundless.

The next case, *Thompson* v. *Stanhope*, which is perhaps even stronger than *Pope* v. *Curl*, came before Lord Bathurst, in 1774. The executors of Lord Chesterfield asked to stop the publication, by the widow of his son, of those celebrated letters which, for a series of years, he had written to her husband; and also the publication of certain character sketches probably not very flattering, which he had drawn in writing of some of his contemporaries. The widow argued that Lord Chesterfield had himself given to her both the letters and the character sketches—and the fact seems to have been admitted. But it was contended, on the

part of the executors that there being no proof of an express
authority to publish, none could be implied from the gift,
and that consequently the exclusive right to control the
publication remained in Lord Chesterfield, and had passed
to his executors. It does not appear, from the report, to have
been claimed that the letters, or character sketches, were
written by Lord Chesterfield with any view to their future
publication, or that the publication of either was intended
by the executors. The publication was stopped by the court.

We come next, after a lapse of nearly forty years, and of
more than seventy from the decision of Lord Hardwicke in
the Pope case to the case of *Lord and Lady Percival* v. *Phipps
and another*, and we find here, not in the decision itself, but
in the somewhat desultory, and wholly extra-judicial remarks
of the Vice-Chancellor, Sir Thos. Plumer, the true and only
source of all the doubts and difficulties that have been permitted to embarrass the question, and have, unfortunately,
led to a conflict of decisions.

The Vice-Chancellor, both upon the hearing and on deliv-
ering his final judgment, unnecessarily chose to discuss the
general question, how far, and in what cases, a court will
interpose to protect the interest of the author of private
letters. And in the course of his observations he lays down,
in positive terms, the novel doctrine, that it is only when the
letters—in his own words—"are stamped with the character
of literary compositions," that the writer can be protected
by an injunction against their publication. And he, in effect,
asserts that the character and value of the letters of Pope
and Lord Chesterfield, as literary compositions, was the true
and only ground of the decisions in those cases, and consequently, that these cases were inapplicable to that which
was before him—it not being intended that such was the
character of Lady Percival's letters.

The assertion is, that some private letters are literary
compositions, and some are not. Those which are, may be
protected as property; those which are not, may be stolen
and published with impunity; the writer has no property,
and sustains no injury.

But we say that every letter is, in the general, and property sense of the term, a literary composition. It is that, and nothing else; and it is so, however defective it may be in sense, grammar or orthography. Every writing in which words are so arranged as to convey the thoughts of the writer to the mind of a reader, is a literary composition; and the definition applies just as certainly to a trivial letter, as to an elaborate treatise, or a finished poem. Literary compositions differ widely in their merits and value, but not at all in the facts from which they derive their common name.

The proposition that in familiar letters, not intended by the writers to be published, there can be no property which a court will protect from invasion, is precisely that which, in *Pope* v. *Curl*, and in *Thompson* v. *Stanhope*, is expressly overruled. There is no evidence that the letters of Pope, and his friends, or those of Lord Chesterfield, were originally written for the press. And in relation to those of Pope, the report shows that the fact was admitted to be otherwise. There is, moreover, a positive absurdity in making the character of any manuscript, as a literary composition, depend upon the extrinsic and accidental fact of the intention to publish. Apply this test, and the plays of Shakespeare are not literary compositions, since there is every reason to believe that not a single play was written with any view to its future publication.

There is the same confusion of ideas and language, in making the character of a manuscript, and the right of property in an author depend upon the accident of its value for publication—its pecuniary value or marketable value. Booksellers are eager to purchase the rights in the autobiography of a shameless adventurer, or self-convicted impostor; but we doubt whether one can be found within the limits of the Union, who, without any hazard or competition, would dare to publish, at his own risk and expense, the Principia of Newton, or the Systeme of La Place, or even a full edition of the prose works of Milton.

Rejecting, then, as we must, the tests "of intended publication," and "pecuniary value," it remains to consider whether the character of letters as literary compositions, and therefore literary property, may be determined by a reference to their contents and intrinsic merits—the merits of language and thought, of style, and sentiments.

It must be admitted that the differences, in these respects, between familiar letters, as between all other productions of the intellect, are wide and strongly marked, and fully justify their distribution by critics into many distinct classes; but we seriously deny, that it is possible to extract from these differences any rule of classification, which a court of justice can be warranted to adopt, as a rule of decision. ◀

Now comes consideration of the point implied by the earlier case: Should judges be obliged to function as critics of literature?

▶ If the question, whether the letters of which the publication is sought to be restrained from the nature of the subjects to which they relate, of the sentiments they convey, or of the style in which they are clothed, deserve to be classed with literary compositions, is to be determined by the Judge to whom the application for relief is made, it is evident that his determination must and will be governed, by his own personal, and it may be, peculiar opinions, taste, studies, and associations. The determinations in such cases will, therefore, be just as various and inconsistent as the literary taste and attainments, and the casual predilections and prejudices of the judges by whom they are pronounced. The letters extolled by one, as full of interest or instruction, will be condemned by another, as utterly worthless. The prohibition granted today will be dissolved, or, in cases not distinguishable, be denied tomorrow; and the question of the rights of property, and its title to protection, will be resolved, not by the application of rules of law to facts, but in the exercise of a discretion, constantly varying and purely arbitrary. The decisions, in most cases, will appear to be, and in many will be, the mere result of accident or ignorance, prejudice or caprice. Whether the letters he has written possess literary merits which render them worthy of publication, is a question which it belongs to the writer alone, and the public, to determine. It is exactly one of those which, from the necessary and total absence of any fixed rules of principles or decision, a court of justice can never rightfully entertain.

It follows, from these remarks, that the test of intrinsic merits must also be rejected. At first view, it seems less unreasonable than that "of intended publication," or "pecuniary value"; but, as it admits no certain definition, and is necessarily shifting, and precarious in its application, it is, in reality, more objectionable than either. Any definite rule is better than an unlimited discretion.

If we were to decide otherwise should a faithless clerk, who has secretly taken copies of the confidential business letters of the merchant who employed him, from motives of revenge, and with the design of blasting the credit and ruining the fortunes of his employer, threaten to publish them, the merchant would have no redress. He cannot say that his letters have value as literary compositions, or that he meant to publish them for his own benefit; he has therefore no property that a court can be required to guard from invasion; and as there is no violation of any of his rights of property, he can recover no damages in an action of law. An indignant public may condemn the vile treachery of the clerk, but it is a treachery that the law refuses to punish. We cannot, however, believe that such is, or ever has been, the doctrine of the law, and that it has found no favor in England, but, on the contrary, has been decisively rejected, the case next to be cited will conclusively show.

In *Gee* v. *Pritchard*, the last of the English cases, it is interesting to observe, with what a gentle, yet firm, hand Lord Eldon sweeps away the unsubstantial theories and distinctions of his Vice-Chancellor, and, scattering doubts that ought never to have been raised, resettles the law, upon its old and true foundations. The case before him on a motion to permit the publication, by Pritchard, of a number of

private and confidential letters, which had been written to
him by Gee in the course of a long and friendly correspondence. Gee was a widow lady, and Pritchard the natural son
of her late husband; and they had lived for many years on
terms of great intimacy and kindness. Disputes, however,
had arisen between them relative to the property left by her
husband; and in consequence of these, at the request of Gee,
he had returned to her the original letters; but he had kept
copies, from which he now claimed the right to publish them,
in vindication of his own proceedings and conduct. In support
of his opinion that Gee had a sufficient property in the original letters to prohibit their publication by Pritchard, Lord
Eldon refers to the language of *Pope* v. *Curl* as proving the
doctrine, that the receiver of letters, although he has a joint
property with the writer, is not at liberty to publish them,
without the consent of the writer; which is equivalent to saying that the latter retains an exclusive right to control the
publication. ◀

After this learned review of the English cases, the court
with that same "gentle and firm hand" it commends in *Gee*
v. *Pritchard,* proceeds to sweep away the narrow decision of
Hoyt v. *MacKenzie* and grant Mr. Woolsey the prohibition
on Judd he has asked for:

▶ We hold, then,
     "that the author of any letter or letters, and his repre-
     sentatives, whether they are literary compositions or
     familiar letters, or letters of business, possesses the sole
     and exclusive right of publishing the same, and that,
     without his consent, the letters cannot be published,
     either by the persons to whom they are addressed, or
     by any other. But that, consistently with this exclusive
     right of the author, the person to whom the letters are
     addressed possesses, by implication, the right of pub-
     lishing them upon occasions which require or justify

the publication. Thus, he may justifiably use or publish them in a suit, when such use is necessary or proper to maintain his action or defence. So, also, if he has been aspersed or misrepresented by the writer of the letters, or accused of improper conduct in a public manner, he may publish such parts of the letter or letters, and no more, as may be necessary to vindicate his character, and free him from unjust obloquy and reproach. But if he attempts to publish the letters, or any parts of them, against the wishes of the writer, and on occasions not justifiable, a court will prevent the publication by an injunction, as a breach of that exclusive property in the letters which the writer retained."

And it is with no ordinary satisfaction that, in closing this discussion, we find ourselves in a condition to affirm that the rules of law relative to the publication of private letters, are in perfect harmony with those of social duty and sound morality, and, in the protection which they afford to individuals, consult and promote the highest interests of society. ◀

This comprehensive and important decision of the New York Court of Appeals helped to clear the decks of past inconsistencies in the law of letters. By deciding that the author of a letter has a right either to permit or withhold its publication, regardless of his intention when he wrote the letter, and regardless also of the pecuniary value or literary merit of the letter, the decision helped pave the way for the development of a specific Right of Privacy in the United States.

But before we leave the subject of personal correspondence and move on to more modern problems, it would be well to note that even in 1962 we have far from settled all the problems of privacy in letters. Surely we want to discourage people from burning letters they receive from important people. It cost a fortune to track down the letters of Jefferson and Madison and the other architects of our Republic. In the days of the quill pen copies were made only on the rarest occasions. But in more recent times, with the advent of the typewriter and carbon paper and the process of facsimile reproduction, letters raise new legal issues. Still substantially unsolved are questions such as: Whose consent is needed, if any, to publish letters, recently found, written by President Cleveland, or Betsy Ross, or F.D.R.? How far back does this right to publish reside in the heirs of the writer? You find a letter written by Lincoln, Washington, or Cleopatra; must you search for heirs to give you permission to publish your great find? In the following chapters of this book you will follow the efforts of the law to answer such practical questions.

Consider this problem, which the courts have scarcely touched upon as yet: You give to the Nantucket Library letters your father received. The letters may have some interest for students of the whaling industry, and your family were whalers. Students of whaling write to the local library for copies. Should the law allow the library to supply copies —even if a thousand libraries throughout the world request copies? In brief, what does the word "publish" mean in this modern world of facsimile and microprint, when ten thousand pages of a book can now be printed on a single small page and read through a magnifying glass or thrown on a screen?

In terms of rules of law we must draw the line between the interests of the original writer of letters, the recipient, and the general overall interest of society in terms of the right to knowledge, both general and specific. Whatever the decision of courts may be, someone could be hurt—either the privacy of the writer or his children or grandchildren, or on the other hand, the appetite of scholars and the public at large for legitimate access to knowledge.

May we not assume that letters never intended to be published have even more historic interest and value than those written with an eye to publication? If so, where do we draw a line or circle in the needed compromise between an individual's desire for privacy and the conflicting interests of posterity? Such is the entrancing problem that gives the law its great value and, at the same time, its romance. Now that you have an insight into what the law of letters meant in the past, why not try to decide what it should be in the future. Your decision may be as good as the next man's, or even the judge's.

Although, as we have said, the problem of letters is still with us, it has given ground in importance during this century to incursions into privacy caused by the constantly expanding mass-communications media. In the following chapters we shall see how, faced with this expansion, American law has extended what was previously a limited Right of Property in private communications into a separate Right of Privacy, a concept that is still growing in order to keep up with the inquisitorial pressures of modern society.

3

Privacy
Comes
of Age

Up to this point the evolution or development of privacy has involved breaches of contract, trust, confidence, and property, with never a specific mention of "privacy" itself. The decisions you have just read show judges, no less sensitive than those of today, searching for certain precedents in the law upon which to base decisions for which there were *no* strict legal precedents. In order to satisfy judicial consciences while at the same time staying within the already established framework of legal principles, these judges took well-established concepts of law and stretched them just a bit. The result, at least sometimes, was the protection of a right that was both more subtle and more profound than any that had existed previously.

These cases, therefore, are important strands in the cable of privacy. They, and many like them, represent in their totality the inexorable march of the judicial process toward a new creation. For this creation to be articulated, however, a catalyst was needed. It came in the last decade of the nineteenth century. On the one hand, the protection of privacy was made more urgent by the introduction on a large scale of instantaneous photography and journalistic sensationalism. Opposed to these forces were man's most imposing and most basic weapons: his intelligence and his ingenuity.

Photography, as originally practiced, was a time-consuming procedure. One sat for a portrait, and the word *sat* cannot be overemphasized. Sitting was not only time-consuming, it was also a physical and emotional trial. Of necessity, portraits were not taken without the full knowledge and cooperation of the subject. With the introduction of flash powder, however, this was all changed. Action could be stopped to the point where exposures were limited only by the speed of the springs actuating the shutter mechanism. With this device, and from a point of vantage, pictures could be taken without either the permission or knowledge of the subject. It was not the taking of the picture but the use that was subsequently made of it that resulted in a significant lawsuit being brought against the photographer.

Instantaneous photography, among other things, aroused man's nosier instincts. It was not surprising, therefore, that newspapers, which formerly devoted most of their space to reporting the news, suddenly found themselves in the entertainment field—the entertainment, moreover, being more in the nature of scandal than of good clean fun.

These impertinences had begun to become all too profitable enterprises, when, in 1890, two young Boston lawyers decided to do something about it. Actually, their decision had been made some years before, but the historic date for their action is 1890. In fact, the date can be pinpointed to the 15th of December, 1890, the date of publication of Volume IV, Number 5, of the *Harvard Law Review*, the now famous issue containing the article "The Right to Privacy" by Samuel D. Warren and Louis D. Brandeis—an article that was so splendidly conceived and executed that Dean Roscoe

Pound was subsequently to say of it that it did nothing less than add a chapter to the law.

Warren and Brandeis had been in the same class (1877) at Harvard Law School, in which they stood, respectively, second and first. Warren, a member of a socially prominent and wealthy Massachusetts family with large paper interests, had entered the employ of an established Boston law firm. Brandeis had stayed on at Harvard for a year's graduate work at law school, at the end of which, after having been admitted to the Missouri bar, he began his legal practice as an associate in the office of a successful St. Louis attorney. By July of 1879, though, he was back in Boston, and the legal partnership of Warren and Brandeis was in business.

In his excellent biography *Brandeis: A Free Man's Life* Alpheus Thomas Mason inserts the following interesting and illuminating footnote to the privacy story: "On January 25, 1883, Warren had married Miss Mabel Bayard, daughter of Senator Thomas Francis Bayard, Sr. They set up housekeeping in Boston's exclusive Back Bay section and began to entertain elaborately. The *Saturday Evening Gazette*, which specialized in 'blue blood items,' naturally reported their activities in lurid detail. This annoyed Warren, who took the matter up with Brandeis. The article ('The Right to Privacy') was the result."

The Warren-Brandeis article, which follows, lies at the very heart of the Right of Privacy. It absorbed and crystallized all that had gone before, and it has imprinted all that has followed with its brilliance, sensitivity, and wisdom. Published in the *Harvard Law Review*, it was obviously addressed to students, scholars, teachers, practitioners and makers of law; in other words it was by professionals for professionals and was written in a thoroughly professional way. Because of its succinctness the article is reprinted here in full. No abridgement or paraphrase can be made without real loss. Each phrase, each sentence, plays an indispensable part in an inexorably logical argument. The article was, it seems, pared to the irreducible minimum by its own authors. The editors of this volume have, however, provided subheads for purposes of guidance and for coffee breaks.

The reader should remember, or be reminded, that two remarkable legal minds were occupied over a period of six years in arranging the words that convey the ideas that constitute this argument. If you spend an hour, or even more, reading and even rereading it, your time will be well invested.

The first section of the Warren-Brandeis article is a succinct account of how broadly the initial and primitive meanings of life, liberty, and property had developed, so that in the case of property it extended its principles to cover the products and processes of the mind.

The Right To Privacy

▶ That the individual shall have full protection in person and in property is a principle as old as the common law; but it has been found necessary from time to time to define anew the exact nature and extent of such protection. Political, social, and economic changes entail the recognition of new rights, and the common law, in its eternal youth, grows to meet the demands of society. Thus, in very early times, the law gave a remedy only for *physical* interference with life and property. Then the "right to life" served only to protect the subject from battery in its various forms; liberty meant freedom from actual restraint; and the right to property secured to the individual his lands and his cattle. Later there came a recognition of man's spiritual nature, of his feelings and his intellect. Gradually the scope of these legal rights broadened; and now the right to life has come to mean the right to enjoy life,—the right to be let alone; the right to liberty secures the exercise of extensive civil privileges;

and the term "property" has grown to comprise every form of possession—intangible, as well as tangible.

Thus, with the recognition of the legal value of sensations, the protection against actual bodily injury was extended to prohibit more *attempts* to do such injury; that is, the putting another in fear of such injury. From the action of battery grew that of assault. Much later there came a qualified protection of the individual against offensive noises and odors, against dust and smoke, and excessive vibration. The law of nuisance was developed. So regard for human emotions soon extended the scope of personal immunity beyond the body of the individual. His reputation, the standing among his fellow-men, was considered, and the law of slander and libel arose. Man's family relations became a part of the legal conception of his life, and the alienation of a wife's affections was held remediable. Occasionally, the law halted —as in its refusal to recognize the intrusion by seduction upon the honor of the family. But even here the demands of society were met. A mean fictional remedy—the loss of services—was ordinarily afforded. Similar to the expansion of the right to life was the growth of the legal conception of property. From corporeal property arose the incorporeal rights issuing out of it; and then there opened the wide realm of intangible property, in the products and processes of the mind, as works of literature and art, goodwill, trade secrets, and trademarks.

This development of the law was inevitable. The intense intellectual and emotional life, and the heightening of sensations which came with the advance of civilization, made it clear to one that only a part of the pain, pleasure, and profit of life lay in physical things. Thoughts, emotions, and sensations demanded legal recognition, and the beautiful capacity for growth which characterizes the common law enabled the judges to afford the requisite protection, without the interposition of the legislature.

Recent inventions and business methods call attention to the next step which must be taken for the protection of the person, and for securing to the individual what Judge Cooley calls the right "to be let alone." ◀

WHISPER IN THE CLOSET—SHOUT FROM THE HOUSETOP

Thomas M. Cooley was the author of *The Elements of Torts*, published in 1878. There, of Personal Immunity, he says: "The right to one's person may be said to be *a right to be let alone*." This seems to be an instance where the definition for a word precedes the word itself.

▶ Instantaneous photographs and newspaper enterprise have invaded the sacred precincts of private and domestic life; and numerous mechanical devices threaten to make good the prediction that "what is whispered in the closet shall be proclaimed from the house tops." For years there has been a feeling that the law must afford some remedy for the unauthorized circulation of portraits of private persons; and the evil of the invasion of privacy by the newspapers, long keenly felt, was recently discussed by an able writer. ◀

The "able writer" was E. L. Godkin, then editor in chief of the (New York) *Evening Post*. An article by him appeared in the July, 1890 issue of *Scribner's Magazine* entilted "The Rights of the Citizen: To his Reputation"—this being one of a series of articles *Scribner's* had run on civil rights. In this particular article the word privacy appears in contexts that cause one to wonder if he and Warren and Brandeis were not in cahoots.

▶ The alleged facts of a somewhat notorious case brought before an inferior court in New York a few months ago, directly involved the consideration of the right of circulating portraits; and the question whether our law will recognize and protect the right to privacy in this and in other respects must soon come before our courts for consideration. ◀

The "somewhat notorious case" was that of *Marion Manola* v. *Stevens & Meyers*. The time was June, 1890. A Warren-Brandeis footnote explains it: The complainant alleged that while she was playing in the Broadway Theatre, in a role which required her appearance in tights, she was, by means of a flash light, photographed surreptitiously and without her consent, from one of the boxes by defendant Stevens, the manager of the "Castle in the Air" company, and defendant Meyers, a photographer. Miss Manola asked the court to restrain Stevens and Meyers from making use of the photographs taken. Surprisingly enough, neither Stevens nor Meyers defended himself, and Miss Manola won.

So an early challenge to invasions of privacy by the camera went by the board through default. But if it went by the board it went, nonetheless, on the record, and Warren and Brandeis wasted no time in adding it to their already potent arsenal for the defense of privacy.

A SUMMARY OF IMPERTINENCES BY THE PRESS

▶ Of the desirability—indeed of the necessity—of some such protection, there can, it is believed, be no doubt. The press is overstepping in every direction the obvious bounds of propriety and of decency. Gossip is no longer the resource of the idle and of the vicious, but has become a trade, which is pursued with industry as well as effrontery. To satisfy a prurient taste the details of sexual relations are spread broadcast in the columns of the daily papers. To occupy the indolent, column upon column is filled with idle gossip, which can only be procured by intrusion upon the domestic circle. The intensity and complexity of life, attendant upon advancing civilization, have rendered necessary some retreat from the world, and man, under the refining influence of culture, has become more sensitive to publicity, so that solitude and privacy have become more essential to the individual; but modern enterprise and invention have, through invasions upon his privacy, subjected him to mental pain and distress, far greater than could be inflicted by mere bodily injury. Nor is the harm wrought by such invasions confined to the suffering of those who may be made the subjects of journalistic or other enterprise. In this, as in other branches of commerce, the supply creates the demand. Each crop of unseemly gossip, thus harvested, becomes the seed of more, and, in direct proportion to its circulation, results in a lowering of social standard and morality. Even gossip apparently harmless, when widely and persistently circulated, is potent for evil. It both belittles and perverts. It belittles by inverting the relative importance of things, thus dwarfing the thoughts and aspirations of a people. When personal gossip attains the dignity of print, and crowds the space available for matters of real interest of the community, what wonder that the ignorant and thoughtless mistake its relative importance. Easy of comprehension, appealing to that weak side of human nature which is never wholly cast down by the misfortunes and frailties of our neighbors, no one can be surprised that it usurps the place of interest in brains capable of other things. Triviality destroys at once robustness of thought and delicacy of feeling. No enthusiasm can flourish, no generous impulse can survive under its blighting influence.

It is our purpose to consider whether the existing law affords a principle which can properly be invoked to protect the privacy of the individual; and, if it does, what the nature and extent of such protection is.

Compare to Feelings Hurt by Libel

Owing to the nature of the instruments by which privacy is invaded, the injury inflicted bears a superficial resemblance to the wrongs dealt with by the law of slander and of libel, while a legal remedy for such injury seems to involve the treatment of mere wounded feelings. The principle on which the law of defamation rests, covers, however, a radically different class of effects from those for which attention is now asked. It deals only with damage to reputation, with the injury done to the individual in his external relations to the community, by lowering him in the estimation of his fellows. The matter published of him, however widely circulated, and however unsuited to publicity, must, in order to be actionable, have a direct tendency to injure him in his intercourse with others, and even if in writing or in print, must subject him to the hatred, ridicule, or contempt of his fellowmen,—the effect of publication upon his estimate of himself and upon his own feelings not forming an essential element in the cause of action. In short, the wrongs and correlative rights recognized by the law of slander and libel are in their nature material rather than spiritual. That branch of the law simply extends the protection surrounding physical property to certain of the conditions necessary or helpful to worldly prosperity. On the other hand, our law recognizes no principle by which compensation can be granted for mere injury to the feelings. However painful the mental effects upon another of an act, though purely wanton or even malicious, yet if the act itself is otherwise lawful, the suffering inflicted is without legal remedy. Injury of feelings may indeed be taken account of in ascertaining the amount of damages when attending what is recognized as a legal injury; but our system, unlike the Roman law, does not afford a remedy even for mental suffering which results from mere contumely and insult, from an intentional and unwarranted violation of the "honor" of another.

It is not however necessary, in order to sustain the view that the common law recognizes and upholds a principle applicable to cases of invasion of privacy, to invoke the analogy, which is but superficial, to injuries sustained, either by an attack upon reputation or by what the civilians called a *violation of honor;* for the legal doctrines relating to infraction of what is ordinarily termed the common-law right to *intellectual and artistic property* are, it is believed, but instances and applications of a general right to privacy, which, properly understood, afford a remedy for the evils under consideration.

THE DOMINION OF MAN'S IDEAS

The common law secures to each individual the right of determining, ordinarily, to what extent his thoughts, sentiments, and emotions shall be communicated to others. Under our system of government, he can never be compelled to express them (except when upon the witness-stand); and even if he has chosen to give them expression, he generally retains the power to fix the limits of the publicity which shall be given them. The existence of this right does not depend upon the particular method of expression adopted. It is immaterial whether it be by word or by sign, in painting, by sculpture, or in music. Neither does the existence of the right depend upon the nature or value of the thought or emotion, nor upon the excellence of the means of expression. The same protection is accorded to a casual letter or any entry in a diary and to the most valuable poem or essay, to a botch or daub and to a masterpiece. In every such case the individual is entitled to decide whether that which is his shall be given to the public. No other has the right to publish his productions in any form, without his consent. This right is wholly independent of the material on which, or the means by which, the thought, sentiment, or emotion is expressed. It may exist independently of any corporeal being, as in words spoken, a song sung, a drama acted. Or if expressed on any material, as a poem in writing, the author may have parted with the paper, without forfeiting any proprietary right in the composition itself. The right is lost only when the author himself communicates his production to the public—in other words, publishes it. It is entirely independent of the copyright laws, and their extension into the domain of art. The aim of those statutes is to secure to the author, composer, or artist the entire profits arising from publication; but the common-law protection enables him to control absolutely the act of publication, and in the exercise of his own discretion, to decide whether there shall be any publication at all. The statutory right is of no value, *unless* there is a publication; the common-law right is lost *as soon as* there is a publication.

KINDS OF PROPERTY

What is the nature, the basis, of this right to prevent the publication of manuscripts or works of art? It is stated to be the enforcement of a right of property; and no difficulty arises in accepting this view, so long as we have only to deal with the reproduction of literary and artistic compositions. They certainly possess many of the attributes of ordinary property: They are transferable; they have a value; and publication or reproduction is a use by which that value is realized. But where the value of the production is found not in the right to take the profits arising from publication, but in the peace of mind or the relief afforded by the ability to prevent any publication at all, it is difficult to regard the right as one of property, in the common acceptation of that term.

A man records in a letter to his son, or in his diary, that he did not dine with his wife on a certain day. No one into whose hands those papers fall could publish them to the world, even if possession of the documents had been obtained rightfully; and the prohibition would not be confined to the publication of a copy of the letter itself, or of the diary entry; the restraint extends also to a publication of the contents. What is the thing which is protected? Surely, not the intellectual act of recording the fact that the husband did not dine with his wife, but that fact itself. It is not the intellectual product, but the domestic occurrence. A man writes a dozen letters to different people. No person would be permitted to publish a list of the letters written. If the letters or the contents of the diary were protected as literary compositions, the scope of the protection afforded should be the same secured to a published writing under the copyright law. But the copyright law would not prevent an enumeration of the letters, or the publication of some of the facts contained therein. The copyright of a series of paintings or etchings would prevent a reproduction of the paintings as pictures; but it would not prevent a publication of a list or even a description of them. Yet in the famous case of *Prince Albert* v. *Strange*, the court held that the common-law rule prohibited not merely the reproduction of the etchings which the plaintiff and Queen Victoria had made for their own pleasure but also "the publishing (at least by printing or writing), a description of them, whether more or less limited or summary, whether in the form of a catalogue or otherwise." Likewise, an unpublished collection of news possessing no element of a literary nature is protected from piracy.

That this protection cannot rest upon the right to literary or artistic property in any exact sense, appears the more clearly when the subject-matter for which protection is invoked is not even in the form of intellectual property, but has the attributes of ordinary tangible property. Suppose a man has a collection of gems or curiosities which he keeps private; it would hardly be contended that any person could publish a catalogue of them, and yet the articles enumerated are certainly not intellectual property in the legal sense, any more than a collection of stoves or of chairs.

The belief that the idea of property in its narrow sense was the basis of the protection of unpublished manuscripts led an able court to refuse, in several cases, prohibitions against the publication of private letters, on the ground that "letters not possessing the attributes of literary compositions are not property entitled to protection"; and that it was "evident the writer could not have considered the letters as of any value whatever as literary productions, for a letter cannot be considered of value to the author which he never would consent to have published." But these decisions have not been followed, and it may now be considered settled that the protection afforded by the common law to the author of any writing is entirely independent of its pecuniary value, its intrinsic merits, or of any intention to publish the same, and, of course, also, wholly independent of the material, if any, upon which, or the mode in which, the thought or sentiment was expressed.

Although the courts have asserted that they rested their decisions on the narrow grounds of protection to property, yet there are recognitions of a more liberal doctrine. Thus in the case of *Prince Albert* v. *Strange*, already referred to, the opinions both of the Vice-Chancellor and of the Lord Chancellor, on appeal, show a more or less clearly defined perception of a principle broader than those which were mainly discussed, and on which they both placed their chief reliance. Vice-Chancellor Knight Bruce referred to stating or publishing of a man that he had "written to particular persons or on particular subjects" as an instance of possibly injurious disclosures as to private matters, that the courts would in a proper case prevent; yet it is difficult to perceive how, in such a case, any right of property, in the narrow sense, would be drawn in question, or why, if such a publication would be restrained when it threatened to expose the victim not merely to sarcasm, but to ruin, it should not equally be enjoined, if it threatened to embitter his life. To deprive a man of the potential profits to be realized by publishing a catalogue of his gems cannot *per se* be a wrong to him. The possibility of future profits is not a right of property which the law ordinarily recognizes; it must, therefore, be an infraction of other rights which constitutes the wrongful act, and that infraction is equally wrongful, whether its results are to forestall the profits that the individual himself might secure by giving the matter a publicity obnoxious to him, or to gain an advantage at the expense of his mental pain and suffering. If the fiction of property in a narrow sense must be preserved, it is still true that the end accomplished by the gossip-monger is attained by the use of that which is another's, the facts relating to his private life, which he has seen fit to keep private. Lord Cottenham stated that a man "is entitled to be protected in the exclusive use and enjoyment of that which is exclusively his," and cited with approval the opinion of Lord Eldon, as reported in a manuscript note of the case of *Wyatt* v. *Wilson*, in 1820, respecting an engraving of George the Third during his illness, to the effect that "if one of the late king's physicians had kept a diary of what he heard and saw, the court would not, in the king's lifetime, have permitted him to print and publish it"; and Lord Cottenham declared, in respect to the acts of the defendants in the case before him, that "privacy is the right invaded." But if privacy is once recognized as a right entitled to legal protection, the interposition of the courts cannot depend on the particular nature of the injuries resulting.

THE RIGHT TO BE LET ALONE

These considerations lead to the conclusion that the protection afforded to thoughts, sentiments, and emotions expressed through the medium of writing or of the arts, so far as it consists in preventing publication, is merely an instance of the enforcement of the more general right of the individual to be let alone. It is like the right not to be assaulted or beaten, the right not to be imprisoned, the right not to be maliciously prosecuted, the right not to be defamed. In each of these rights, as indeed in all other rights recognized by the law, there inheres the quality of being owned or possessed—and (as that is the distinguishing attribute of property) there may be some propriety in speaking of those rights as property. But, obviously, they bear little resemblance to what is ordinarily comprehended under that term. The principle which protects personal writings and all other personal productions, not against theft and physical appropriation, but against publication in any form, is in reality not the principle of private property, but that of an inviolate personality.

If we are correct in this conclusion, the existing law affords a principle which may be invoked to protect the privacy of the individual from invasion either by the too enterprising press, the photographer, or the possessor of any other modern device for recording or reproducing scenes or sounds. For the protection afforded is not confined by the authorities to those cases where any particular medium or form of expression has been adopted, nor to products of the intellect. The same protection is afforded to emotions and sensations

expressed in a musical composition or other work of art as
to a literary composition; and words spoken, a pantomime
acted, a sonata performed, is no less entitled to protection
than if each had been reduced to writing. The circumstances
that a thought or emotion has been recorded in a permament
form renders its identification easier, and hence may be important from the point of view of evidence, but it has no
significance as a matter of substantive right. If, then, the
decisions indicate a general right to privacy for thoughts,
emotions, and sensations, these should receive the same protection, whether expressed in writing, or in conduct, in con-
versation, in attitudes, or in facial expression.

It may be urged that a distinction should be taken between
the deliberate expression of thoughts and emotions in literary
or artistic compositions and the casual and often involuntary
expression given to them in the ordinary conduct of life. In
other words, it may be contended that the protection afforded is granted to the conscious products of labor, perhaps
as an encouragement to effort. This contention, however
plausible, has, in fact, little to recommend it. If the amount
of labor involved be adopted as the test, we might well find
that the effort to conduct one's self properly in business and
in domestic relations had been far greater than that involved
in painting a picture or writing a book; one would find that
it was far easier to express lofty sentiments in a diary than
in the conduct of a noble life. If the test of deliberateness of
the act be adopted, much casual correspondence which is now
accorded full protection would be excluded from the benefi-
cent operation of existing rules. After the decisions denying the distinction attempted to be made between those
literary productions which it was intended to publish and
those which it was not, all considerations of the amount of
labor involved, the degree of deliberation, the value of the
product, and the intention of publishing must be abandoned,
and no basis is discerned upon which the right to restrain
publication and reproduction of such so-called literary and
artistic works can be rested, except the right to privacy, as
a part of the more general right to the immunity of the person,—the right to one's personality. ◀

As must by now be obvious to the reader, here is a work of profound importance, a spurt of legal imagination which takes us far beyond what at the time were considered by many to be immutable principles of law and logic. Here are Warren and Brandeis in 1890, ambushing from the previous "literary property" cases the perhaps unspoken elements that bound them all together at that time, and molding these elements into a new legal principle that deftly expresses what all the inadequate fumblings of the past had not been able or inclined to do.

Having shown that there was an element common to the old cases which could not be explained in terms of "property," Warren and Brandeis now turn to a series of cases that attempted to get at a concept of privacy by use of the then well-established doctrines of contract and breach of trust or confidence.

▶ It should be stated that, in some instances where protection has been afforded against wrongful publication, the jurisdiction has been asserted, not on the ground of property, or at least not wholly on that ground, but upon the ground of an alleged breach of an implied contract or of a trust or confidence.

Four Important Cases

1. Thus in *Abernethy* v. *Hutchinson* (1825), where a distinguished surgeon sought to restrain the publication in the "Lancet" of unpublished lectures which he had delivered at St. Bartholomew's Hospital in London, Lord Eldon doubted whether there could be property in lectures which had not been reduced to writing, but granted the restraint on the ground of breach of confidence, holding "that when persons were admitted as pupils or otherwise, to hear these lectures, although they were orally delivered, and although the parties might go to the extent, if they were able to do so, of putting down the whole by means of short-hand, yet they could do

that only for the purposes of their own information, and could not publish, for profit, that which they had not obtained the right of selling."

2. In *Prince Albert* v. *Strange* (1849), Lord Cottenham, while recognizing a right of property in the etchings which of itself would justify the prohibition of the publication, stated, after discussing the evidence, that he was bound to assume that the possession of the etchings by Strange had "its foundation in a breach of trust, confidence, or contract" and that upon such ground also Albert's right to the prohibition was fully sustained.

3. In *Tuck* v. *Priester* (1887), the plaintiffs were owners of a picture, and employed Priester to make a certain number of copies. He did so, and made also a number of other copies for himself, and offered them for sale in England at a lower price. Subsequently, the plaintiffs registered their copyright in the picture, and then brought suit for an injunction and damages. The Lords Justices differed as to the application of the copyright acts to the case, but held unanimously that independently of those acts, the plaintiffs were entitled to an injunction and damages for breach of contract.

4. In *Pollard* v. *Photographic Co.* (1888), a photographer who had taken a lady's photograph under the ordinary circumstances was restrained from exhibiting it, and also from selling copies of it, on the ground that it was a breach of an implied term in the contract, and also that it was a breach of confidence. Mr. Justice North interjected in the argument of the lady's counsel the inquiry: "Do you dispute that if the negative likeness were taken on the sly, the person who took it might exhibit copies?" and counsel for the lady answered: "In that case there would be no trust or consideration to support a contract." Later, the photographer's counsel argued that "a person has no property in his own features; short of doing what is libelous or otherwise illegal, there is no restriction on the photographer's using his negative." But the court, while expressly finding a breach of contract and of trust sufficient to justify its interposition, still seems to have felt the necessity of resting the decision

also upon a right of property, in order to bring it within the
line of those cases which were relied upon as precedents.

MORALITY, PRIVATE JUSTICE AND CONVENIENCE

This process of implying a term in a contract or of implying a trust (particularly where the contract is written, and
where there is no established usage or custom), is nothing
more nor less than a judicial declaration that public morality,
private justice, and general convenience demand the recognition of such a rule, and that the publication under similar
circumstances would be considered an intolerable abuse. So
long as these circumstances happen to present a contract
upon which such a term can be engrafted by the judicial
mind, or to supply relations upon which a trust or confidence
can be erected, there may be no objection to working out the
desired protection through the doctrines of contract or of
trust. But the court can hardly stop there. The narrower
doctrine may have satisfied the demands of society at a time
when the abuse to be guarded against could rarely have arisen
without violating a contract or a special confidence; but now
that modern devices afford abundant opportunities for the
perpetration of such wrongs without any participation by the
injured party, the protection granted by the law must be
placed upon a broader foundation. While, for instance, the
state of the photographic art was such that one's picture
could seldom be taken without his consciously "sitting" for
the purpose, the law of contract or of trust might afford the
prudent man sufficient safeguards against the improper circulation of his portrait; but since the latest advances in
photographic art have rendered it possible to take pictures
surreptitiously, the doctrines of contract and of trust are
inadequate to support the required protection, and other laws
must be resorted to. The right of property in its widest sense,
including all possession, including all rights and privileges,
and hence embracing the right to an inviolate personality,
affords alone that broad basis upon which the protection
which the individual demands can be rested.

Thus, the court, in searching for some principle upon

which the publication of private letters could be enjoined,
naturally came upon the ideas of a breach of confidence, and
of an implied contract; but it required little consideration to
discern that this doctrine could not afford all the protection
required, since it would not support the court in granting a
remedy against a stranger; and so the theory of property in
the contents of letters was adopted. Indeed, it is difficult to
conceive on what theory of the law the casual recipient of a
letter, who proceeds to publish it, is guilty of a breach of
contract, express or implied, or of any breach of trust, in the
ordinary acceptation of that term. Suppose a letter has been
addressed to him without his solicitation. He opens it, and
reads. Surely, he has not made any contract; he has not
accepted any trust. He cannot, by opening and reading the
letter, have come under any obligation save what the law
declares; and, however expressed, that obligation is simply
to observe the legal right of the sender whatever it may be,
and whether it be called his right of property in the contents
of the letter, or his right to privacy.

What About Trade Secrets?

A similar groping for the principle upon which a wrongful
publication can be enjoined is found in the law of trade
secrets. There, injunctions have generally been granted on
the theory of a breach of contract, or of an abuse of confidence. It would, of course, rarely happen that any one
would be in the possession of a secret unless confidence had
been reposed in him. But can it be supposed that the court
would hesitate to grant relief against one who had obtained
his knowledge by an ordinary trespass,—for instance, by
wrongfully looking into a book in which the secret was
recorded, or by eavesdropping? Indeed, in *Yovatt* v. *Winyard* (1820), where an injunction was granted against making any use of or communicating certain recipes for veteri-
nary medicine, it appeared that Winyard, while in Yovatt's
employ, had surreptitiously got access to his book of recipes,
and copied them. Lord Eldon "granted the injunction, upon

the ground of there having been a breach of trust and confidence"; but it would seem to be difficult to draw any sound legal distinction between such a case and one where a mere stranger wrongfully obtained access to the book.

Rights Against the World

We must therefore conclude that the rights, so protected, whatever their exact nature, are not rights arising from contract or from special trust, but are rights as against the world; and, as above stated, the principle which has been applied to protect these rights is in reality not the principle of private property, unless that word be used in an extended and unusual sense. The principle which protects personal writings and any other productions of the intellect or of the emotions, is the right to privacy, and the law has no new principle to formulate when it extends this protection to the personal appearance, sayings, acts, and to personal relations, domestic or otherwise. ◀

Having thus finished their analysis of prior cases by concluding that the majority of them reflect the existence of something which may be called a Right to Privacy, Warren and Brandeis then attempt to determine the extent of this right.

▶ If the invasion of privacy constitutes a legal *injuria*, the elements for demanding redress exist, since already the value of mental suffering, caused by an act wrongful in itself, is recognized as a basis for compensation.

The right of one who has remained a private individual, to prevent his public portraiture, presents the simplest case for such extension; the right to protect one's self from pen portraiture, from a discussion by the press of one's private affairs, would be a more important and far-reaching one. If casual and unimportant statements in a letter, if handiwork, however inartistic and valueless, if possessions of all sorts are protected not only against reproduction, but against description and enumeration, how much more should the acts and sayings of a man in his social and domestic relations be guarded from ruthless publicity. If you may not reproduce a woman's face photographically without her consent, how much less should be tolerated the reproduction of her face, her form, and her actions, by graphic descriptions colored to suit a gross and depraved imagination.

The right to privacy, limited as such right must necessarily be, has already found expression in the law of France.

It remains to consider what are the limitations of this right to privacy, and what remedies may be granted for the enforcement of the right. To determine in advance of experience the exact line at which the dignity and convenience of the individual must yield to the demands of the public welfare or of private justice would be a difficult task; but the more general rules are furnished by the legal analogies already developed in the law of slander and libel, and in the law of literacy and artistic property.

1. The right to privacy does not prohibit any publication of matter which is of public or general interest.

In determining the scope of this rule, aid would be afforded by the analogy, in the law of libel and slander, of cases which deal with the qualified privilege of comment and criticism on matters of public and general interest. There are of course difficulties in applying such a rule; but they are inherent in the subject-matter, and are certainly no greater than those which exist in many other branches of the law—for instance, in that large class of cases in which the reasonableness or unreasonableness of an act is made the test of liability. The design of the law must be to protect those persons with whose affairs the community has no legitimate concern, from being dragged into an undesirable and undesired publicity and to protect all persons, whatsoever their position or station, from having matters which they may properly prefer to keep private, made public against their will. It is the unwarranted invasion of individual privacy which is reprehended, and to be, so far as possible, prevented. The distinction, however, noted in the above statement is obvious and fundamental. There are persons who may reasonably claim as a right, protection from the notoriety entailed by being made the victims of journalistic enterprise. There are others who, in varying degrees, have renounced the right to live their lives screened from public observation. Matters which men of the first class may justly contend, concern themselves alone, may in those of the second be the subject of legitimate interest to their fellow-citizens. Peculiarities of manner and person, which in the ordinary individual should be free from comment, may acquire a public importance, if found in a candidate for political office. Some further discrimination is necessary, therefore, than to class facts or deeds as public or private according to a standard to be applied to the fact or deed *per se*. To publish of a modest and retiring individual that he suffers from an impediment in his speech or that he cannot spell correctly, is an unwarranted, if not an unexampled, infringement of his rights, while to state and comment on the same characteristics found in a would-be congressman could not be regarded as beyond the pale of propriety.

The general object in view is to protect the privacy of private life, and to whatever degree and in whatever connection a man's life has ceased to be private, before the publication under consideration has been made, to that extent the protection is to be withdrawn. Since, then, the propriety of publishing the very same facts may depend wholly upon the person concerning whom they are published, no fixed formula can be used to prohibit obnoxious publications. Any rule of liability adopted must have in it an elasticity which shall take account of the varying circumstances of each case,—a necessity which unfortunately renders such a doctrine not only more difficult of application, but also to a certain extent uncertain in its operation and easily rendered abortive. Besides, it is only the more flagrant breaches of decency and propriety that could in practice be reached, and it is not

perhaps desirable even to attempt to repress everything
which the nicest taste and keenest sense of the respect due
to private life would condemn.

In general, then, the matters of which the publication
should be repressed may be described as those which concern
the private life, habits, acts, and relations of an individual,
and have no legitimate connection with his fitness for a
public office which he seeks or for which he is suggested, or
for any public or quasi-public position which he seeks or for
which he is suggested, and have no legitimate relation to or
bearing upon any act done by him in a public or quasi-
public capacity. The foregoing is not designed as a wholly
accurate or exhaustive definition, since that which must
ultimately in a vast number of cases become a question of
individual judgment and opinion is incapable of such definition; but it is an attempt to indicate broadly the class of
matters referred to. Some things all men alike are entitled
to keep from popular curiosity, whether in public life or not,
while others are only private because the persons concerned
have not assumed a position which makes their doings legitimate matters of public investigation.

2. The right to privacy does not prohibit the communication of any matter, though in its nature private, when the
publication is made under circumstances which would render
it immune from attack according to the law of slander and
libel.

Under this rule, the right to privacy is not invaded by any
publication made in a court of justice, in legislative bodies,
or the committees of those bodies; in municipal assemblies,
or the committees of such assemblies, or practically by any
communication made in any other public body, municipal or
parochial, or in any body quasi-public, like the large voluntary associations formed for almost every purpose of benevolence, business, or other general interest; and (at least in
many jurisdictions) reports of any such proceedings would
in some measure be accorded a like privilege. Nor would the

rule prohibit any publication made by one in the discharge of some public or private duty, whether legal or moral, or in conduct of one's own affairs, in matters where his own interest is concerned.

3. The law would probably not grant any redress for the invasion of privacy by oral publication in the absence of special damage.

The same reasons exist for distinguishing between oral and written publications of private matters, as is afforded in the law of defamation by the restricted liability for slander as compared with the liability for libel. The injury resulting from such oral communications would ordinarily be so trifling that the law might well, in the interest of free speech, disregard it altogether.

4. The right to privacy ceases upon the publication of the facts by the individual, or with his consent.

This is but another application of the rule which has become familiar in the law of literary and artistic property. The cases there decided establish also what should be deemed a publication,—the important principle in this connection being that a private communication or circulation for a restricted purpose is not a publication within the meaning of the law.

5. The truth of the matter published does not afford a defense.

Obviously this branch of the law should have no concern with the truth or falsehood of the matters published. It is not for injury to the individual's character that redress or prevention is sought, but for injury to the right of privacy: for the former, the law of slander and libel provides perhaps a sufficient safeguard. The latter implies the right not merely to prevent inaccurate portrayal of private life, but to prevent its being depicted at all.

6. The absence of "malice" in the publisher does not afford a defense.

Personal ill-will is not an ingredient of the offense any more than in an ordinary case of trespass to person or property. Such malice is never necessary to be shown in an action for libel or slander at common law, except in rebuttal of some defense, e.g., that the occasion rendered the communication immune from attack, or, under the statutes in this State and elsewhere, that the statement complained of was true. The invasion of the privacy that is to be protected is equally complete and equally injurious, whether the motives by which the speaker or writer was actuated are, taken by themselves, culpable or not; just as the damage to character, and to some extent the tendency to provoke a breach of the peace, is equally the result of defamation without regard to the motives leading to its publication. Viewed as a wrong to the individual, this rule is the same pervading the whole law of torts, by which one is held responsible for his intentional acts, even though they are committed with no sinister intent; and viewed as wrong to society, it is the same principle adopted in a large category of statutory offenses.

ALL RIGHTS SHOULD CARRY A REMEDY

The remedies for an invasion of the right of privacy are also suggested by those administered in the law of defamation, and in the law of literary and artistic property, namely:—

1. An action for damages in all cases. Even in the absence of special damages, substantial compensation could be allowed for injury to feelings as in the action of slander and libel.

2. An injunction, in perhaps a very limited class of cases.

Should It Be a Crime?

It would doubtless be desirable that the privacy of the individual should receive the added protection of the criminal law, but for this, legislation would be required. Perhaps it would be deemed proper to bring the criminal liability for such publication within narrower limits; but that the community has an interest in preventing such invasions of privacy, sufficiently strong to justify the introduction of such a remedy, cannot be doubted. Still, the protection of society must come mainly through a recognition of the rights of the individual. Each man is responsible for his own acts and omissions only. If he condones what he reprobates, with a weapon at hand equal to his defense, he is responsible for the results. If he resists, public opinion will rally to his support. Has he then such a weapon? It is believed that the common law provides him with one, forged in the slow fire of the centuries, and today fitly tempered to his hand. The common law has always recognized a man's house as his castle, impregnable, often, even to its own officers engaged in the execution of its commands. Shall the courts thus close the front entrance to constituted authority, and open wide the back door to idle or prurient curiosity? ◀

The appeal of Warren and Brandeis was to logic, not to fancy. It was their claim that the seed of the principle for which they argued so persuasively lay in the past; they were merely bringing it to maturity. As we have seen, they were to some extent correct in this claim. Like all prophets, while they had one foot in the past they were extending the other into the future. But judges, and many other men of legal bent, are notoriously wary of newfangled notions.

There is no doubt that the article was widely read and energetically discussed when it appeared. But it was some time before the principles it propounded gained a significant foothold in the law. And even then reasonable men differed widely about how much this so-called Right of Privacy owed to history and how much to imagination. Was it really, as Warren and Brandeis maintained, a crystallization of legal precedents, or was it, as many felt, merely a statement of What Ought to Be—a legal invention?

There is little doubt that the article partook both of the past and of the future. But as this country moved into the twentieth century, the extent to which lawyers and judges emphasized one or the other of these positions determined in large part whether it would be the courts or the legislatures that would eventually be the guardians of our privacy.

Because we live in a country with, now, fifty-one different legal systems (one for each state and one for the federal government) the blessings of legal uniformity often give way to what are perhaps the more important blessings of legal variety. It is not surprising, therefore, that different courts in different states reached different conclusions about the persuasiveness of the Warren-Brandeis article and the plea for privacy. There were some judges who felt that the cases Warren and Brandeis used to prove their point didn't prove it at all. And there were some who thought they did. There were some judges who felt that a Right of Privacy did in fact exist—not, however, as a result of past cases but rather as a manifestation of natural law. And there were those who didn't give a hoot about natural law, and thought Warren and Brandeis were just a couple of young conjurers. And so on.

As we shall see, sides were taken early in the game. And by and large they are still the sides today, more sophisticated and multifaceted perhaps, but no less imposing and varied.

4

A Picture,
a Statue,
a Gravestone,
and a Five-Cent Cigar

Nᴏᴛ surprisingly, a lawyer was quick to tempt the court with the Warren-Brandeis theory. During the year 1891—within twelve months of its appearance—the article was successfully cited in a suit heard by a New York court. Without permission, a medicine manufacturer used the name and a reproduction of the signature of a well-known physician in connection with the promotion of one of the manufacturer's products. In his argument for a restraining judgment, the doctor's lawyer said that the manufacturer's acts constituted "an unwarrantable invasion of the reasonable right of privacy," and referred the court specifically to the Warren-Brandeis article. Historically, this was victory Number One for privacy *as* privacy. The planted seed had sprouted.

Two years later, there was another test of privacy. It, too, took place in New York City. In 1893 a newspaper, *Der*

Wächter, was published in New York City. An actor by the name of Marks (judicial opinions seldom give human details such as first name, age, and the like) was at that time dividing his loyalties between the stage and the law. In fact, he was a law student preparing for admission to the bar. Another actor by the name of "Mogulesko" was, so the judge held, "equally well known."

A newspaper devised a plan by which pictures of the two actors were to be published with an invitation to the readers to vote to determine—in a prepoll but lottery age—who was the more popular of the two. When informed of the contest, Marks declined to consent to the use of his name or picture for any such purpose. The newspaper was not deterred, and went on with the contest. Doubtless it had benefit of legal counsel who advised that there was no law in New York that could stop them. If so, their counsel reckoned without due consideration for the newly sprouted concept and principle of privacy, whereas the counsel for Marks did.

The action was specifically one of the Right of Privacy, and was based on, leaned on, and depended upon the Warren and Brandeis article. That the judge was favorably impressed by this argument is clear to see in the construction of his decision:

▶ The action may seem novel, but there can be no question about Marks' right to relief irrespective of the amount of damages he might recover at law. If a person can be compelled to have his name and profile put up in this manner for public criticism, to test his popularity with certain people, he could be required to submit to the same test as to his *honesty* or *morality*, or any other virtue or vice he was supposed to possess, and the victim selected would either have to vindicate his character in regard to the virtue or vice selected, or be declared inferior to his competitor, a comparison which might prove most odious. Indeed, he might be placed in competition with a person whose association might be peculiarly offensive as well as detrimental to him. Such a wrong is not without its remedy. No newspaper or institution, no matter how worthy, has the right to use the name or picture of anyone for such a purpose without his consent. An individual is entitled to protection in person as well as property, and now the right to life has come to mean the privilege to enjoy life, without the publicity or annoyance of a lottery contest waged without authority, on the result of which is made to depend, in public estimation at least, the worth of private character or value of ability. Games of chance have always been discountenanced by the law, and when they are used as the pretended means of testing private character or ability, they become impositions on the public and frauds upon the individuals affected.

"PEACE OF MIND"

The courts will in such cases secure to the individual what has been aptly termed the right "to be let alone." The law affords a remedy for the unauthorized circulation of portraits of private persons, and the principle has been even extended to an actress whose picture was taken surreptitiously and without her consent by means of a flash light.

Private rights must be respected as well as the wishes and sensibilities of people. When they transgress the law, invoke its aid or put themselves up as candidates for public favor, they warrant criticism, and ought not to complain of it. But where they are content with the privacy of their homes they are entitled to peace of mind and cannot be suspended over the press-heated gridiron of excited rivalry and voted for against their will and protest. The right of Marks to relief seems too clear, both upon principle and authority, to require further discussion. ◀

Note well that this decision says in passing, "An individual is entitled to protection in *person as well as property*." Then consider the very beginning of the Warren and Brandeis article: "That the individual shall have full protection *in person and in property* is a principle as old as the common law." Then the judge, in deciding in Marks' favor, says, "the right of life has come to mean the privilege to enjoy life." And at the end of the first Warran and Brandeis paragraph you will find the words, "Gradually the scope of these legal rights broadened; and now the right to life has come to mean the right to enjoy life." And, finally, the judgment says, "The courts will in such cases secure to the individual what has been aptly termed the right 'to be let alone.'" This reference to this Cooley phrase of 1878 is also contained in the Warren and Brandeis first paragraph. Who could doubt, at this point, that the sprouted seed was not flourishing?

More than any other of the original colonies, Massachusetts has in many ways preserved a cultural continuity with the mother country. We find in the scores of privacy cases an interesting one in Massachusetts that touches on the sensitivity of the family of a well-known inventor, the demands of history, the contractual rights of a photographer, prior waiver of anonymity, and other intriguing facets of the Right of Privacy. It presents a point of view differing from other decisions not so much in result as in philosophy. The opinion is also of interest because it was uttered by a federal —not a state court—judge, since the case touched both on Massachusetts and Rhode Island.

CORLISS v. E. W. WALKER Co. (Massachusetts, 1894)

▶ As the case was first presented, it appeared that the print of George H. Corliss to be inserted in a biographical sketch about to be published by the Walker Co. was taken from a photograph obtained from Mrs. Corliss by the Walker Co.

upon certain conditions, which they had failed to comply with. It now appears that the Walker Co. obtained two photographs of Mr. Corliss, and that the one received from Mrs. Corliss was returned to her, while the other, from which the print was actually taken, was purchased for the Walker Co. at a studio in Providence without the knowledge of Mrs. Corliss several months before.

The question resolves itself into the broad proposition of how far an individual, in his lifetime, or his heirs at law after his death, have the right to control the reproduction of his picture or photograph. The photograph obtained by the Walker Co. was a copy of an original taken by Mr. Heald, of Providence, for Mr. Corliss, in September, 1885. Mr. Corliss engaged Mr. Heald, in the ordinary way, to take his photograph, and paid for the pictures which he ordered. The contention of Mrs. Corliss is that Mr. Heald had no right to make prints from the original negative, other than those which Mr. Corliss ordered, and that neither Mr. Heald nor any one else had the right to reproduce copies from any of the photographs ordered by Mr. Corliss, and that to do so would be a breach of contract or a violation of confidence, for which relief can be had in a court. In support of this position, Mrs. Corliss says that Mr. Corliss never authorized Mr. Heald to make any prints from the negative, except those he ordered, and that after his death, in February, 1888, Mrs. Corliss obtained the original negative, and forbade Mr. Heald from exhibiting in his studio any pictures of Mr. Corliss.

Was Corliss a Public or Private Person?

I believe the law to be that a private individual has a right to be protected in the representation of his portrait in any form; that this is a property as well as a personal right; and that it belongs to the same class of rights which forbids the reproduction of a private manuscript or painting, or the publication of private letters, or of oral lectures delivered by a teacher to his class, or the revelation of the contents of a merchant's books by a clerk. But, while the right of a private individual to prohibit the reproduction of his picture or photograph should be recognized and enforced, this right may be surrendered or dedicated to the public by the act of the individual, just the same as a private manuscript, book, or painting becomes (when not protected by copyright) public property by the act of publication. The distinction in the case of a picture or photograph lies, it seems to me, between public and private characters. A private individual should be protected against the publication of any portraiture of himself, but where an individual becomes a public character the case is different. A statesman, author, artist, or inventor, who asks for and desires public recognition, may be said to have surrendered this right to the public. When any one obtained a picture or photograph of such a person, and there is no breach of contract or violation of confidence in the method by which it was obtained, he has the right to reproduce it, whether in a newspaper, magazine, or book. It would be extending this right of protection too far to say that the general public can be prohibited from knowing the personal appearance of great public characters. Such characters may be said, of their own volition, to have dedicated to the public the right of any fair portraiture of themselves.

In this sense, I cannot but regard Mr. Corliss as a public man. He was among the first of American inventors, and he sought public recognition as such.

Further, it does not seem that Mr. Corliss, personally, ever objected to the reproduction of his picture, but, on the contrary, that he permitted thousands of his pictures to be circulated. Ten thousand pictures of Mr. Corliss were sold or given away, without objection on his part, at the time of the Centennial Exhibition, in 1876. In 1886 there was published in Providence, by J. A. and R. A. Reid, about 10,000 copies of a book called "Providence Plantations," in which a picture of Mr. Corliss appears, which is a reprint from the Heald photograph, now in controversy. His picture also was printed in Harper's Weekly of March 3, 1888, and in the Scientific American of June 2, 1888. I am aware that

Mrs. Corliss says that she wrote a letter, at the request of her husband, to the Messrs. Reid, forbidding the insertion of the picture in the "Providence Plantations," and that she also declares that the publication in the Harper's Weekly and Scientific American were authorized by the family; but, whatever may be the position now taken by the plaintiffs, there is no substantial evidence that Mr. Corliss, in his lifetime, ever prohibited the reproduction and circulation of his picture.

Upon the facts as now presented, and for the reasons given, I am of opinion that the Walker Co. has a right to insert in the biographical sketch of Mr. Corliss published by them a print of his photograph. ◀

So Mrs. Corliss lost because her husband was too well known. The reasoning of the appellate court in this case is worth remembering because, in many ways, it was far ahead of its time. By recognizing a Right of Privacy but at the same time carving out an exception for so called "public figures," it recognized a pattern in these cases that is now followed in most states.

But what if Mr. Corliss had not been a public personage of such magnitude? Suppose, even, that he was, in the words of that Steig cartoon, merely "a great human being" in the eyes of his family? Should the shield of protection he might have had in his lifetime also be available to the surviving members of his family?

In most societies, and certainly in ours, men cherish the intimacy of their relations with loved ones recently deceased. Therefore it is not surprising that very early in the development of the Right of Privacy in this country we find men seeking the protection of this right not for themselves, but for deceased relatives they loved and admired. The next few cases will show varieties within this area of sensitivity and the extent to which courts felt they could, or could not, insulate private memories from public appropriation.

Once, a client died and left by will $10,000 for a hospital
bed in perpetuity. The hospital director was grateful, but
apologetically explained that the upkeep of a bed in perpetuity had climbed to $20,000. Interest on that amount was
needed to carry the upkeep year after year. So a wise lawyer
wrote as follows to the hospital: "I can give you a choice.
One-half of a bed for perpetuity or a whole bed for half of
perpetuity—take your choice but don't use up too much of
perpetuity to make up your mind."

Where the family is the root of a culture, or where death
assumes different contours than it does in our society, the
law of privacy may be very different. Law will interpret
attitudes from the womb to the tomb in perpetuity if the
people of a society so desire. That such desires do not always
keep pace with the judicial guess of current popular demands is wholesome, for who can be thought fit to make
early appraisals in a changing dervish of attitudes—in the
exciting shift from thin to thick skins—or vice versa? Few
judges pretend that they can be prophets in a changing
world.

Only recently it was urged that money be raised in the
United States to erect a statue of Winston Churchill in
Grosvenor Square, London, to face the statue of F.D.R.
contributed by the people of England. These two men should
face each other for future generations. As a matter of taste
Winston Churchill was asked if he approved the idea. The reply was not unexpected: Statues are not fittingly erected during the lifetime of the subject. But in the eyes of the law
problems must be forseeable. Since marble is used to portray
a person usually only after death, whose privacy is scarred
and who, if anyone, has the right to object? In a real sense the
issue is sharpened if the proposed portrait in stone is to be one
of a group of people. Or, if you please, statues sitting together,
such as President Truman and General MacArthur—both for
peace but bitter opponents on the means of attaining it. Liv-

ing people, like Sir Winston, are around to object when people want to erect statues of them. But what about those deceased? Should their relatives or friends be able to object when someone, even for the noblest of reasons, wants to cast their image in bronze or marble and stand it up somewhere? And should it make any difference if the statue is to be placed in the company of others identified with particular causes or beliefs—perhaps antithetical causes or beliefs? Is there, in short, a kind of guilt by association for statues, the existence of which gives some representative of the deceased a right of action? As notions of the Right of Privacy were developed, they had to accommodate themselves to problems of this kind, problems that arose because of the special mystique in our culture that ties the dead to the living by an often unbreakable grip of sentiment.

In 1895, before laws were passed that established a Right of Privacy in New York, the New York Court of Appeals had to decide a "statue" case. We shall separate the facts from the decisions that followed. After reading the facts, it might be intriguing for the reader to formulate his own decree and also the reasons therefor.

One tip might be allowed. The court divided, and there will follow the prevailing opinion and the equally tight reasoning of the minority jurist.

PHILIP SCHUYLER v. ERNEST CURTIS, ALICE DONLEVY AND OTHERS (1895)

▶ Mr. Schuyler brought this action against members of an association called "The Woman's Memorial Fund" to restrain them from making a statue or bust of the late Mrs. Mary M. Hamilton Schuyler in any form, and from causing the same to be made or exhibited; also from receiving or soliciting subscriptions for the purpose of defraying the cost and expenses of making such bust or procuring it to be made, and

also to restrain them from making use of the name of Mrs.
Mary M. Hamilton Schuyler or circulating any description
of her in any way in connection with the "Woman's Memorial
Fund Association."

THE CLAIM OF MR. SCHUYLER

Philip Schuyler was the nephew and later stepson of the
late Mrs. Mary Hamilton Schuyler. Mrs. Schuyler died in
May, 1877, leaving no children. Her husband died in July,
1890, and her only brother had died in December, 1889. The
only immediate relatives, now living, of the second Mrs.
Schuyler are certain nephews and nieces, an uncle and an
aunt, all of whom approve of the commencement and maintenance of this action. The avowed object of the Woman's
Memorial Fund was the completion of two sculptures to
honor "Woman as the Philanthropist" and "Woman as the
Reformer," to be placed on exhibition at the Columbian Exposition of 1893. This Fund in May, 1891, publicly announced that "as the typical Philanthropist, Mary M.
Hamilton, who died Mrs. G. L. Schuyler, has been chosen
as the subject of the statue," and about that time the Fund
began to send printed circulars to that effect and to solicit
subscriptions for the purpose of carrying out this project,
and public announcement was made that a contract had
been entered into with the defendant Hartley, a professional
sculptor, for the execution of a statue of Mrs. Schuyler to
be placed on exhibition as stated.

It was also announced that the Fund intended to place
the statue on exhibition at the same time and place as a
statue of Miss Susan B. Anthony, whom the Fund had chosen
as the subject of the statue to be designated the "Representative Reformer." George L. Schuyler, the husband, and Alexander Hamilton, the brother, of the deceased Mrs. Schuyler,
were living in New York at the time when the Fund claims
to have originated the plan for making the statue but no
application was made to either for his consent to the making
of the statue and neither of them ever authorized anyone to

make it. Subsequent to the deaths of the husband and brother of Mrs. Schuyler, and in May, 1891, Philip Schuyler first heard of the contemplated action of the Memorial Fund Association and he, in behalf of himself and also of the other relatives of Mrs. Schuyler, requested the Fund to abandon the making of such statue and the circulation of subscription papers for the purpose of collecting money toward defraying the cost and expenses of procuring the statue. The Fund refused and continued to circulate such subscription papers widely throughout the United States, and they were printed in some of the New York City newspapers.

The lower court decided that these acts have exposed the name and the memory of Mrs. Mary M. Hamilton Schuyler to adverse comment and criticism of a nature peculiarly disagreeable to her relatives and have caused disagreeable notoriety for which they are in no way responsible; that such comment has been made in the public prints and elsewhere; that annoyance and pain have been caused thereby to Philip Schuyler and to the immediate relatives of Mrs. Schuyler; that he and they have been greatly distressed and injured thereby and by the notoriety incident thereto; and that such notoriety and adverse comment and criticism are wholly due to the unauthorized acts of the Fund. The court decided that the acts of the Fund constituted an unlawful interference with the right of privacy, and that the surviving relatives of the deceased Mary Schuyler were specially injured by the acts.

It was, therefore, adjudged in the lower courts that Philip Schuyler was entitled to judgment perpetually prohibiting the Fund from making or causing to be made a statue of Mrs. Schuyler in any form and from exhibiting any statue of her and from receiving subscriptions for the purposes stated.

More Evidence at the Trial

Upon the trial evidence was given which showed that Mrs. Schuyler in her lifetime was a very charitable woman; was a member of many private charitable associations; that in 1852 she was one of the founders of the School of Design for Women in the City of New York and one of its managers until it was adopted by the Cooper Institute; that some of the female defendants were members of the School of Design for Women and had frequently met Mrs. Schuyler at its meetings and were on terms of some intimacy with her so far at least as her interest in and her attendance at the meetings of the "Ladies Art Association" called for; that the "Ladies Art Association" was founded about 1867, partly at the suggestion of Mrs. Schuyler made to some of the defendants who were members of the School of Design for Women, the object of the Association being to help ladies support themselves and to give them adequate education in art and design, and the Association is a reputable and well-known organization in New York City, and Mrs. Schuyler evinced considerable interest in it during her life; that the "Woman's Memorial Fund Association" was composed largely of members of the "Ladies Art Association," and it was publicly announced that the statue in question was to be placed after the exposition in the rooms or studio of the Association, there to remain permanently; that Mrs. Schuyler was prominently identified with the U. S. Sanitary Commission during the late war; and also that she was one of the vice-regents for the State of New York of the Mt. Vernon Association which was organized for the purpose of securing the preservation of the home of Washington. These several facts were proved and uncontradicted, but the lower court said they were immaterial. ◀

So stated the sympathetic lower court. Now consider the facts for yourself. Try to put yourself in Philip's position and see whether you too would, or should, feel aggrieved if someone tried to immortalize in stone or bronze the likeness of your famous parent or grandparent without your consent. Opinions may vary, and there may be a lot of good logic on both sides. There usually is in the law. . . .

Now that you have reached your own verdict, read what the Court of Appeals, the highest New York court, thought of the lower court's opinion. Of the court's seven judges, six of them felt this way:

▶ This action is of a nature somewhat unusual and depends for its support upon an application of certain principles which are themselves not very clearly defined or their boundaries very well recognized or plainly laid down. Briefly described the action is founded upon an alleged violation of what is termed the right of privacy. The alleged violation of this right, so far as regards Philip Schuyler, consists of an attempt on the part of certain reputable women without the sanction of Philip Schuyler or other immediate members of the family, to do honor to the memory of a woman who was Philip Schuyler's aunt and who, at the time of the commencement of this action, had been dead for fourteen years. A statue, of a most costly and meritorious kind, to be made out of appropriate material and by an artist of the first rank, was contemplated as the means of doing this honor to the memory of this woman.

It may, perhaps, be somewhat difficult for the ordinary mind to perceive any reason for Philip Schuyler's distress arising out of this contemplated action by women of respectability who are desirous of honoring the memory of a woman whom they regarded in life as a friend and benefactor of their sex. Objection has, however, been made to the carrying out of this project.

In order to determine whether there has been a violation of the right of privacy it is necessary to know something about the right itself and its proper limitations. It is not necessary, however, in the view which we take of this case, to attempt to lay down precise and accurate rules which shall apply to all cases touching upon this alleged right. If the facts in any case fail to furnish any clear or sure foundation for a reasonable man to claim that any injury to his feelings has been or would be caused by the action taken, or to be taken, by another, then we can at least say in such a case that there has not been and cannot be any such real mental distress or injury as a court ought to recognize as within judicial relief. For the purpose we have in view it is unnecessary to wholly deny the existence of the right of privacy to which Philip Schuyler appeals as the foundation of his cause of action. It may be admitted that courts have power in some cases to enjoin the doing of an act where the nature or character of the act itself is well calculated to wound the sensibilities of an individual, and where the doing of the act is wholly unjustifiable, and is, in legal contemplation, a wrong, even though the existence of no property, as that term is usually used, is involved in the subject.

The Court Looks Again at the Facts in the Case

We enter upon this examination with an admission for the purposes of this case that Philip Schuyler occupies such a relationship to the deceased that he might maintain an action to prevent the painting of a picture or the making of a statue of the deceased which would be regarded as inappropriate by reasonable people because the use for which it was destined or the place where it was to be kept was obviously improper, or because the thing itself, portrait or bust or statue, was not of that degree of merit, all the circumstances considered, which might reasonably and properly be insisted upon by those to whom the life and memory of the deceased were most dear. Many other cases can be imagined where the ulterior purpose of the individuals engaged in the matter would be so manifestly improper, if not illegal, that no statue or picture of a reputable individual, alive or dead, ought to be permitted to be made for such purpose. These are merely imaginary cases, alluded to only for the purpose of accentuating our ideas as to some of the circumstances in which courts might be called upon to act on the part of a living relative of one who was long since dead.

To Restate Mr. Schuyler's Grievances

In the present case the grounds of Mr. Schuyler's objection are not very many. They are these:

1. The persons concerned in getting up the proposed statue were not the friends of Mrs. Mary Schuyler and did not know her.

2. They were proceeding with their plan without consulting with any immediate members of the Schuyler-Hamilton family and without their consent to the making of any statue.

3. The circulars issued by or in behalf of the Fund contained a statement that Mrs. Schuyler was the founder of or the first woman in the enterprise for securing the home of Washington, and that this statement was inaccurate because a prominent woman in South Carolina was in fact such founder and justly entitled to the honor arising therefrom. This mistake, it was asserted, had caused adverse comment in the newspapers as to the attitude of the family in permitting such a claim to be made when they must have known it was without foundation.

4. It was disagreeable to Mr. Schuyler because the making of such a statue would have been disagreeable and obnoxious to his aunt were she living. She had a great dislike to have her name brought into public notoriety of any kind, as she was a singularly sensitive woman and of a very retiring nature, anxious to keep her name from the public prints or newspapers.

5. Mrs. Mary Schuyler had not been personally acquainted with Susan B. Anthony, and he was quite sure she had not sympathized with or approved the position taken by Miss Anthony upon the question of the proper sphere of woman and her treatment by the law, and it was disagreeable and annoying to have the memory of Mrs. Schuyler joined with principles of which she did not approve.

These are substantially all the objections taken by Mr. Schuyler regarding the proposed action of the defendants. He said he did not claim that the Fund, in any of its actions or in any of its published notices, threw any discredit, disgrace or ridicule upon Mrs. Schuyler's memory, and he did not think it wished to do so in any way. The chief reason for bringing this action was to establish a principle that the

right of privacy should be respected, and he was willing to
bring such an action for the purpose of maintaining that
principle.

The Court Is Not Impressed

After taking all these objections into careful consideration, we cannot say that we are in the least degree impressed
with their force. The first ground of objection, even if well
founded in fact, is not of the slightest importance. Whether
the defendants were friends or not of Mrs. Schuyler in her
lifetime does not seem to us to have any legitimate effect upon
the question. If the motive were to do honor to a good
woman, and if the work were to be done in an appropriate
way, the relations towards the deceased of those who proposed to render this mark of honor to her memory as one
of the benefactors of her sex, would be a matter of very
small moment, entitled to no consideration whatever. It
appears, however, that there was enough personal intercourse between Mrs. Schuyler and some of the women to
account for the affection in which her memory is held and
for their desire to give some practical evidence of their
feelings.

The second ground of objection we think is equally un-
tenable. The fourth ground may properly be considered as
a part of it. It is true that these members have assumed to
take the preliminary steps leading to the making of the
proposed statue without having consulted with or obtained
the consent of the relatives of the deceased. The whole of
Philip Schuyler's claim of the right of privacy in this case
rests upon the lack of this consent. It is stated that Mrs.
Schuyler was not in any sense a public character during her
life, and consequently had not surrendered to any extent
whatever her own right of privacy. This right, it is claimed,
not having been surrenderd by any act of the deceased in
her lifetime, descends unimpaired to her immediate relatives
as the proper representatives of her feelings and her rights.
Whatever the rights of a relative may be, they are not in

such a case as this, rights which once belonged to the deceased, and which a relative can enforce in her behalf and
in a mere representative capacity, as, for instance, an execu-
tor or administrator, in regard to assets of deceased. ◀

Having disposed (rather quickly) of the argument that
it makes a difference whether those who erect a statue are
"deserving" of the honor, the majority of the court now turns
to the crux of Schuyler's case and proceeds to make it clear
that it is not any right belonging to Mary Schuyler that is
involved; rather, the question is whether Philip and the
other heirs have been injured in a way the law does not
allow. This is an important point to keep in mind when reading cases *that go beyond the grave.* Even today, although our
laws of privacy have expanded, there is a strong reluctance
on the part of legislatures and courts to carry on past the
grave and allow to a "ghost" the legal rights of the living.

WHO IS PHILIP SCHUYLER, ANYWAY?

▶ It is not a question of what right of privacy Mrs. Schuyler had in her lifetime. Mr. Philip Schuyler does not represent that right. Whatever right of privacy Mrs. Schuyler
had dies with her. Death deprives us all of rights in the
legal sense of that term, and, when Mrs. Schuyler died, her
own individual right of privacy, whatever it may have been
expired at the same time. The right which survived (however extensive or limited) was a right pertaining to the
living only. It is the right of privacy of the living which it
is sought to enforce here. That right may, in some cases,
be itself violated by improperly interfering with the character or memory of a deceased relative, but it is the right of
the living and not that of the dead which is recognized. A
privilege may be given the surviving relatives of a deceased
person to protect his memory, but the privilege exists for

the benefit of the living, to protect their feelings and to prevent a violation of their own rights in the character and memory of the deceased.

A woman like Mrs. Schuyler may very well in her lifetime have been most strongly averse to any public notice, even if it were of a most flattering nature, regarding her own works or position. She may have been (and the evidence tends most strongly to show that she was) of so modest and retiring a nature that any publicity, during her life, would have been to her most extremely disageeable and obnoxious. All these feelings died with her. It is wholly incredible that any individual could dwell with feelings of distress or anguish upon the thought that, after his death, those whose welfare he had toiled for in life would inaugurate a project to erect a statue in token of their appreciation of his efforts and in honor of his memory. This applies as well to the most refined and retiring woman as to a public man. It is, therefore, impossible to credit the existence of any real mental injury or distress to a surviving relative grounded upon the idea that the action proposed in honor of his ancestor would have been disagreeable to that ancestor during his life.

We cannot assent to the proposition that one situated as Mr. Schuyler in this case can properly prevent such action as the Fund proposes on the ground that as mere matter of fact his feelings would be thereby injured. We hold that in this class of cases there must in addition be some reasonable and plausible ground for the existence of this mental distress and injury. It must not be the creation of mere caprice or of pure fancy, or the result of a supersensitive and morbid mental organization, dwelling with undue emphasis upon the exclusive and sacred character of this right of privacy. Such a class of mind might regard the right as interfered with and violated by the least reference even of a complimentary nature to some illustrious ancestor without first seeking for and obtaining the consent of his descendants. Feelings that are thus easily and unnaturally injured and distressed under such circumstances are much too sensitive to be recognized by any purely earthly tribunal. A proposed act

which a court will prohibit because it would be a violation of
a legal right, must, among other conditions, be of such
a nature as a reasonable man can see might and probably
would cause mental distress and injury to any one possessed of ordinary feeling and intelligence, situated in like
circumstances as the complainant, and this question must
always to some extent be one of law.

If the circumstances be such that it is to a court inconceivable that the feelings of any sane and reasonable person
could be injured by the proposed act, then it is the duty of
the court to say so and to refuse to prevent its performance.

WHAT IF MRS. SCHUYLER WERE ALIVE?

If the defendants had projected such a work in the
lifetime of Mrs. Schuyler, it would perhaps have been a
violation of her individual right of privacy, because it might
be contended that she had never occupied such a position
toward the public as would have authorized such action by
any one so long as it was in opposition to her wishes. The
fact that Mrs. Schuyler is dead alters the case, and the
plaintiff and other relatives must show some right of their
own violated, and that proof is not made by evidence that
the proposed action of the defendants would have caused
Mrs. Schuyler pain if she were living. A shy, sensitive,
retiring woman might naturally be extremely reluctant to
have her praises sounded, or even appropriate honors accorded her while living, and the same woman might, upon
good grounds, believe with entire complacency and satisfaction that after her death a proposition would be made
and carried out by her admirers to do honor to her memory
by the erection of a statue or some other memorial.

For these reasons we are of the opinion that regarding the
facts thus far discussed, it was not necessary for the defendants to procure the consent of Philip Schuyler or other
immediate relatives of the deceased. We think that so long
as the real and honest purpose is to do honor to the memory
of one who is deceased, and such purpose is to be carried out

in an appropriate and orderly manner, by reputable individuals and for worthy ends, the consent of the descendants
of such deceased person is not necessary, and they have no
right to prevent, for their own personal gratification, any
action of the nature described. ◀

After disposing of Philip's third objection, namely, that
his aunt-stepmother never was the founder of the Mt. Vernon Association, with a few words to the effect that the mistake was unintentional and would have been corrected
immediately if it had been brought to the attention of the
Fund (and still could be corrected, for that matter), the
majority turns to consider Philip's unfortunately prophetic
plea of "guilt by association":

▶ Whether Mrs. Schuyler sympathized with the work or the
views of Miss Anthony we must say seems to us utterly foreign to the subject. There was no proposition looking towards the placing the statues of these two ladies together as
representatives of the same ideas, or as in any way, even the
remotest, united in the same works, or in inculcating the
same principles in regard to the rights of women. The objection seems to rest wholly upon the proposition that these
two proposed statues were to be exhibited in the same room
of a building in the Chicago fair grounds—one as the representative of a class of women philanthropists and the other
as the representative of a class of women reformers. The
placing of the statues in the same room for exhibition by the
same association does not in our view tend in the slightest
degree to confuse the identity of Mrs. Schuyler, or to lead
in any way to the supposition that she was in sympathy with
or believed in the correctness of the principles which have
been advocated by Miss Anthony.

The fact, if it be a fact, that Mrs. Schuyler did not
sympathize with what is termed the "Woman's Rights"
movement is of no importance here. The proposed placing

of the two statues would, if carried out, have had no tendency
to show that Mrs. Schuyler did so sympathize. Many of us
may, and probably do, totally disagree with these advanced
views of Miss Anthony in regard to the proper sphere of
women, and yet it is impossible to deny to her the possession
of many of the ennobling qualities which tend to the making
of great lives. She has given the most unselfish devotion of
a long life to what she has considered would tend most for
the benefit and practical improvement of her sex, and she
has thus lived almost literally in the face of the whole world,
and during that period there has never been a single shadow
of any dark or ugly fact connected with her or her way of
life to dim the lustre of her achievements and of her efforts.
Although we may utterly fail to sympathize with these efforts or achievements, it is plain enough that no one will
have reasonable ground for objection to the placing of a
bust of his or her own ancestor in the same room with the
bust of such a woman and under such circumstances as were
originally contemplated by these defendants. This ground
of objection, however, time has itself rendered valueless. ◀

Gallant gentlemen! Miss Anthony, after all, was a nice
and proper lady, even if a bit cracked. What lady, or even
gentleman, reading this opinion today doesn't have to smile
at these Victorian anachronisms that do seem to fill our lawbooks in one way or another. Our law, seeking stability and
guidance more often than invention, has made the past its
legacy. But let us proceed with these Victorian gentlemen
to their conclusion. Ask yourself: Should the statue at least
have to *look* like Mrs. Schuyler? Now listen to the court's
answer and its conclusion:

▶ It was urged that the proposed statue would be a fraud
upon the public because there was no portrait, likeness or
statue of Mrs. Schuyler accessible to the Association from
which any possible likeness of the deceased could be secured.

The idea of an actual likeness was early abandoned, and it was stated that the statue would be an ideal one and not a likeness. The court below has not found any fraud and we are not of the opinion that any was shown.

While not assuming to decide what this right of privacy is in all cases, we are quite clear that such right would not be violated by the proposed action of the Fund. Mr. Schuyler's cause of action is, we think, wholly fanciful. The Fund's contemplated action is not such as might be regarded by reasonable and healthy minds as in the slightest degree distressing or tending in the least to any injury to those feelings of respect and tenderness for the memory of the dead which most of us possess, and which ought to be considered as a proper subject of recognition and protection by civilized courts.

Upon the whole we are of the opinion that Philip Schuyler has made a mistake in his choice of this case as an appropriate one in which to ask for the enforcement of the right of privacy. ◀

Obviously, the majority thought that Philip was too sensitive about the whole thing. Do you agree? Ask yourself also whether the court would be likely to reach the same result if the people who wanted to put up the statue were rather less respectable than those of the Woman's Memorial Fund? And what, do you think, George Washington would have said had he known what these ladies wanted to do to his beloved Mt. Vernon? No matter; for those of you who disagree with the majority opinion we now present the minority —of one:

GRAY, J. (dissenting):

▶ I must emphatically dissent from the decision of this court that there was no ground shown in this case for the equitable relief which was granted below. That a precisely analogous case may not have arisen heretofore furnishes no reason against the assumption of jurisdiction. This right of the court to act is determined by the particular circumstances of each particular case and depends upon the existence of a state of facts which demonstrates a wrongful act performed, or threatened to be performed, to the prejudice of some right of property and for which there is no adequate remedy at law.

Upon the findings in this case, I think we are bound to say that the purpose of the Fund was to commit an act which was an unauthorized invasion of Philip Schuyler's right to the preservation of the name and memory of Mrs. Schuyler intact from public comment and criticism. As the representative of all her immediate living relatives, it was competent for him to maintain an action to preserve them from becoming public property; as would be the case if a statue were erected by strangers, for public exhibition under such classification, with respect to the characteristic virtues of the deceased, as they judged befitting.

I cannot see why the right of privacy is not a form of property, as much as is the right of complete immunity of one's person. If it is a property right with reference to the publication of a catalogue of private etchings and entitled to be protected against invasion, as Lord Cottenham held in *Prince Albert* v. *Strange*, why is it not such with reference to name and reputation? We have some illustrations of the exercise by courts of their peculiar powers in cases which have been cited, in principle not unlike this; where the publication of one's letters and the sales of photographic portraits have been enjoined, besides the case of the publication of the catalogue referred to. These decisions are authority for the doctrine that courts will interfere to prevent what are deemed to be violations of personal legal rights, and the only limitation upon the application is that the legal right which is to be protected shall be one cognizable as property, but not necessarily corporeal property. The Fund was a voluntary, unincorporated association; whose object was to erect a statue of Mrs. Schuyler as the "typical philanthropist," and

subscriptions were solicited from the public to create a fund
for that purpose. It was determined by the trial court that
the acts of the defendants "have exposed the name and the
memory of Mrs. Schuyler to adverse comment and public
criticism of a nature peculiarly disagreeable to her relatives,
and have caused disagreeable notoriety, for which they are
in no way responsible." It was determined that "annoyance
and pain have been caused thereby to Mr. Schuyler and to
the immediate relatives of Mrs. Schuyler," to their great distress and injury, by the notoriety incident thereto.

Is Our Interest in Rights or Feelings?

However opinions may differ with respect to the substantial nature of the injury to the feelings of Mrs. Schuyler's
relatives, we have the finding by the trial judge that it was
in fact caused, and we should not say that it was merely
fanciful. The theory of the case, which calls for relief, is not
that of a mere protection to wounded feelings; but the protection of a right which those who represent the deceased
have to her name and memory as a family heritage and which
had not become the public property. Why is that not a legal
and an exclusive interest and why are its possessors not entitled to be protected by the law from a notoriety which
invites public criticism of the memory and reputation of the
deceased relative? And if it be true that there is no known
application at law of the principle, does not that natural
justice with which equity is synonymous require that equity
supply the deficiency, or enlarge the operation of legal principles, and grant the shelter of the law to the name and
memory of the deceased, at the instance of her relatives?

Was Mrs. Schuyler a Public or Private Person?

The evidence does not establish that Mrs. Schuyler was a
public character, nor that she was in such public station,
or so prominent in public works, as to make her name and
memory public property. That she was engaged, throughout

her life, in acts of benevolence and beneficence, may be perfectly true; but she was never a public character and in no just sense can it be said that, because of what she chose to do in the private walks of life, she dedicated her memory to the state or nation as public property. To hold that, by reason of her constant and avowed interest in philanthropical works, unconnected with public station, the right accrued to an association of individuals, strangers to her blood, to erect a statue of her, typifying a human virtue, through contributions solicited from the general public, is, in my judgment, to assert a proposition at war with the moral sense and I believe it to be in violation of the sacred right of privacy; whose mantle should cover not only the person of the individual, but every personal interest which he possesses and is entitled to regard as private, when through no act of his, nor by any peculiar circumstances, has the public acquired any right in them. Unless equity does interfere, the right of privacy will be lost and that will become the property of the public, which, our sentiments and reason and our sense of justice tell us, is the private property of the relatives of the deceased person. That Philip Schuyler is entitled, if any one is, to a remedy, has been heretofore mentioned and it is the determination of the trial court, and that that remedy may be preventive in its character seems to me to be within the reason and principle upon which equity proceeds.

Not Interested in Libel, if Any, by Statue

It is not necessary that the proposed statue of Mrs. Schuyler should be libelous in character. The wrong consists not in that fact, but in the unauthorized acts of the Fund, which will invite adverse comment and public criticism upon the life and character of the deceased, bring her name and memory into more or less unenviable notoriety and inflict upon her immediate relatives and representatives more or less injury in their feelings and their desires for that privacy, which, in their private station of life, they have the right to enjoy.

The threatened offense is of a permanent and continuing nature and, in many senses, differs from cases of mere libelous publications. I think that a case was made out where equity was unfettered in its exercise by any legal principle and where the decree of the court below should be affirmed. ◀

In this short but well reasoned dissent, Judge Gray attempts, like many before and after him, to draw an analogy between property in letters and privacy and to lead from the one into the other.

The reasoning of the majority of the court in the case of Mary Schuyler's statue is still followed today in New York. What Judge Gray was attempting in the Schuyler case went even beyond the Warren-Brandeis argument, and has proved, at least to date, much less successful.

Intangible values assume greater importance as man climbs the cultural ladder. The more the family declines as a social instrument of discipline and unity, the more sentiment and sentimentality seem to accrue to the idea of "family." And we don't mean merely a commercially prescribed show of affection such as Mother's Day or Father's Day. Particularly in the hurly-burly of big-city life do we find deep wells of yearned-for intimacy among men and women who are too often suspect by their more gregarious neighbors if they express their affections in quiet, often secret, ways.

It is natural that Commerce and Press in their tasteless zeal should try to penetrate these private nooks where intimate relations thrive. That being so, the law finds itself called upon to consider new demands for privacy—for a child, a pet, a deceased parent, innumerable other subjects of pride or love.

As a people we suffer from the absence of tradition. Buildings are not proof against wrecking crews long enough for us to love them. And the less we are supported by the continuity of life through tradition, the greater our affection and regard for what represents more than the confined lineaments of our own personalities.

GRAVES, PRIVACY AND PERPETUITY

For most people in our culture, burial is the apogee of personal privacy. Cemeteries and tombstones are public only in the sense that it is rare for a family to possess its own private back-yard burial ground. And still those interesting and intimate gravestones found along the eastern seaboard, dating back to our earliest history, are also part of our public heritage. Recorders of our early history read the stone carvings and regard the early headstones almost as if they were artifacts.

Surely if a body is buried in a plot your family owns, a suit will be justified if it is moved without permission. This in a way is as if someone, uninvited, tampered with the bed in your home. Cases have come into courts for removal of buried bodies, often because of congestion in religiously or privately owned cemeteries. We can find no cases involving tampering with ashes placed in urns at crematories, but such litigation may well have taken place. And in India, where bodies are burned or left for vultures to eat, the feelings—that is, in a sense, the law—must travel a totally different path than in our culture where the cost of birth and death, from baby carriage to coffin, is a mighty burden.

The reason for our reference to this macabre facet of the Right to Be Let Alone is that it points up an untidy bit of the law of privacy—untidy for those who believe that law can be less haphazard than life itself.

In 1856 one Jacob Jacobus bought in the city of Augusta, Georgia, a cemetery plot. The lot, or square as it was called, was paid for and surrounded by a row of brick. In 1856 a

son Harold died and was buried there, and in 1858 Harold's
sister Irene was interred next to Harold. Jacob, the father,
died in 1862, and his wife followed in 1894. Harold's bones
and those of his sister lay undisturbed until 1895. At that
time some officials of the Congregation of the Children of
Israel *without permission* removed the headstones, opened
the caskets of Harold and Irene, exposed the remains to the
view of people(that is, the gravediggers), and reinterred the
bodies in another *part* of the burial grounds. The court said
in its opinion that the other *part* was "obscure"—which
raises the query: What if the new resting-place were more
stylish or had a better view or was more favorable in the eyes
of worshipers or presumably of God? After the Congregation
had sold the original Jacobus plot to another person, who was
subsequently buried there, a lawsuit was begun. Now the
Congregation was in trouble.

A suit was brought by the three living children of Jacob
and his wife Manahn. They claimed they had suffered "chagrin, mortification, insult and injury"—an insult, they said,
of such nature that "money cannot repair it and time cannot
eradicate it." These are human but dogmatic words, for time
does eradicate, as man knows, everything—if you give it
enough time. They asked that the bodies be returned to the
family plot, which meant, of course, that the Congregation
would no doubt face a new lawsuit from the family of the
persons then occupying the space.

The law of corpses is wide and handsome but varied, extending in some cultures even to the need of criminal statutes to penalize necrophilia (sexual relationship with a
corpse). But we need not here be concerned with property
rights or even injured feelings and chagrin. The Congregation could meet the money claim of $250, asked for as
"exemplary damages." Our concern goes to the problem of
who should have the right to sue. If a great-great-grandchild,
living emotionally and deeply in his ancestral past, were to

bring suit, would the court say there is no limit to the valid claim on his emotions over the decades? Against this poser, estimate for yourself how many Americans have died since 1585 (the date of the earliest settlements); how many had headstones; and how few markers remain. . . .

In a previous case that arose in Kentucky, a judge held: "The right of possession of a cemetery plot will continue as long as the cemetery continues to be used."

The gist of the decision in the Jacobus case, on the point of interest to those concerned with privacy, relates to the length of time that injured feelings persist, from generation to generation. For some reason not yet satisfactorily developed by the courts, the feelings hurt by finding a dead father's picture on a cigar band are treated differently from the chagrin occasioned by the removal of the gravestone and remains of a loved one recently deceased.

In *Jacobus* v. *Children of Israel*, as the case is headlined, the decision in 1899 concludes:

▶ If these gravestones were erected by Jacob Jacobus to mark and designate the graves of his children, then if they had been injured or removed during his lifetime, he would have had a right of action against whoever inflicted the injury. While it is not distinctly averred that he did erect them, we think it is a fair presumption that he did, from the fact that he was the father of these infant children, purchased the lot, and had their bodies interred therein. After his death, the *right* to sue for a trespass, that is—defacing or removing the gravestones—was in the heirs of the persons to whose memory the stones were erected, that is—the heirs at law of the children whose remains were interred in the graves. Whether the people bringing this case, or either of them, were in life at the time that either of these children died, does not appear from the petition; but if they were not, the father and mother became heirs at law of the deceased children, and at the time the stones were removed by the defendant the plaintiffs were the heirs at law of both the father and the mother. So the right of action belonging to the heirs at law of these children, for the trespass committed by the removal of the gravestones, was in the plaintiffs at the time this injury was inflicted. This is clear when we consider that a monument or gravestone which designated the grave of a particular person was considered by the early law in the nature of a family heirloom, and for this reason the law, after the death of the person who erected it, gave to the heirs at law of the person in whose memory the stone was set up the right to maintain an action against anyone who injured or removed it. ◄

A GOOD FIVE-CENT CIGAR

Even though commerce has been stopped from playing fast and loose with the names and likenesses of living people, there are still problems concerning the commercial use of the names and features of the dead.

With the advertising fraternity in our society destroying so much of the taste of the marketplace, we must come to grips with the testimonial printed without permission. In its basic terms we have solved the problem either by statute, as in New York State, or by court construction, as in Georgia. But what if you wake up and find your dead mother's or father's face on a package of rat poison? Or suppose you and your family were drys and you find your dead father's picture on a gin bottle?

The kind of world of "privacy in the law" that you desire can be reached only by following the thoughtful philosophy of judges, particularly those with whom you may disagree.

For example, consider yet another case: a dead relative's portrait and name appear on a cigar band without his prior or your present consent—and for all you know, it may be an inferior brand of cigar! Here is how a court in Michigan handled the situation:

ATKINSON v. JOHN E. DOHERTY & Co. (Michigan, 1899)

▶ The late Col. John Atkinson was a well-known lawyer and politician. After his death, a manufacturer of cigars brought out an article that it named the John Atkinson cigar, and sought to put it upon the market under a label bearing that name and a likeness of Col. John Atkinson. The widow of Col. Atkinson filed a bill to restrain this, and upon the hearing the circuit court refused the restraint and the widow has appealed.

WHAT'S IN A NAME?

As a rule, names are received at the hands of parents,—surnames by inheritance, and first names at their will. But this is not an invariable rule, for many names are adopted or assumed by those who bear them. But in neither case is the right to the use of a name exclusive. A disreputable person or criminal may select the name of the most exemplary for his child, or for his horse or dog or monkey. We have never heard this questioned. No reason occurs to us for limiting the right to apply a name, though borne by another person, to animate objects. Why not a John Atkinson wagon, as well as a John Atkinson Jones or horse or dog? Society understands this, and may be depended upon to make proper allowances in such cases; and although each individual member may, in his own case, suffer a feeling of humiliation when his own name or that of some beloved or respected friend is thus used, he will usually, in the case of another, regard it as a trifle. We feel sure that society would not think the less of Col. John Atkinson if cigars bearing his name were sold in the shops. Nor are his friends brought into disrepute thereby. So long as such use does not amount to libel, we are of the opinion that Col. John Atkinson would himself be remediless, were he alive, and the same is true of his friends who survive.

It is urged in this case that the connection of the name with cigars wounds the feelings of the widow, and extreme and improbable illustrations of the possibilities of a rule which should permit the indiscriminate use of names of deceased persons are given. We appreciate the indelicacy of the man who should join the funeral procession of Col. John Atkinson in a carriage bearing the legend, "The Col. John Atkinson cigar," and we can readily understand that it would annoy the friends of the deceased. The sentiment which prompts the feeling of annoyance at such an act is aroused by any aspersion of the dead. It is natural and commendable, as are all recognitions of the proprieties of life; but it does not follow that such an act is an actionable wrong, or that a court will intervene to prevent it, though we are quite sure that the disapproval of society would ordinarily have the latter effect.

Stress is laid upon the fact that the picture of Col. John Atkinson is to be displayed upon this label. It is claimed that a man has no right to print and circulate pictures of another, except by his consent, or where, by reason of his celebrity, the public has an interest in him. This is a proposition of modern origin, and is said to have the support of some cases. We will examine the authorities that have been cited, and such as we have been able to find. ◀

Note here that the Michigan court, in this well-written and cogent opinion, goes even further afield from the protection of privacy than did the New York Court of Appeals in the *Schuyler* case. Not only does the court say that Colonel Atkinson's widow has no legal cause to complain, it indicates also that the colonel himself, were he alive, would have to suffer the fate of the cigar, whether a good smoke or no.

After a brief excursion into past authorities the court turns an icy glance upon the Warren-Brandeis article. Says the judge:

▶ In 1890 prominence was given to this subject by an article in the Harvard Law Review entitled, "The Right to Privacy," in which the writers urge the "right to be let alone," and the necessity for the protection of citizens against invasions of their domestic affairs through the newspaper, the camera, and numerous mechanical devices, "which (they say) threaten to make good the prediction that 'what is whispered in the closet shall be proclaimed from the housetops.' " The right to privacy in a broader sense than before known to the common law is asserted. The article cites a number of cases, some of them relating to pictures, and criticizes the courts for basing their decisions upon property or contract rights. These cases relate to letters, diaries, and other private writings, paintings, sculptures, music, etc. In this connection the case of *Prince Albert* v. *Strange,* is cited, wherein the defendant was restrained from publishing some etchings made by their majesties, the king and queen. The burden of the article is to establish a right of privacy which shall be recognized and protected by the courts, and it is urged that "in such right, as in the right not to be assaulted or beaten (i.e., the right to be let alone)," there inheres the quality of being owned or possessed; and, as that is the distinguishing attribute of property, there may be some propriety in speaking of those rights as property, though it is admitted that they bear little resemblance to what is ordinarily comprehended under that term. Notwithstanding the unanimity of the courts in resting the decisions adverted to upon property rights, the authors assert that "it is in reality not the principle of private property, but that of an inviolate personality."

In April, 1894, a case was decided involving pictures; namely, *Murray* v. *Engraving Co.* (New York). It was decided that:

A parent cannot maintain an action to enjoin the unauthorized publication of the portrait of an infant child, and for damages for injury to his sensibilities caused by the invasion of his child's privacy; for the law takes no cognizance of a sentimental injury, independent of a wrong to person or property. Nor can such suit be maintained upon the ground that the parent had caused the portrait to be painted, and that the publication is an invasion of his proprietary rights, where it appears that he had given the portrait to his wife.

The law may be made uncertain by adopting the opinions of law writers which have not the authority of adjudicated cases behind them. There is perhaps no more dangerous practice than that, unless it be the kindred one of basing a legal principle upon anything but a decided case.

We may search the law books published before 1860 in vain for the assertion of any such right as that claimed, or the denial of the right to publish the truth, for any lawful purpose and in a decent manner, either orally, in writing, or by pictures. What is a picture? It is one of the ways of representing a person or thing. It attempts imitation, rather than description. Pictures antedated letters, and their use was probably one of the earliest methods of communicating thought and perpetuating events. Pantomime and pictures are intelligible to all people, while the same cannot be said of written or even spoken language. This generation owes much to the picture-writing of the ancient Egyptian priests. It is a pleasure to look upon a friend. Crowds travel far to see men of celebrity or notoriety. We learn of places and things from pictures. They impart information to those who cannot or will not read, and many times more rapidly and effectually than written description would do to those who can and will. The picture is today an important extension of alphabets, which for a time largely superseded their use; and, if written language were to be deprived of their aid, literature would receive a serious blow. When it can be used, the picture is a much more satisfactory method than the use of the alphabet alone, of conveying an understanding of material objects, animate and inanimate.

IMPERTINENCE AND THE LAW IN MICHIGAN IN 1899

We are not satisfied that the homes and landscapes are so entirely within the control of owners that one commits an unlawful invasion of the right of privacy in looking upon their beauties, or by sketching or even photographing them, or that one has a right of action either for damages or to restrain the possessor of a camera from taking a snap shot at the passer-by for his own uses. If we admit the impertinence of the act, it must also be admitted that there are many impertinences which are not actionable, and which courts will not restrain. As the right alleged is not a property right, and does not spring from any contract, it must follow that relief must be in an action for damages for a breach of duty upon an actionable wrong, or a suit to prevent a threatened injury. In either case such action must be based upon an act done or threatened which the law looks upon as a wrong and, if the act complained of is one which is not in the law denominated a wrong, there is no legal remedy.

All men are not possessed of the same delicacy of feeling, or the same consideration for the feelings of others. These things depend greatly upon the disposition and education. Some men are sensitive, some brutal. The former will suffer keenly from an act or a word that will not affect the latter. Manifestly, the law cannot make a right of action depend upon the intent of the alleged wrongdoer, or upon the sensitiveness of another. Although injuries to feelings are recognized as a ground for increasing damages, the law has never given a right of action for an injury to feelings merely. Slander and libel are based upon an injury to reputation, not the feelings; and although many offensive things may be said that injure feelings and shock and violate the moral sense, even though they be untruthful, they are not necessarily actionable. To make them so, they must be of such an atrocious character that the law will presume an injury to reputation, or special damage to property interests must be alleged and proved. What becomes of the innumerable cases of ill-natured and perhaps insulting and immoral things that may be said about persons? The answer is that in an enlightened effort to preserve the liberties of men, upon the one hand, and to prevent invasion of their liberties, upon the other, it has been found that a line of demarkation must be drawn, which affords a practical balance and satisfactory test of liability. Mr. Bishop, by his "Diagram of Crime," has made plain the fact that there are many wrongs against the public that are not indictable, because too small for the law to notice. The same is true of private wrongs. Hence, that which would be slanderous if said in the presence of a third person is not actionable if addressed to the object of the remark in private. The law does not discriminate between persons who are sensitive and those who are not, and the brutality of the remark makes no difference. Yet the alleged "right to privacy" is invaded.

The wisdom of the law has been vindicated by experience. This "Law of Privacy" seems to have obtained a foot hold at one time in the history or our jurisprudence,—not by that name, it is true, but in effect. It is evidenced by the old maxim, "The greater the truth, the greater the libel," and the result has been the emphatic expression of public disapproval, by the emancipation of the press, and the establishment of freedom of speech, and the abolition in most of our States of the maxim quoted, by constitutional provisions; the limitation upon the exercise of these rights being the law of slander and libel, whereby the publication of an untruth that can be presumed, or shown to the satisfaction, not of the one who complains, but of others (i.e., an impartial jury), to be injurious, not alone to the feelings, but to the reputation, is actionable. Should it be thought that it is a hard rule that is applied in this case, it is only necessary to call attention to the fact that a ready remedy is to be found in legislation. We are not satisfied, however, that the rule is a hard one, and think that the consensus of opinion must be that the complainant contends for a much harder one. The law does not remedy all evils; it cannot, in the nature of things; and deliberation may well be used in considering the propriety of an innovation such as this case suggests.

We do not wish to be understood as belittling the complaint. We have no reason to doubt the feeling of annoyance alleged. Indeed, we sympathize with it, and marvel at the impertinence that does not respect it. We only say that it is one of the ills that, under the law, cannot be redressed. ◀

Although one may feel frustrated by the court's refusal to stretch a little bit in order to satisfy a complaint with which it is in sympathy, one should not dismiss the court's well-reasoned opinion as being merely hardhearted. The court is quite right in placing privacy and freedom of speech and press in opposition to one another. What you give to the one you take away from the other. As is so often the case, the level at which a balance is struck depends upon the scales that are used. In this case, the court felt angry, but not angry enough to tip the balance in favor of privacy. As we have seen, other courts have felt differently; but rather than consider this opinion to be misanthropic let us turn now to a similar situation in New York. We shall see that Michigan and New York can sometimes be closer together than geography would indicate.

5

The Sad Plight of Abigail

T_{HE} time has come (it is 1902) for us to consider the poignant case of Abigail, a young, innocent girl of breeding with whose tender sensibilities gross liberties were taken. In terms of formal prosaic law, Abigail is remembered fondly as *Roberson* v. *Rochester Folding Box;* but to legal students, scholars, and professional practitioners she is universally known simply as "Abigail," and properly so. Abigail's impact upon the tortuous course of privacy legislation was considerable. Her case touched off the public, the law, the press, the legislature, and had a permanently curtailing and chastizing effect on overzealous economic enterprise and commercial impertinence. It was indeed a pivotal case. Try to think yourself back to 1902. Instantaneous photography was, as one of the judges said, a modern invention. Moreover, our economy of distribution of goods had not begun to use advertising on any national scale such as now saturates our culture.

The facts involved in Abigail Roberson's grievance against the Rochester Folding Box Company and the Franklin Mills

Company were not in dispute. So we suggest that you first
read the facts and then try to decide what your decision
might have been—in 1902. And if your guess proves to be
less than "accurate" (as determined by the court), be re-
lieved, for out of seven judges in the highest court of the
Empire State, the vote was 4 to 3.

The Agreed-Upon Facts of the Case

▶ The Franklin Mills Co. was engaged in a general milling
business and in the manufacture and sale of flour. Without
the knowledge or consent of young Abigail Roberson or her
parents, Franklin Mills Co., knowing that they had no right
or authority so to do, had obtained, printed, sold and circulated about 25,000 lithographic prints, photographs and
likenesses of Abigail. Above the portrait there were printed,
in large plain letters, the words, "Flour of the Family," and
below the portrait in large capital letters, "Franklin Mills
Flour," and in the lower right-hand corner in smaller capital
letters, "Rochester Folding Box Co., Rochester, N.Y.";
upon the same sheet were other advertisements of the flour
of the Franklin Mills Co.; those 25,000 likenesses of Abigail
were conspicuously posted and displayed in stores, ware-
houses, and even in saloons and other public places; they
were seen by friends of Abigail and other people with the
result that she claimed she had been greatly humiliated by
the scoffs and jeers of persons who have recognized her face
and picture on this advertisement and her good name had
been attacked, causing her great distress and suffering both
in body and mind; she was made sick and suffered a severe
nervous shock, was confined to her bed and compelled to
employ a physician. Abigail asked damages in the sum of
$15,000, and she asked that the Flour Company be pre-
vented from making, printing, publishing, circulating, or
using in any manner any likenesses of her.

It will be observed that there is no complaint made that
Abigail was libeled by this publication of her portrait. The

likeness is said to have been a very good one, and one that
her friends and acquaintances were able to recognize; indeed,
her grievance is that a good portrait of her, and, therefore,
one easily recognized, had been used to attract attention
toward the Flour Company advertisement. Such publicity,
which some find agreeable, was to Abigail very distasteful,
and because of the advertiser's impertinence in using her picture without her consent for its own business purposes, she
claimed she had suffered mental distress. Others might have
appreciated the compliment to their beauty implied in the
selection of the picture for such purposes; but it was distasteful to her. ◀

The Highest Court Looks for the Law to Be Applied

The majority of the court stated:

▶ There is no precedent for such an action to be found in
the decisions of this court; indeed the learned judge who
wrote the very able and interesting opinion in the court
below said, while upon the threshold of the discussion of the
question: "It may be said in the first place that the theory
upon which this action is predicated is new, at least in instance if not in principle, and that few precedents can be
found to sustain the claim made by Abigail, if indeed it can
be said that there are any authoritative cases establishing
her right to recover in this action." Nevertheless, the court
below reached the conclusion that Abigail had a good cause
of action against the Flour Company, because it had invaded
what is called a "right of privacy"—in other words, the right
to be let alone. Mention of such a right is not to be found
in Blackstone, Kent or any other of the great commentators
upon the law. Not so far as the learning of counsel or the
courts in this case have been able to discover, does its existence
seem to have been asserted prior to about the year 1890,
when it was presented with attractiveness and no inconsider-

able ability in the Harvard Law Review in an article by Warren and Brandeis entitled, "The Right to Privacy."

The so-called right of privacy is, as the phrase suggests, founded upon the claim that a man has the right to pass through this world, if he wills, without having his picture published, his business enterprises discussed, his succesful experiments written up for the benefit of others, or his eccentricities commented upon either in handbills, circulars, catalogues, periodicals or newspapers, and, necessarily, that the things which may not be written and published of him must not be spoken of him by his neighbors, whether the comment be favorable or otherwise. While most persons would much prefer to have a good likeness of themselves appear in a responsible periodical or leading newspaper rather than upon an advertising card or sheet, the doctrine which the courts are asked to create for this case would apply as well to the one publication as to the other, for the principle which a court is asked to assert in support of a recovery in this action is that the right of privacy exists and is enforceable, and that the publication of that which purports to be a portrait of another person, even if obtained upon the street by an impertinent individual with a camera, will be restrained on the ground that an individual has the right to prevent his features from becoming known to those outside of his circle of friends and acquaintances.

A MASS OF LAWSUITS IF ABIGAIL WINS?

If such a principle be incorporated into the body of the law through the instrumentality of a court, the attempts logically to apply the principle will necessarily result, not only in a vast amount of litigation, but in litigation bordering upon the absurd, for the right of privacy, once established as a legal doctrine, cannot be confined to the restraint of the publication of a likeness but must necessarily embrace as well the publication of a word-picture, a comment upon one's looks, conduct, domestic relations or habits. And were the right of privacy once legally asserted it would necessarily be held to include the same things if spoken instead of printed, for one, as well as the other, invades the right to be absolutely let alone. An insult would certainly be in violation of such a right and with many persons would more seriously wound the feelings than would the publication of their picture. And so we might add to the list of things that are spoken and done day by day which seriously offend the sensibilities of good people to which the principle which Abigail seeks to have imbedded in the doctrine of the law would seem to apply.

Abigail Should Ask the Legislature to Enact a New Law

The legislative body could very well interfere and arbitrarily provide that no one should be permitted for his own selfish purpose to use the picture or the name of another for advertising purposes without his consent. In such event no embarrassment would result to the general body of the law, for the rule would be applicable only to cases provided for by the statute. The courts, however, being without authority to legislate, are required to decide cases upon principle, and so are necessarily embarrassed by precedents created by an extreme, and, therefore, unjustifiable application of an old principle.

It is undoubtedly true that in the early days of England the judges were accustomed to deliver their judgments without regard to principles or precedents and in that way the process of building up the system of law went on, the judge disregarding absolutely many established principles of the common law. In no other way could the system of jurisprudence have been commenced and continued so as to arrive at its present proportions. In their work the judges were guided not only by what they regarded as the eternal principles of absolute right, but also by their individual consciences, but after a time when the period of infancy was passed and an orderly system of equitable principles, doctrines and rules began to be developed out of the increasing mass of precedents, this theory of a personal conscience was abandoned; and "the conscience" came to be regarded, and has so continued to the present day, as a metaphorical term, designating the common standard of civil right and expediency combined, based upon general principles and limited by established doctrines to which the court appeals, and by which it tests the conduct and rights of suitors—a juridical and not a personal conscience.

The importance of observing the spirit of this rule cannot be overestimated, for, while justice in a given case may be worked out by a decision of the court according to the notions of right which govern the individual judge or body of judges comprising the court, the mischief which will finally result may be almost incalculable under our system which makes a decision in one case a precedent for decisions in all future cases which are akin to it in the essential facts.

So in a case like the one before us, which is concededly new to this court, it is important that the court should have in mind the effect upon future litigation and upon the development of the law which would necessarily result from a step so far outside of the beaten paths of law assuming—what I shall attempt to show in a moment—that the right of privacy as a legal doctrine enforceable in equity has not, down to this time, been established by decisions. ◀

It is said of perhaps the most important judge this country ever had, Chief Justice John Marshall, that after listening to argument in a case he would say to his assistant: "Storey, here is my decision. Now find me the precedents to support it." Judges often follow this procedure, but very few of them have as good a batting average as Marshall's. Perhaps the fault is not with the system, but with the players—the judges themselves. Here we see the spokesman for the majority of the judges of the New York Court of Appeals practicing a bit of "decide now, prove later." Having stated in terms that are hard to miss that he really can't find a trace of the

Right of Privacy in the past cases and that, anyway, can you imagine the flood of litigation which the enunciation of such a right would loose on the courts, he now turns majestically to a disclosure of his reasons, much as a magician might explain to his audience (if he so chose) How It Was Done.

THE COURT LOOKS AT THE EARLY CASES

▶ The history of the phrase "right of privacy" in this country seems to have begun in 1890 in a clever article in the Harvard Law Review, in which a number of English cases were analyzed, and, reasoning by analogy, the conclusion was reached that—notwithstanding the unanimity of the courts in resting their decisions upon property rights in cases where publication is prevented by injunction—in reality such prevention was due to the necessity of affording protection to thoughts and sentiments expressed through the medium of writing, printing and the arts, which is like the right not to be assaulted or beaten; in other words, that the principle, actually involved though not always appreciated, was that of an inviolate personality, not that of private property.

The first case is *Prince Albert* v. *Strange*. The queen and the prince, having made etchings and drawings for their own amusements decided to have copies struck off from the etched plates for presentation to friends and for their own use. The workman employed, however, printed some copies on his own account, which afterwards came into the hands of Strange, who purposed exhibiting them, and published a descriptive catalogue. An examination of the opinion of the vice-chancellor discloses that he found two reasons for granting the injunction, namely, that the property rights of Prince Albert had been infringed, and that there was a breach of trust by the workman in retaining some impressions for himself. The opinion contained no hint whatever of a right of privacy separate and distinct from the right of property.

In *Gee* v. *Pritchard* (1818) B attempted to print a private letter written him by A, and he was restrained on the ground that the property of that private letter remained in A, B having it only for the qualified purpose for which it was sent to him, the basis of the decision, therefore, being the idea of A's property in the thing published, as being the produce of his mind, written by him and put into the hands of B for a limited purpose only.

The same judge, Lord Eldon, in *Abernethy* v. *Hutchinson* (1825), also restrained the publication in the "Lancet" of lectures delivered at a hospital by the plaintiff. The court expressed a doubt in that case whether there could be property in lectures which had not been reduced to writing, but granted the injunction on the ground that it was a breach of confidence on the part of a pupil who was admitted to hear the lectures to publish them, inasmuch as they were delivered for the information of the pupils and not for sale and profit by them.

In *Duke of Queensberry* v. *Shebbeare* (1758) the Earl of Clarendon delivered to one Gwynne an original manuscript of his father's, "Lord Clarendon's History." After Gwynne's death his administrator sold it to Shebbeare, and the court, upon the application of the personal representative of Lord Clarendon, restrained its publication on the ground that they had a property right in the manuscript which it was not intended that Gwynne should have the benefit of by multiplying the number of copies in print for profit.

In not one of these cases, therefore, was it the basis of the decision that the defendant could be restrained from performing the act he was doing or threatening to do on the ground that the feelings of the plaintiff would be thereby injured; but, on the contrary, each decision was rested either upon the ground of breach of trust or that plaintiff had a property right in the subject of litigation which the court could protect.

A more recent English case, is more nearly in point and negates the contention that one may restrain an unauthorized publication which is offensive to him—namely, *Dockrell*

v. *Dougall* (1898). In that case the owner of a medicine called "Sallyco" published the following substantially true but unauthorized statement about plaintiff: "Dr. Morgan Dockrell, physician to St. John's Hospital, London, is prescribing Sallyco as an habitual drink. Dr. Dockrell says nothing has done his gout so much good." In the course of the opinion the court said, in effect, that an injunction should not be granted in every such case where it can be shown that the use of one's name is unauthorized and is calculated to injure him in his profession, and stated the proper rule to be that "In order that one may be restrained from using another's name the use of it must be such as to injure the person's reputation or property."

In the Murray case, in 1894, it is held that a parent cannot maintain an action to prevent an unauthorized publication of the portrait of an infant child, and for damages for injuries to his sensibilities caused by the invasion of his child's privacy, because "the law takes no cognizance of a sentimental injury, independent of a wrong to person or property."

PUBLIC AND PRIVATE CHARACTERS

Outside of the State of New York the question seems to have been presented in two other cases in this country. The Corliss case (1894) was an action to prevent the publication of the biography and picture of Mr. Corliss. The learned court, although deciding against Mr. Corliss for other reasons, expressed the opinion that a private individual has the right to be protected from the publication of his portrait in any form. This suggestion merits discussion and an examination of that which it promulgates as doctrine discloses what we deem a fatal objection to the establishment of a rule of privacy. The learned judge says: "I believe the law to be that a private individual has a right to be protected in the representation of his portrait in any form; that this is a property as well as a personal right, and that it belongs to the same class of rights which forbids the reproduction of a private manuscript or painting, or the publication of private letters, or of oral lectures delivered by a teacher to his class, or the revelation of the contents of a merchant's book by a clerk. . . . But, while the right of a private individual to prohibit the reproduction of his picture or photograph should be recognized and enforced, this right may be surrendered or dedicated to the public by the act of the individual, just the same as a private manuscript, book or painting becomes (when not protected by copyright) public property by the act of publication. The distinction in the case of a picture or photograph lies, it seems to me, between public and private characters. A private individual should be protected against the publication of any portrait of himself, but where an individual becomes a public character the case is different. A statesman, author, artist or inventor, who asks for and desires public recognition, may be said to have surrendered his right to the public."

This distinction between public and private characters cannot possibly be drawn. On what principle does an author or artist forfeit his right of privacy and a great orator, a great preacher, or a great advocate retain his? Who can draw a line of demarcation between public characters and private characters, let that line be as wavering and irregular as you please? In the very case then before the judge, what had Mr. Corliss done by which he surrendered his right of privacy? In what respect did he by his inventions "ask for and desire public recognition" any more than a banker or merchant who prosecutes his calling? Or is the right of privacy the possession of mediocrity alone, which a person forfeits by giving rein to his ability, spurs to his industry or grandeur to his character? A lady may pass her life in domestic privacy when, by some act of heroism or self-sacrifice, her name and fame fill the public ear. Is she to forfeit by her good deed the right of privacy she previously possessed? These considerations suggest the answer we would make to the position of the learned judge and at the same time serve to make more clear what we have elsewhere attempted to point out, namely, the absolute impossibility of dealing with this subject save by legislative enactment, by which may be drawn arbitrary distinctions which no court would promulgate as a part of general jurisprudence.

I do not say that, even under the existing law, in every case of the character of the one before us, or indeed in this case, a party whose likeness is circulated against his will is without remedy. By section 245 of the New York Penal Code any *malicious* publication by picture, effigy or sign which exposes a person to contempt, ridicule or obloquy is a libel, and it would constitute such at common law. Malicious in this definition means simply intentional and willful. There are many articles, especially of medicine, whose character is such that using the picture of a person, particularly that of a woman, in connection with the advertisement of those articles might justly be found by a jury to cast ridicule or obloquy on the person whose picture was thus published. The manner or posture in which the person is portrayed might readily have a like effect. In such cases both a civil action and a criminal prosecution could be maintained. But there is no allegation in the complaint before us that this was the tendency of the publication complained of, and the absence of such an allegation is fatal to the maintenance of the action, treating it as one of libel.

The judgment of the lower court in favor of Abigail Roberson should be reversed. ◀

So said the majority of the judges of the New York Court of Appeals. But, as with most legal (and human) problems, there is reason and subtle discourse on both sides. And even judges, sitting together on the same bench, hearing the same arguments of learned counsel, and researching the same questions of law, may differ. It is not surprising, therefore, to note that cases are often won or lost by the thin margin of a judicial whisper. So it was with Abigail's case. Here, now, is the conflicting opinion of the dissenting minority, speaking through one of its members:

▶ That the individual has a right to privacy, which he can enforce and which the law will protect against the invasion of, is a proposition which is not opposed by any decision in this court and which, in my opinion, is within the field of accepted legal principles. In the present case, we may not say that Abigail's complaint is fanciful, or that her alleged injury is, purely, a sentimental one. Her objection to acts of the Flour Company is not one born of caprice; nor is it based upon its act being merely "distasteful" to her. We are bound to assume, and I find no difficulty in doing so, that the conspicuous display of her likeness, in various public places, has so humiliated her by the notoriety and by the public comments it has provoked, as to cause her distress and suffering, in body and in mind, and to confine her to her bed with illness.

I am not of the opinion that the gravity of the injury need be such as to be capable of being estimated by money damages. If the right of privacy exists I think that relief, preventing the continuance of its invasion by the Flour Company, will not depend upon Abigail's ability to prove substantial pecuniary damages and, if the court finds the Flour Company acted without justification and for selfish gain and purpose, and in a way as is reasonably calculated to wound the feelings and to subject Abigail to the ridicule, or to the contempt of others; that her right to the relief will follow; without considering how far her sufferings may be measurable by a pecuniary standard.

WHY NOT A RIGHT OF PRIVACY?

The right of privacy, or the right of the individual to be let alone is a personal right, which is not without judicial recognition. It is the complement of the right to the immunity of one's person. The individual has always been entitled to be protected in the exclusive use and enjoyment of that which is his own. The common law regarded his person and property as inviolate, and he has the absolute right to be let alone. The principle is fundamental and

essential in organized society that every one, in exercising
a personal right and in the use of his property, shall respect
the rights and properties of others. He must so conduct himself, in the enjoyment of the rights and privileges which
belong to him as a member of society, so that he shall prejudice no one in the possession and enjoyment of those which
are exclusively his. When, as here, there is an alleged invasion of some personal right, or privilege, the absence of exact
precedent and the fact that early commentators upon the
common law have no discussion upon the subject are of no
material importance in awarding equitable relief.

TIME MARCHES ON—WHY NOT THE LAW?

That the exercise of the preventive power of a court is
demanded in a novel case, is not a fatal objection. In the
social evolution, with the march of the arts and sciences and
in the resultant effects upon organized society, it is quite
intelligible that new conditions must arise in personal relations, which the rules of the common law, cast in the rigid
mould of an earlier social status, were not designed to meet.
It would be a reproach to law if it were powerless to extend
the application of the principles of law, or of natural justice,
in remedying a wrong, which, in the progress of civilization,
has been made possible as the result of new social, or commercial conditions.

As I have suggested, that the exercise of this peculiar
preventive power of a court is not found in some precisely
analogous case, furnishes no valid objection, at all, to the
action by a court, if the particular circumstances of the case
show the performance, or the threatened performance of an
act which is wrongful, because it is invasion, in some novel
form, of another's right to something as to which the law
provides no adequate remedy. It would be a justifiable exercise of power, whether the principles of interference be
rested upon analogy to some established common-law principle, or whether it is one of natural justice. In an article in
the Harvard Law Review, of December 15, 1890, which

contains an impressive argument upon the subject of the "right of privacy," it was well said by the authors "that the individual shall have full protection in person and in property is a principle as old as the common law; but it has been found necessary from time to time to define anew the exact nature and extent of such protection.* * * The right to life has come to mean the right to enjoy life—the right to be let alone; the right to liberty secures the exercise of extensive civil privileges; and the term 'property' has grown to comprise every form of possession—intangible, as well as tangible."

Instantaneous Photography and the Law

Instantaneous photography is a modern invention and affords the means of securing a portraiture of an individual's face and form. Although a species of aggression, I concede it to be an irremediable and irrepressible feature of the social evolution. But, if it is to be permitted that the portraiture may be put to commercial, or other, uses for gain, by the publication of prints therefrom, then an act of invasion of the individual's privacy results, possibly more formidable and more painful in its consequences, than an actual bodily assault might be. Security of person is as necessary as the security of property; and for that complete personal security, which will result in the peaceful and wholesome enjoyment of one's privileges as a member of society, there should be afforded protection, not only against the scandalous portraiture and display of one's features and person, but against the display and use thereof for another's commercial purposes or gain. The proposition is, to me, an inconceivable one that these defendants may, unauthorizedly, use the likeness of this young woman upon their advertisement, as a method of attracting widespread public attention to their wares, and that she must submit to the mortifying notoriety, without right to invoke the exercise of the preventive power of a court of equity.

Such a view, as it seems to me, must have been unduly

influenced by a failure to find precedents in analogous cases, or some declaration by the great commentators upon the law of a common-law principle which would, precisely, apply to and govern the action; without taking into consideration that, in the existing state of society, new conditions affecting the relations of persons demand the broader extension of those legal principles, which underlie the immunity of one's person from attack. ◀

Having taken judicial notice of the fact that times had changed, a thought to which the majority had perhaps given too little consideration, the writer for the minority now attempts to draw a parallel between the early cases dealing with "property" of an inorganic nature and the "property" in Abigail's face—just the kind of distinction that would have made Warren and Brandeis smile with satisfaction:

▶ I think that the majority's view is unduly restricted too, by a search for some property, which has been invaded by the defendant's acts. Property is not, necessarily, the thing itself, which is owned; it is the right of the owner in relation to it. The right to be protected in one's possession of a thing, or in one's privileges, belonging to him as an individual, or secured to him as a member of the commonwealth, is property, and as such entitled to the protection of the law. The protective power of the law is not exercised upon the tangible thing, but upon the right to enjoy it; and, so, it is called forth for the protection of the right to that which is one's exclusive possession, as a property right. It seems to me that the principle, which is applicable, is analogous to that upon which courts have interfered to protect the right of privacy, in cases of private writings, or of other unpublished products of the mind. The writer, or the lecturer, has been protected in his right to a literary property in a letter, or a lecture, against its unauthorized publication; because it is property, to which the right of privacy attaches.

I think that this young woman has the same property in the right to be protected against the use of her face for the Flour Company's commercial purposes, as she would have, if they were publishing her literary compositions. The right would be conceded, if she had sat for her photograph; but if her face, or her portraiture, has a value, the value is hers exclusively; until the use be granted away to the public. Any other principle of decision, in my opinion, is as repugnant to law as it is shocking to reason.

It would be, in my opinion, an extraordinary view which, while conceding the right of a person to be protected against the unauthorized circulation of an unpublished lecture, letter, drawing, or other ideal property, yet, would deny the same protection to a person, whose portrait was unauthorizedly obtained, and made use of, for commercial purposes. The injury to the plaintiff is irreparable; because she cannot be wholly compensated in damages for the various consequences entailed by defendants' acts. The only complete relief is an order restraining their continuance. Whether, as incidental to that relief, she should be able to recover only nominal damages is not material; for the issuance of the restraining order does not, in such a case, depend upon the amount of the damages in dollars and cents.

A careful consideration of the question presented upon this appeal leads me to the conclusion that the judgment of the lower court should be followed and the Flour Company directed to stop using Abigail's picture. ◀

This was, alas for Abigail, only the opinion of a minority of the learned judges. The majority, as we have seen, had decided otherwise. So, despite the plea of the minority, Abigail lost and the advertisers of all commodities were, for the time being, given a green light to use anyone's name and picture to market their wares, at least in New York.

Abigail, however, was not the only one who had suffered. There had been, it seems, a series of similar outrages about that time and the *New York Times* decided something should be done. Nor did it make any bones about *what* should be done. In the process, as you will see, the *Times,* on August 23, 1902, took the author of the majority decision briskly to task:

THE RIGHT OF PRIVACY

▶ Several glaring illustrations have of late been furnished of the amazing opinion of Judge Parker of the Court of Appeals of this State, that the right to privacy is not a right which in the State of New York anybody is bound to respect, or which the courts will lend their aid to enforce. We happen to know that that decision excited as much amazement among lawyers and jurists as among the promiscuous lay public.

The present President of the United States has been so much annoyed by photographers who have attended his down-sittings and his uprisings and spied out all his ways, for the purpose of making permanent pictorial record of the same, that it is reported that only his respect for the dignity of his office has upon one or two occasions prevented him from subjecting the impertinent offender to the appropriate remedy, which is all that the Court of Appeals has left, of personal chastisement.

Mr. J. PIERPONT MORGAN, we read, was so beset by "Kodakers" lying in wait to catch his emergence from his office on the day of his return from Europe that he was actually held a prisoner for some time.

Both the President of the United States and so very leading a figure in the industrial and financial world as Mr. MORGAN are necessarily public characters. Moreover, they are reasonably thick-skinned citizens who do not partake the characteristics of the shrinking violet. When they revolt from the continuous ordeal of the camera, it is shown that there is something very irritating to normal nerves in chronic "exposure." But take the case of that young woman in Newport whose portrait was flaunted in all the illustrated newspapers for no other reason than that she had at one time been betrothed to a young gentleman who committed suicide in circumstances necessarily very painful and horrible to her, and rendered far more so by this wanton invasion of her privacy and her grief. If that young woman had happened to be the daughter of Judge PARKER, we are of the opinion that the incident might have induced his Honor to reconsider with some care the decision that no private person had any rights which the purveyors of publicity were bound to respect.

In this series of events we can see political evolution at work. We can see the effect of public opinion upon law and institutions in the making. For all these things appeal to the decent and unsophisticated human mind as outrages. And the highest legal authority in the greatest State in the Union assures us that they are outrages for which the law provides no remedy. So much the worse for the law, say all the decent people. If there be, as Judge PARKER says there is, no law now to cover these savage and horrible practices, practices incompatible with the claims of the community in which they are allowed to be committed with impunity to be called a civilized community, then the decent people will say that it is high time that there were such a law. In some way they will see to it that there is such a law, and the Court of Appeals will not be left to shadowy analogies and precedents for its conclusion that these outrages are legally unpreventible and unpunishable. It will have the advantage of a clear and explicit statute to construe. ◀

The first effect of this editorial was, surprisingly, an article in the *Columbia Law Review*, late in the same year, by Judge O'Brien, one of the four who had voted against Abigail. That the article was the direct result of the *Times* editorial was obvious enough; it began by reprinting the editorial *in toto*. It then proceeded to point out the obvious irony of a newspaper championing, of all things, the Right of Privacy!

"It is only a short time," said Judge O'Brien, "since a bill was introduced into the Senate of this state and passed for the very purpose of prohibiting the use of pictures and photographs without the consent of the person represented. The opposition of the press not only defeated the bill, but went so far as to demand the retirement of its author to private life."

But as for "the right of privacy," the judge adds, while it "represents an attractive idea to the moralist and social reformer . . . to the lawmaker who seeks to embody the right in a statute the subject is surrounded with some serious difficulties. It is quite impossible to define with anything like precision what the right of privacy is or what its limitations are, if any; how or when the right is invaded or infringed, or what remedy can be applied if any."

The New York State Legislature, however, felt differently. On the basis of the public disapproval of the *Roberson* decision, triggered and catalyzed by the *Times*, the legislators passed in the following year an act that made it illegal to do what had been done to Abigail. It was a privacy law, all right—but a limited one, that prevented only the unauthorized use of names and photographs.

6

New York and Georgia Disagree

THE Privacy Law was included as part of the New York Civil Rights Law in 1903. The statute created a Right of Privacy that the courts had to recognize. This law, which remains virtually unchanged, reads as follows:

▶ 50. *Right of Privacy.*
A person, firm or corporation that uses for advertising purposes, or for the purposes of trade, the name, portrait or picture of any living person without having first obtained the written consent of such person, or if a minor of his parent or guardian, is guilty of a misdemeanor. ◀

The second section referred also to privacy in relation to advertising purposes or purposes of trade, but indicated that a remedy other than jail or a fine, as provided in Section 50, was needed. So the legislature, also in 1903, said that the abused person could sue for money damages or sue to stop the use of the name, portrait, or picture—that is, ask a court for an injunction directed against the invader of his privacy. In fact, he could use both the civil and criminal remedies:

▶ 51. *Action for injunction and for damages.*

Any person whose name, portrait or picture is used within this state for advertising purposes or for the purposes of trade without the written consent first obtained as above provided may maintain an equitable action in the Supreme Court of this state against the person, firm or corporation so using his name, portrait or picture, to prevent and restrain the use thereof; and may also sue and recover damages for any injuries sustained by reason of such use and if the defendant shall have knowingly used such person's name, portrait or picture in such manner as is forbidden or declared to be unlawful by the last section (section 50), the jury, in its discretion, may award exemplary damages. ◀

Thus the Abigails of the future were safe—as far as the privacy of their name and face was concerned, anyway—and provided they lived in New York.

In 1911 a special amendment was passed to protect those who "practice the profession of photography." This amendment was added to Section 51, and reads as follows:

▶ But nothing contained in this act shall be so construed as to prevent any person, firm or corporation, practicing the profession of photography, from exhibiting in or about his or its establishment specimens of the work of such establishment, unless the same is continued by such person, firm or corporation after written notice objecting thereto has been given by the person portrayed. ◀

This section was to answer the question: How does one choose a photographer without looking at some samples of his previous jobs?

By 1921 a further change was needed. This related to the name, portrait, or picture of a manufacturer himself—or even a dealer. New York also thought it wise to recognize the abandonment by an author or composer or artist of his complete anonymity when he put his created wares on the market. This change was added also as an addition to Section 51, and goes like this:

▶ Nothing contained in this act shall be so construed as to prevent any person, firm or corporation from using the name, portrait or picture of any manufacturer or dealer in connection with the goods, wares and merchandise manufactured, produced or dealt in by him which he has sold or disposed of with such name, portrait or picture used in connection therewith; or from using the name, portrait or picture of any author, composer or artist in connection with his literary, musical or artistic productions which he has sold or disposed of with such name, portrait or picture used in connection therewith. ◀

So the legislature acted; but, as with most lawmaking, the passing of a law does not necessarily put an end to the problems that instigated it. Indeed, the passing of a law often marks the beginning of new problems.

The New York Court of Appeals is a highly respected judicial body, and the decision of a majority of its judges in the *Roberson* case remained an imposing, if not persuasive, argument against the existence of a Right of Privacy. There are, however, other courts perhaps less august but equally important, and other judges perhaps less well paid but equally scholarly. Very often in our happily varied separate state cultures the most helpful reflective judicial wisdom arises not in big cities but in the grass roots of moderate-sized communities. Perhaps the judicial mind is more inventive, in historic terms, in the communities where the

pace of life is on the moderate side and where time permits
for backward glances to appraise steps of forward mood.

While New York (judicially but nonetheless coldly) says
to beautiful Miss Roberson, "Sorry, but the court can't write
a new law; you'll have to wait for your elected representatives in the legislature to define your new rights and remedies," it is heartwarming to find another state in our federal
system relating history and law and life to give relief to a
citizen who simply wants to be let alone.

Abigail's drama now repeats itself, but with variations.
The time is 1904. The place is Georgia. An established artist
is the complainant. In lieu of a flour company and a box
manufacturer, we have an insurance company and a photographer. And we have advertisements in a newspaper
rather than posters. Otherwise, however, the plot is the
same.

Fourteen years after Warren and Brandeis wrote their
article, a judge of a city court in Atlanta wrote what we
believe to be one of the most comprehensive and scholarly
reviews of the problem of privacy up to that time. The
case: *Pavesich* v. *New England Life Insurance Co.* The
question: Is there a Right of Privacy as a matter of court-
made law, or must Pavesich be brushed aside until the legislature of Georgia enacts a law that creates a Right of Privacy
—as eventually had to be done in New York?

Paolo Pavesich brought an action against the New England Mutual Life Insurance Company, Thomas B. Lumpkin,
its general agent, and J. Q. Adams, a photographer. The
allegations of the petition were as follows:

▶ In an issue of the Atlanta Constitution, a newspaper published in the City of Atlanta, there appeared a likeness of
Pavesich, which would be easily recognized by his friends and
acquaintances, placed by the side of the likeness of an ill-
dressed and sickly looking person. Above the likeness of

Pavesich were the words, "Do it now. The man who did."
Above the likeness of the other person were the words, "Do
it while you can. The man who didn't." Below the two pictures were the words, "Their two pictures tell their own
story." Under Pavesich's picture the following appeared:
"In my healthy and productive period of life I bought insurance in the New England Mutual Life Insurance Co., of
Boston, Mass., and to-day my family is protected and I am
drawing an annual dividend on my paid-up policies." Under
the other person's picture was a statement to the effect that
he had not taken out insurance, and now realized his mistake.
The statements were signed, "Thomas B. Lumpkin, General
Agent." The picture was made from the negative without
Pavesich's consent, at the request of the insurance company,
through its agent Lumpkin. Paolo Pavesich was an artist by
profession, and the publication was peculiarly offensive to
him. The statement attributed to him in the publication was
false and malicious. He never made any such statement and
never had a policy of life insurance with that insurance company. The publication was malicious and tended to bring
him into ridicule before the world, and especially with his
friends and acquaintances who knew that he had no policy
in that company. The publication was a trespass upon
Pavesich's right of privacy, and was caused by breach of
confidence and trust reposed in Adams, the photographer. ◀

Here is the court's opinion:

▶ We will first deal with the claim of damages on account of
an alleged violation of Pavesich's right of privacy. The question, therefore, to be determined is whether an individual has
a right of privacy which he can enforce and which the courts
will protect against invasion. It is to be conceded that prior
to 1890 every adjudicated case, both in this country and
England, which might be said to have involved a right of
privacy, was not based upon the existence of such right, but

was founded upon a supposed right of property, or a breach of trust or confidence, or the like; and that therefore a claim to a right of privacy, independent of a property or contractual right or some right of a similar nature, had, up to that time never been recognized in terms in any decision.

LEGAL PRECEDENT VERSUS PUBLIC GOOD

The entire absence for a long period of time, even for centuries, of a precedent for an asserted right should have the effect to cause the courts to proceed with caution before recognizing the right, for fear that they may thereby invade the province of the lawmaking power; but such absence, even for all time, is not conclusive of the question as to the existence of the right. The novelty of the complaint is no objection when an injury cognizable by law is shown to have been inflicted on the plaintiff. In such a case although there be no precedent, the common law will judge according to the law of nature and the public good. Where the case is new in principle, the courts have no authority to give a remedy, no matter how great the grievance; but where the case is only new in instance, and the sole question is upon the application of a recognized principle to a new case, it will be just as competent to courts of justice to apply the principle to any case that may arise two centuries hence as it was two centuries ago.

MAN VERSUS SOCIETY

The individual surrenders to society many rights and privileges which he would be free to exercise in a state of nature, in exchange for the benefits which he receives as a member of society. But he is not presumed to surrender all those rights, and the public has no more right, without his consent, to invade the domain of those rights which it is necessarily to be presumed he has reserved than he has to violate the valid regulations of the organized government under which he lives. The right of privacy has its foundation in the instincts of nature. It is recognized intuitively, consciousness being the witness that can be called to establish its existence. Any person whose intellect is in a normal condition recognizes at once that as to each individual member of society there are matters private and there are matters public so far as the individual is concerned. Each individual as instinctively resents any encroachment by the public upon his rights which are of a private nature as he does the withdrawal of those of his rights which are of a public nature. A right of privacy in matters purely private is therefore derived from natural law. This idea is embraced in the Roman's conception of justice, which was not simply the external legality of acts, but the accord of external acts with the precepts of the law prompted by internal impulse and free volition. It may be said to arise out of those laws sometimes characterized as immutable, because they are natural, and so just at all times, and in all places, that no authority can either change or abolish them. It is one of those rights referred to by some law-writers as absolute; such as would belong to their persons merely in a state of nature, and which every man is entitled to enjoy, whether out of society or in it.

Among the absolute rights referred to by the commentator just cited is the right of personal security and the right of personal liberty. In the first is embraced a person's right to a legal and uninterrupted enjoyment of his life, his limbs, his body, his health, and his reputation and in the second is embraced the power of locomotion, of changing situation, or moving one's person to whatsoever place one's own inclination may direct, without imprisonment or restraint, unless by due court of law. While neither Sir William Blackstone nor any of the other writers on the principles of the common law have referred in terms to the right of privacy, the illustrations given by them as to what would be a violation of the absolute rights of individuals are not to be taken as exhaustive, but the language should be allowed to include any instance of a violation of such rights which is clearly within the true meaning and intent of the words used to declare the principle. When the law guarantees to one the right to the enjoyment of his life, it gives to him something more than the mere right to breathe and exist. While of course the most flagrant violation of this right would be deprivation of life, yet life itself may be spared and the enjoyment of life entirely destroyed.

WHAT LIBERTY MEANS

An individual has a right to enjoy life in any way that may be most agreeable and pleasant to him, according to his temperament and nature, provided that in such enjoyment he does not invade the rights of his neighbor or violate public law or policy. The right of personal security is not fully accorded by allowing an individual to go through his life in possession of all of his members and his body unmarred; nor is his right to personal liberty fully accorded by merely allowing him to remain out of jail or free from other physical restraints. The liberty which he derives from natural law, and which is recognized by municipal law, embraces far more than freedom from physical restraint. The term liberty is not to be so dwarfed, but is deemed to embrace the right of a man to be free in the enjoyment of the faculties with which he has been endowed by his Creator, subject only to such restraints as are necessary for the common welfare. Liberty, in its broad sense, as understood in this country, means the right, not only of freedom from servitude, imprisonment, or restraint, but the right of one to use his faculties in all lawful ways, to live and work where he will, to earn his livelihood in any lawful calling, and to pursue any lawful trade or avocation.

Liberty includes the right to live as one will, so long as that will does not interfere with the rights of another or of the public. One may desire to live a life of seclusion; another may desire to live a life of publicity; still another may wish to live a life of privacy as to certain matters and of publicity as to others. One may wish to live a life of toil where his work is of a nature that keeps him constantly before the public gaze; while another may wish to live a life of research and contemplation, only moving before the public at such times and under such circumstances as may be necessary to his actual existence. Each is entitled to a liberty of choice as to his manner of life, and neither an individual nor the public has a right to arbitrarily take away from him his liberty.

All will admit that the individual who desires to live a life of seclusion cannot be compelled, against his consent to exhibit his person in any public place, unless such exhibition is demanded by the law of the land. He may be required to come from his place of seclusion to perform public duties,— to serve as a juror and to testify as a witness, and the like; but when the public duty is once performed, if he exercises his liberty to go again into seclusion, no one can deny him the right. One who desires to live a life of partial seclusion has a right to choose the times, places, and manner in which and at which he will submit himself to the public gaze. Subject to the limitation above referred to, the body of a person cannot be put on exhibition at any time or at any place without his consent. The right of one to exhibit himself to the public at all proper times, in all proper places, and in a proper manner is embraced within the right of personal liberty. The right to withdraw from the public gaze at such times as a person may see fit, when his presence in public is not demanded by any rule of law is also embraced within the right of personal liberty. Publicity in one instance and privacy in the other is each guaranteed. If personal liberty embraces the right of publicity, it no less embraces the correlative right of privacy; and this is no new idea in Georgia law. The right of privacy within certain limits is a right derived from natural law, recognized by the principles of municipal law, and guaranteed to persons in this State by the constitutions of the United States and of the State of Georgia, in those provisions which declare that no person shall be deprived of liberty except by due process of law. ◀

The concept of "natural law," something absolute and immutable, handed down to us by a "brooding omnipresence in the sky" is no longer in vogue in legal circles or, for that matter, in modern nonlegal circles. It is therefore with a certain amount of condescension that we listen to the Georgia court make its point. However, since we have derived most of our liberties from certain eighteenth century gentlemen who believed firmly in natural law, we must realize that sound principles of jurisprudence (and just plain prudence) have often been served up under that no longer palatable label of "natural law." So when we evaluate this opinion, let's look beyond the characterizations to the substance. When we do, we see that this fellow is a pretty sound and farsighted thinker. Perhaps sensing our reserve, however, the court now turns from philosophy to history, with a few well-chosen words about Roman law:

▶ While in reaching the conclusion just stated we have been deprived of the benefit of the light that would be shed on the question by decided cases and utterances of law-writers directly dealing with the matter, we have been aided by many side-lights in the law. The ancient law also recognized that a person had a legal right "to be let alone," so long as he was not interfering with the rights of other individuals or of the public. This idea has been carried into the common law, and appears from time to time in various places, a conspicuous instance being in the case of private nuisances resulting from noise which interferes with one's enjoyment of his home, and this too where the noise is the result of the carrying on of a lawful occupation. Even in such cases where the noise is unnecessary, or is made at such times that one would have a right to quiet, the courts have interfered in behalf of the person complaining. It is true that these cases are generally based upon the ground that the noise is an invasion of a property right, but there is really no injury to the property, and the gist of the wrong is that the individual is disturbed in his right to have quiet.

Under the Roman law, to enter a man's house against his

will, even to serve a summons, was regarded as an invasion of his privacy. This conception is the foundation of the common-law maxim that every man's house is his castle. Where this maxim was applied, one of the points resolved was that the house of every one is to him as his castle and fortress, as well for his defence against injury and violence as for his repose. Eavesdroppers, or such as listen under walls or windows or the eaves of a house to hearken after discourse, and there-upon to frame slanderous and mischievous tales, were a nuisance at common law and indictable, and were required, in the discretion of the court, to find people to guaranty their good behavior. A common scold was at common law indictable as a public nuisance to her neighborhood. And the reason for the punishment of such a character was not the protection of any property right of her neighbors, but the fact that her conduct was a disturbance of their right to *quiet* and *repose*, the offense being complete even when the party indicted committed it upon her own premises. In-stances might be multiplied where the common law has both tacitly and expressly recognized the right of an individual to repose and privacy. ◀

But this court, like Warren and Brandeis before it, is more interested in nudging the future than in nurturing the past. And so it leaves ancient law and precedents and moves on to contest the "parade of horribles" the majority in the *Roberson* case claimed would result from judicial recogni-tion of a Right of Privacy. In so doing, it embarks upon an adventure in jurisprudence that surveys both the limits and the balances of a newly created right—and gives us all an example of first-rate legal trailblazing. The *Roberson* major-ity claimed that to recognize a right of privacy would be to create a right without limits, to open the floodgate of un-warranted litigation, and to encroach upon the freedom of speech and press. Here is the Georgia court's answer to this claim:

▶ The right of privacy, however, like every other right that rests in the individual, may be waived by him. The effect of his waiver will not be such as to bring before the public those matters of a purely private nature which express law or public policy demands shall be kept private. The most striking illustration of a waiver is where one either seeks or allows himself to be presented as a candidate for public office. He thereby waives any right to restrain or impede the public in any proper investigation into the conduct of his private life which may throw light upon his qualifications for the office or the advisability of imposing upon him the public trust which the office carries. But even in this case the waiver does not extend into those matters and transactions of private life which are wholly foreign and can throw no light whatever upon the question as to his competency for the office or the propriety of bestowing it upon him. One who holds public office makes a waiver of a similar character, that is, that his life may be subjected at all times to the closest scrutiny in order to determine whether the rights of the public are safe in his hands; but beyond this the waiver does not extend. So it is in reference to those belonging to the learned professions, who by their calling place themselves before the public and thereby consent that their private lives may be scrutinized for the purpose of determining whether it is to the interest of those whose patronage they seek to place their interests in their hands. In short, any person who engages in any pursuit or occupation or calling which calls for the approval or patronage of the public submits his private life to examination by those to whom he addresses his call, to any extent that may be necessary to determine whether it is wise and proper and expedient to accord him the approval or patronage which he seeks.

A Liberty of Privacy

It may be said that to establish a liberty of privacy would involve in numerous cases the perplexing question to determine where this liberty ended and the rights of others and of the public began. This affords no reason for not recognizing the liberty of privacy and giving to the person aggrieved legal redress against the wrong-doer in a case where it is clearly shown that a legal wrong has been done. It may be that there will arise many cases which lie near the border line which marks the right of privacy on the one hand and the right of another individual or of the public on the other. But this is true in regard to numerous other rights which the law recognizes as resting in the individual. In regard to cases that may arise under the right of privacy, as in cases that arise under other rights where the line of demarcation is to be determined, the safeguard of the individual on the one hand and of the public on the other is the wisdom and integrity of the judiciary. Each person has a liberty of privacy, and every other person has as against him liberty in reference to other matters, and the line where these liberties impinge upon each other may in a given case be hard to define; but that such a case may arise can afford no more reason for denying to one his liberty of privacy than it would to deny to another his liberty, whatever it may be. The courts may proceed in cases involving the violation of a right of privacy as in other cases of a similar nature, and the juries may in the same manner proceed to a determination of those questions which the law requires to be submitted for their consideration. With honest and fearless trial judges to pass in the first instance upon the question of law as to the existence of the right in each case, whose decisions are subject to review by the court of last resort, and with fair and impartial juries to pass upon the questions of fact involved and assess the damages in the event of a recovery, whose verdict is, under our law, in all cases subject to supervision and scrutiny by the trial judge, who may, within the limits of a legal discretion, control their findings, there need be no more fear that the right of privacy will be the occasion of unjustifiable litigation, oppression, or wrong than that the existence of many other rights in the law would bring about such results.

The liberty of privacy exists, has been recognized by the

law, and is entitled to continual recognition. But it must be kept within its proper limits, and its exercise must be made to accord with the right of those who have other liberties, as well as the rights of any person who may be properly interested in the matters which are claimed to be of purely private concern. Publicity in many cases is absolutely essential to the welfare of the public. Privacy in other matters is not only essential to the welfare of the individual, but also to the well-being of society. The law stamping the unbreakable seal of privacy upon communications between husband and wife, attorney and client, and similar provisions of the law, is a recognition, not only of the right of privacy, but that for the public good some matters of private concern are not to be made public even with the consent of those interested. It therefore follows from what has been said that a violation of the right of privacy is a direct invasion of a legal right of the individual.

Free Speech versus the Right to Be Let Alone

The stumbling block which many have encountered in the way of a recognition of the existence of a right of privacy has been that the recognition of such right would inevitably tend to curtail the liberty of speech and of the press. The right to speak and the right of privacy have been coexistent. Each is a natural right, each exists, and each must be recognized and enforced with due respect for the other. The right to convey one's thoughts by writing or printing grows out of but does not enlarge in any way the natural right of speech; it simply authorizes one to take advantage of those mediums of expression which the ingenuity of man has contrived for broadening and making more effective the influences of that which was formerly confined to mere oral utterances. The right to speak and write and print has been, at different times in the world's history, seriously invaded by those who, for their own selfish purposes, desired to take away from others such privileges, and consequently these rights have been the subject of provisions in the constitutions of the

United States and of this State. The right preserved and guaranteed against invasion by these constitutions is the right to utter, to write, and to print one's sentiments, subject only to the limitation that in so doing he shall not be guilty of an abuse of this privilege by invading the legal rights of others.

To make intelligent, forceful, and effective an expression of opinion it may be necessary to refer to the life, conduct, and character of a person; and so long as the truth is adhered to, the right of privacy of another can not be said to have been invaded by one who speaks or writes or prints, provided the reference to such person and the manner in which he is referred to is reasonably and legitimately proper in an expression of opinion on the subject that is under investigation. It will therefore be seen that the right of privacy must in some particulars yield to the right of speech and of the press. It is well recognized that slander is an abuse of the liberty of speech, and that a libel is an abuse of the liberty to write and print; but it is nowhere expressly declared in the law that these are the only abuses of such rights. And that the law makes the truth in suits for slander and in prosecutions and suits for libel a complete defence may not necessarily make the publication of the truth the legal right of every person, nor prevent it from being in some cases a legal wrong. The truth may be spoken, written, or printed about all matters of a public nature, as well as matters of a private nature in which the public has a legitimate interest. The truth may be uttered and printed in reference to the life, character, and conduct of individuals whenever it is necessary to the full exercise of the right to express one's sentiments on any and all subjects that may be proper matter for discussion. But there may arise cases where the speaking or printing of the truth might be considered an abuse of the liberty of speech and of the press; as, in a case where matters of purely private concern, wholly foreign to a legitimate expression of opinion on the subject under discussion, are injected into the discussion for no other purpose and with no other motive than to annoy and harass the individual referred to. Such cases might be of rare occurrence; but if such should arise, the party aggrieved may not be without a remedy.

The right of privacy is unquestionably limited by the right to speak and print. It may be said that to give liberty of speech and of the press such wide scope as has been indicated would impose a very serious limitation upon the right of privacy; but if it does, it is due to the fact that the law considers that the welfare of the public is better served by maintaining the liberty of speech and of the press than by allowing an individual to assert his right of privacy in such a way as to interfere with the free expression of one's sentiments and the publication of every matter in which the public may be legitimately interested. In many cases the law requires the individual to surrender some of his natural and private rights for the benefit of the public; and this is true in reference to some phases of the right of privacy as well as other legal rights. Those to whom the right to speak and write and print is guaranteed must not abuse this right; nor must one in whom the right of privacy exists abuse this right. The law will no more permit an abuse by the one than by the other. Liberty of speech and of the press is and has been a useful instrument to keep the individual within limits of lawful, decent, and proper conduct; and the right of privacy may be well used within its proper limits to keep those who speak and write and print within the legitimate bounds of the constitutional guaranties of such rights. One may be used as a check upon the other; but neither can be lawfully used for the other's destruction.

This Court Also Read the "Harvard Law Review" of 1890

An article in Harvard Law Review appeared in 1890 and was written by Samuel D. Warren and Louis D. Brandeis. The article attracted much attention at the time. It was conceded by the authors that there was no decided case in which the right of privacy was distinctly asserted and recognized, but it was asserted that there were many cases from which it would appear that this right really existed, although the judgment in each case was put upon other grounds when the complaining party was granted the relief it asked for.

It must be conceded that the numerous cases decided before 1890, in which the court has interfered to restrain the publication of letters, writings, papers, etc., have all been based either upon the recognition of a right of property or upon the fact that the publication would be a breach of contract, confidence, or trust. It is well settled that if any contract, or property right, or trust relation has been violated, damages are recoverable. There are many cases which sustain such a doctrine. ◀

After citing the history of many of these cases, some of which appear in this volume, the judge faces the *Roberson* decision head-on, and concludes that the dissenting opinion of that court of seven judges would have been the proper one:

▶ The effect of the reasoning of the learned minority is to establish conclusively the correctness of the conclusion which we have reached, and we prefer to adopt it as our own. The decision of the Court of Appeals of New York in the *Roberson* case gave rise to numerous articles in the different law magazines of high standing in the country, some by the editors and others by contributors. In some the conclusion of the majority of the court was approved; in others the views of the dissenting judges were commended; and in still others the case and similar cases were referred to as apparently establishing that the claim of the majority was correct, but regret was expressed that the necessity was such that the courts could not recognize the right asserted. An editorial in the American Law Review said: The decision under review shocks and wounds the ordinary sense of justice of mankind. We have heard it alluded to only in terms of regret.

The Judge Considers Mr. Pavesich

As we have already said, cases may arise where it is difficult to determine on which side of the line of demarcation, which separates the right of privacy from the well-established right of others, they are to be found; but we have little difficulty in arriving at the conclusion that the present case is one in which it has been established that the right of privacy has been invaded, and invaded by one who can not claim exemption under the constitutional guaranties of freedom of speech and of the press. The form and features of Pavesich are his own. The insurance company and its agent had no more authority to display them in public for the purpose of advertising the business in which they were engaged than they would have had to compel Pavesich to place himself upon exhibition for this purpose. The latter procedure would have been unauthorized and unjustifiable, as every one will admit; and the former was equally an invasion of the rights of his person. Nothing appears from which it is to be inferred that Pavesich has waived his right to determine for himself where his picture should be displayed in favor of the advertising right of the insurance company.

Special Rights for an Artist

The mere fact that he is an artist does not of itself establish a waiver of this right, so that his picture might be used for advertising purposes. If he displayed in public his works as an artist, he would of course subject his works and his character as an artist, and possibly his character and conduct as a man, to such scrutiny and criticism as would be legitimate and proper to determine whether he was entitled to rank as an artist and should be accorded recognition as such by the public. But it is by no means clear that even this would have authorized the publication of his picture. The constitutional right to speak and print does not necessarily carry with it the right to reproduce the form and features of an individual.

SPECIAL RIGHTS AS A PUBLIC PERSON?

Pavesich was in no sense a public character, even if a different rule in regard to the publication of one's picture should be applied to such characters. It is not necessary in this case to hold, nor are we prepared to do so, that the mere fact that a man has become what is called a public character, either by aspiring to public office, or by holding public office, or by exercising a profession which places him before the public, or by engaging in a business which has necessarily a public nature, gives to every one the right to print and circulate his picture.

SPECIAL RIGHTS AS A POLITICAL PERSON?

It may be that the aspirant for public office, or one in official position, impliedly consents that the public may gaze not only upon him but upon his picture; but we are not prepared now to hold that even this is true. It would seem to us that even the President of the United States in the lofty position which he occupies has some rights in reference to matters of this kind, which he does not forfeit by aspiring to or accepting the highest office within the gift of the people of the several States. While no person who has ever held this position, and probably no person who has ever held public office, has ever objected, or ever will object, to the reproduction of his picture in reputable newspapers, magazines, and periodicals, still it cannot be that the mere fact that a man aspires to public office or holds public office subjects him to the humiliation and mortification of having his picture displayed in places where he would never go to be gazed upon, at times when and under circumstances where, if he were personally present, the sensibilities of his nature would be severely shocked. If one's picture may be used by another for advertising purposes, it may be reproduced and exhibited anywhere. If it may be used in a newspaper, it may be used on a poster or a placard. It may be posted upon the walls of private dwellings or upon the streets. It may ornament the bar of the saloon-keeper, or decorate the walls of a brothel. By becoming a member of society, neither man nor woman can be presumed to have consented to such uses of the impression of their faces and features upon paper or upon canvas. The conclusion reached by us seems to be so thoroughly in accord with natural justice, with the principles of the law of every civilized nation, and especially with the elastic principles of the common law, and so thoroughly in harmony with those principles as molded under the influence of American institutions, that it seems strange to us that not only four of the judges of one of the most distinguished and learned courts of the Union, but also lawyers of learning and ability, have found an insurmountable stumbling-block in the path that leads to a recognition of the right which would give to persons like the plaintiff in this case, and the young woman in the Roberson case, redress for the legal wrong, or, what is by some of the law-writers called, the outrage, perpetrated by the unauthorized use of their pictures for advertising purposes.

What we have ruled can not be in any sense construed as an abridgment of the liberty of speech and of the press as guaranteed in the constitution. Whether the reproduction of a likeness of another which is free from caricature can in any sense be declared to be an exercise of the right to publish one's sentiments, certain it is that one who, merely for advertising purposes and from mercenary motives, publishes the likeness of another without his consent, can not be said, in so doing, to have exercised the right to publish his sentiments.

ADVERTISING VERSUS IDEAS

There is in the publication of one's picture for advertising purposes not the slightest semblance of an expression of an idea, a thought, or an opinion, within the meaning of the constitutional provision which guarantees to a person the right to publish his sentiments on any subject. Such conduct

is not embraced within the liberty to print, but is a serious
invasion of one's right of privacy, and may in many cases,
according to the circumstances of the publication and the
uses to which it is put, cause damages to flow which are irreparable in their nature. The knowledge that one's features
and form are being used for such a purpose and displayed
in such places as such advertisements are often liable to be
found brings not only the person of an extremely sensitive
nature, but even the individual of ordinary sensibility, to a
realization that his liberty has been taken away from him,
and, as long as the advertiser uses him for these purposes,
he can not be otherwise than conscious of the fact that he is,
for the time being, under the control of another, that he is
no longer free, and that he is in reality a slave without hope
of freedom, held to service by a merciless master; and if a
man of true instincts, or even of ordinary sensibilities, no one
can be more conscious of his complete enthrallment than he is.

So thoroughly satisfied are we that the law recognizes
within proper limits, as a legal right, the right of privacy,
and that the publication of one's picture without his consent
by another as an advertisement, for the mere purpose of
increasing the profits and gains of the advertiser, is an invasion of this right, that we venture to predict that the day will
come when the American bar will marvel that a contrary view
was ever entertained by judges of eminence and ability. ◀

So the majestic process of law proceeds along one path in
Georgia and another in New York. Several states to this day
hold that there is no Right of Privacy; others follow the
Georgia approach and by court decision have declared for
the Right to Be Let Alone. Utah, for example, took an interesting tack: it extended the Right of Privacy to public institutions, and even protected the rights of deceased persons.
Still other states left it to the legislature to protect a person's
Right to Be Let Alone. But even among the states that have
widened their law to cover protection of privacy there is

great diversity as to the scope of this new legal right—as we shall see later in this book.

It is good that judges should not all see eye to eye. It would be frightening if at the start of every new legal concept all judicial minds should be in agreement. It takes time, except under dictatorships, to find a basic philosophy judges may wisely use as a springboard for their own personal conclusions.

7

The
Acid Test:
Privacy Is
Constitutional

Our Constitution is the matrix of our law-life. Each of the states, of course, has its separate constitution. The District of Columbia, managed by the Congress under the federal Constitution, is governed by acts of Congress.

The greatest contribution we have made to the history of government may lie in the fact that we are a *federal* government. The federal Constitution is the residuary of those powers and duties that the people have turned over to their federal government. Each state is subject to those basic federal constitutional provisions. Each state, however, also has its own constitution to provide for its people.

Constitutional law, national or state, is of the highest order of law, dealing primarily with the basic problems and fundamental rights of man. The Founding Fathers saw to it that no demagogue could easily change the basis of our legal life as expressed in the Constitution. To amend this root, or

149

matrix, of law in our nation a two-thirds vote of the United States Senate and of the House of Representatives or a two-thirds vote of the states is required. A majority vote is not deemed sufficient, and even after the Congress has so adopted an amendment it must still be accepted by three-fourths of the states before the amendment becomes law.

We have added only twenty-two amendments to our federal constitution in the past 170 years. In truth, there are only twenty amendments that have been duly voted, approved by the states, and are still in existence. The discrepancy is explained by the fact that in 1919 we adopted the Prohibition Amendment but in 1933 repealed it by the Twenty-first Amendment.

In 1787, when we organized our nation, there existed in England, and in the colonies, a large amount of law made by judges when deciding cases. The decisions written by the judges were called the "common law," and were handed down in England and the colonies from time immemorial. The *Pavesich* case is a good example of such "judge-made" law. Of course, the decisions of courts must conflict in no way with the state or federal constitutions, which are, in effect, the guidelines for all legal behavior in our culture.

There is another category of lawmaking ordinarily called statutory law. Statutes are enacted by the Congress or the state legislatures. Usually such law is accomplished by a majority vote, although under the Constitution there is a special provision that treaties, for example, require a two-thirds vote of the United States Senate. Statutory law is more fluid and experimental than constitutional law, and it is more readily repealed or changed. But statutes enacted by Congress or the state legislatures must not interfere with or conflict with the basic law; that is, the provisions of the state or federal constitutions.

When judges make law by deciding a particular case or controversy, they must always make sure that their opinions and final decisions do not undermine or run counter to the constitutional law. We are living under a unique experiment. Our government concept is threefold: executive, legislative, and judicial. Since our structure is based on these three divisions of power, someone had to have a final word, and the Founding Fathers decided that the final word should rest, in a sense, with the judges. Therefore the United States Supreme Court has the final say on the constitutionality of a statute, or even the decision of a lower court. Hence the courts have the duty of finding out if the state legislature or the Congress has voted for something that conflicts with a constitutional provision.

Of course, in the final analysis the people can override even the Supreme Court of the United States. They always have the power, through an act of Congress and its adoption by three-quarters of the states, to amend the Constitution. Likewise, state constitutions can be amended by the people of a state, thus changing their basic idea of the law as incorporated in the constitution.

Whenever a new legal right is created, some citizen is likely to go to court to find out if the legislature, for example, has voted for a statute that runs counter to the state or federal consitution. Also, when a court declares that certain rights do not exist with the people, the legislature can be heard to say that the rights *do* exist, and then, as in the case of the creation of the Right of Privacy, the court in the final analysis must determine whether the new statute is in conflict with the concepts of freedom and liberty as set forth in the Constitution.

In Georgia, as we have seen, the Right of Privacy was established by judicial decision. In New York, however, a statute was needed. Since judges themselves, under our system of government, are empowered to decide whether something is constitutional, one cannot claim that a particular judicial decision is, strictly speaking, *un*constitutional.

All one can say is that the judge *misinterpreted* the constitution. But where, as in New York, a statute is needed to declare the existence of a particular right, that statute is immediately open to a court test of its constitutionality. And that is precisely what happened in New York.

The reader will recall that in the *Roberson* case the New York court recognized no Right of Privacy as such. The legislature then passed a law creating and setting forth such a right and providing punishment for its invasion. The final act in the process occurred when the highest court of the State of New York was asked in the case of *Rhodes* v. *Sperry and Hutchinson* to decide whether the privacy statute was constitutional. Did it conflict with the constitution of the State of New York?

In 1904 one Aida T. Rhodes had her picture taken, for her own use, only to have the photographer, a Mr. Young, exhibit the pictures in the office of the Sperry and Hutchinson Company. It seems that Mr. Young had a deal going with Sperry and Hutchinson, and the latter, seeking to call attention to Young's work, exhibited pictures of Aida and others as a kind of advertisement for Young's work. The S. & H. office was visited daily by many people, and Aida's photographs were prominently displayed. Needless to say, Aida had never consented to their use in this manner. She was offended, and started a suit. Note that this was not a case where the photographer showed the results of his artistry in his own studio.

Aida was lucky. Her case came up two years after Abigail's and therefore one year after the New York legislature had passed its statute on privacy. She sued Sperry and Hutchinson under the new law and won $1,000 in damages. But Sperry and Hutchinson didn't let the matter rest there. They decided to appeal the case to the highest court in New York (which happened to be the same court that had, prior to the statute, denied relief to Abigail Roberson). Only, this time the situation was different. Now there *was* a statute on the books protecting the lady. Sperry and Hutchinson claimed, however, that the statute was unconstitutional because it deprived them of liberty (the right to exhibit the pictures) and property (the $1,000) without "due process of law." Which is to say that the statute was "unreasonable" because it didn't follow the previous cases.

So the issue in the case of Aida Rhodes was for the court to decide if the privacy law passed by the New York legislature and duly signed by the governor of the state was constitutional—that is, did not violate the safeguards of constitutional law.

By the time the Rhodes case got to the Court of Appeals, it was 1908. This time the Court of Appeals stood firm and united. All seven judges agreed that the law was constitutional because it is the essence of laws passed by the legislature that they do not have to follow prior judicial decisions. In fact, statutes are often enacted in order to change prior judicial rules. Nor did the court think that the privacy laws violated anyone's constitutional liberty or property. Here are excerpts of the court's *unanimous* opinion:

▶ In the case of *Roberson* v. *Rochester Folding Box Co.* this court determined that in the absence of any statute on the subject the right of privacy as an enforceable legal doctrine did not exist in this state so as to enable a woman to prevent the use of her portrait by others for advertising purposes without her consent. In the prevailing opinion in that case, however, Chief Judge Parker suggested that the right of privacy to that extent might properly be protected by an act of the legislature, saying: "The legislative body could very well interfere and arbitrarily provide that no one should be permitted for his own selfish purpose to use the picture or the name of another for advertising purposes without his consent."

The Privacy Law of 1903 was passed at the very next session of the legislature after this judicial utterance was made public and there can be little doubt that its enactment was prompted by the suggestion which I have quoted.

It is contended that this law violates the State Constitution: (1) Because it deprives persons of liberty without due process of law; and (2) Because it deprives persons of property without due process of law.

As to the first objection, it is to be observed that the statute does not deny the right of any person to make such use of his own portrait as he may see fit. The legislature has not undertaken to restrict his liberty in this respect to any extent whatever. It is only the use of his name or picture by others and for particular purposes that is affected by the statute. Unless we are bound to assume that there is an inherent right in the public at large to use the names and portraits of others for advertising or trade purposes without their consent, the legislative restriction of their liberty imposed by this act is not an exercise of power which affords the basis of any valid objection in a court of justice. The statute merely recognizes and enforces the right of a person to control the use of his name or portrait by others so far as advertising or trade purposes are concerned. This right of control in the person whose name or picture is sought to be used for such purposes is not limited by the statute. The requirement of his written consent in order to effectuate a valid transfer of the privilege of thus using his name or portrait is not liable to constitutional objection.

The power of the legislature in the absence of any constitutional restriction to declare that a particular act shall constitute a crime or be the subject of a suit for damages cannot be questioned, where the right established or recognized and sought to be protected is based upon an ethical sanction. Such is the character of the right of privacy preserved by legislation protecting persons against the unauthorized use of their names or portraits in the form of advertisements or trade notices. It is a recognition by the law-making power of the very general sentiment which pre-

vailed throughout the community against permitting advertisers to promote the sale of their wares by this method,
regardless of the wishes of the persons thereby affected.
There was a natural and widespread feeling that such use
of their names and portraits in the absence of consent was
indefensible in morals and ought to be prevented by law.
Hence the enactment of this statute.

THE LAW DOES NOT OBJECT TO NEW CONCEPTS

It is not a valid objection to the act of 1903 that it creates
a right of action and imposes a liability unknown to the
prior law. There is no such limit to legislative power. The
legislature may alter or repeal the prior law.

ADVERTISING HAS NO SACRED IMMUNITIES

It appears to be conceded by counsel that the requirement
of a written consent to authorize the use of one's name or
portrait by others for advertising or trade purposes is de-
nounced as an interference with personal liberty "without
due process of law." I am unable to see that this requirement
is any more objectionable than was that in the statute under
consideration in the case under what is commonly known as
the Bottling Act. That statute declared it to be unlawful for
any person to fill with beverages or medicine any marked
bottle without the written consent of the person or corporation whose mark or device had been placed upon the bottle,
and it was construed to be constitutional in all respects.

MINOR FANCIFUL OBJECTIONS

There is considerable discussion in the briefs submitted
upon this appeal as to the relative rights of photographers
and those who procure their photographs to be taken; but
these matters are immaterial to the real issues presented by
this record and we do not deem it necessary to discuss them.
Many possible inconveniences are also suggested as liable to

occur in consequence of the enforcement of the act of 1903 some of which seem quite fanciful and hardly likely to arise; but however this may be, they cannot be permitted to affect the disposition of the question before us. In my opinion the statute is in all respects constitutional. ◀

8

Show Biz
and the
World of Letters

THE cases we have discussed up to now have all a certain
old-fashioned flavor. Their emphasis upon the written word
on the one hand, and upon homespun sentimentalities on the
other, strikes a somewhat archaic note amidst the shrill
sounds of our own atomic age. And yet, as we have seen,
they all represent important stages in the progressive development of a right carved by necessity and imagination from
the solid and seemingly unyielding granite of legal precedent. These early cases formed the axis upon which all later
developments of the Right of Privacy have turned, and we
therefore thought it important to present them chronologi-
cally in order to show clearly the lines of construction of a
legal right.

Only after having paid the early cases proper obeisance,
as now, can we view with understanding those more recent
cases in the law of privacy which have set the standards of
present behavior in this field. Undoubtedly, in the near
future these so-called "recent" cases will also seem old-

fashioned, for the law, although essentially a conservative tool of man, eventually follows society in its headlong dash through time.

As the law of privacy developed in the twentieth century, judges had to decide whether the protection previously granted to individuals under decided cases and legislative enactments was to be extended to cover rapidly developing media of communication and entertainment. New considerations became important. Should a distinction be made between fictional and nonfictional portrayals in books and periodicals? How valid is the assumption that the one is made purely for profit and the other is a public service? How should the ever-increasing thirst of the public for news and information be balanced against the sometimes desperate desire for privacy on the part of the individual? How, in a society which has become continually subject to an avalanche of words and pictures through a variety of communications media, should we regard the specific reference to an individual without his consent?

As it grew, the law of privacy spread its protection over ever-widening areas of human endeavor. And with growth came sophistication. As judges wrestled with the meaning of statutes or prior court decisions, terms were defined more precisely, and areas of protection were broken down into their component parts. No longer did privacy follow a straight line of development, but rather veered now this way, now that as it turned to confront new problems. Law began to be made by subject matter rather than by chronology.

As we present our next cases, therefore, we shall follow only a casual chronology and place more emphasis than previously upon the development of specific *areas* of the Right to Be Let Alone.

It is not surprising that many of the leading cases that had to contend with these problems arose in New York. Not only is New York the center of commerce of our nation; it is also the center of our communications complex. And it is, or should be, the maxim of an injured party to sue his oppressor in the place where he keeps his assets.

In 1913 New York was also the center of the motion-picture industry. It is thus understandable that the first (and probably most important) case to decide whether a fictionalized motion-picture photoplay was subject to the prohibitions of the privacy laws arose in New York. Before reading the case the reader should remember that in 1903 New York had passed laws that protected the privacy of an individual's name or picture from certain unauthorized uses by others. The questions were: Did the prohibition apply to fiction in general and to fictionalized motion pictures in particular?

JOHN R. BINNS v. THE VITAGRAPH COMPANY OF AMERICA (1913)

▶ The Vitagraph Co. is a corporation engaged in the business of manufacturing, leasing, licensing, selling, distributing, displaying and circulating photographic films for use in motion picture machines. On January 23, 1909, the steamships *Republic* and *Florida* came into collision at sea. The *Republic* was equipped with machines for sending and receiving messages by wireless telegraphy and Binns, a British subject, was the operator of said machine. Immediately following the collision he sent a danger signal consisting of the letters "C.Q.D.," which were received by a wireless operator on the steamship *Baltic* and by such an operator at Siasconset, on Nantucket Island. Messages were thereafter exchanged, between Binns on the *Republic* and the operator on the *Baltic* and at Siasconset. The messages sent by Binns resulted in the *Baltic* going to the rescue of the passengers on the other steamships and the passengers and crew of the

Republic were removed to the *Baltic* and transported to New York. Binns was the first man to use wireless telegraphy at a time when its use resulted in saving hundreds of lives.

Soon after the day of the collision the Vitagraph Company proceeded to make a series of pictures entitled "C.Q.D. or Saved by Wireless; A True Story of the Wreck of the *Republic*." These pictures, with the exception perhaps of one or more taken of the *Baltic* as it entered the harbor of New York, were manufactured or made up in the Vitagraph studio by the use of scenery prepared for the purpose and of actors employed to impersonate Binns and others. A series of picture films were thus prepared from which moving pictures could be produced for public exhibition. Such pictures were exhibited in many places in this state. The series of pictures commenced with a sub-series entitled "John R. Binns the Wireless Operator in his Cabin aboard the S.S. Republic." This sub-series was followed by others, the last one of the series being entitled "Jack Binns and his Good American Smile." The picture of Binns appeared in the series five times and his name was used in the sub-titles six or more times. This action is brought to prevent the use of Binns' picture and name and to recover damages for the injuries received by him by reason of such use. It is not claimed that Binns ever consented in writing or otherwise to the use of his picture and name. Further facts appear in the opinion.

The lower court found that Vitagraph used Binns' name and picture for the purpose of trade and advertising. This action is brought pursuant to the Civil Rights Law (the New York Privacy Laws previously referred to in this volume).

Prior to the passage of this law it was definitely determined in this state that the right of privacy as a legal doctrine did not exist to prevent the use of a portrait for advertising purposes (*Roberson* v. *Rochester Folding Box Company*). The statute now recognizes and enforces the right of a person to control the use of his name or portrait by others so far as advertising or trade purposes are concerned.

The statute is very general in its terms, but when a living

person's name, portrait or picture is used, it is not necessarily and at all times so used either for advertising purposes, or for the purposes of trade. The statute does not prohibit every use of the name, portrait or picture of a living person. It would not be within the evil sought to be remedied by that statute to construe it so as to prohibit the use of the name, portrait or picture of a living person in truthfully recounting or portraying an actual current event as is commonly done in a single issue of a regular newspaper. It is not necessary now to attempt to define what is, or is not within its prohibitive provisions. In the case before us the series of pictures were not true pictures of a current event but mainly a product of the imagination, based, however, largely upon such information relating to an actual occurrence as could readily be obtained. The method used in designing and preparing the pictures is described by one of the officers of the Vitagraph Company as follows: "Our method of reproducing current events which I have described as news matters, is by getting all the data, all the matter in hand, from every reliable source and weave it into what we call a picture story. That story is produced by first being written just as a playwright writes a play or an author writes a story."

The same witness, referring to the series of pictures relating to the wreck of the *Republic*, testified: "It was under my supervision. I was in collaboration with one of our stage directors, the author of the text that accompanied the picture. We purchased all the newspapers we could find, everything that had any bearing on the story, and we sat down and wrote out what we called a scenario.* * * We produced in our studio the interiors of the captain's cabin; the wireless operator's room on the *Republic;* the wireless operator's room on the *Baltic* and the operator's room at Siasconset.* * * We assigned various actors and actresses in our employ to take the various parts.* * * The part of Mr. Binns was assigned to one of our actors.* * * We have to use our imagination largely in those cases."

After the negative films for the pictures under consideration so made were completed, a large number of picture films were manufactured. Vitagraph filed one set, which it defined as a "photograph," with the librarian of Congress, and a copyright was issued to it for the title to the picture story. The picture films ready for use in moving picture shows, and of course including Binns' name and picture, were with others described at length in circulars and pamphlets, and such circulars and pamphlets were sent throughout this and other states to those engaged in the business of exhibiting pictures to the public.

About February 20, following the collision, the picture films were placed upon the market and were thereafter used in moving picture shows pursuant to leases from and other agreements with the defendant. Binns' name was prominent in the advertisements put out by Vitagraph describing its manufactured product, and the purpose of the advertisements was to extend Vitagraph's business and add to its profits by increasing the demand for such pictures, and thus multiplying the number of leases or other agreements by which the pictures and films were put upon the market. The use of the name and picture of Binns by Vitagraph in the picture films, and pursuant to leases and agreements with Vitagraph in the moving picture shows was commercial. Such use was in the language of the opinion in the *Roberson* case: "For his (its) own selfish purposes."

A picture within the meaning of the New York Privacy Law is not necessarily a photograph of the living person, but includes any representation of such person. The picture represented by Vitagraph to be a true picture of Binns and exhibited to the public as such, was intended to be, and it was, a representation of Binns. Vitagraph is in no position to say that the picture does not represent Binns or that it was an actual picture of a person made up to look like and impersonate Binns.

It is not necessary in this opinion to discuss the question whether a person, firm or corporation would be liable under the statute for making and using a picture of a living person when it is included in a picture of an actual event in which such person was an actor, and such picture is a mere incident to the actual event portrayed. The use of Binns' name and picture as shown by the testimony in this case was not a mere incident to a general picture representative of the author's understanding of what occurred at the wreck of the *Republic*. The first picture of the series was essentially a picture of Binns, although included therewith was a place having relation to the other parts of the pictures exhibited— but the last picture of the series had no connection whatever with any other place or person or with any event. His alleged personal movements as exhibited in the now well-known form of moving pictures had no relation to the other pictures, and it was not designed to instruct or educate those who saw it. Vitagraph used Binns' alleged picture to amuse those who paid to be entertained. If the use of Binns' name and picture as shown in this case is not within the terms of the statutes, then the picture of any individual can be similarly made and exhibited for the purpose of showing his peculiarities as of dress and walk, and his personal fads, eccentricities, amusements and even his private life. By such pictures an audience would be amused and the maker of the films and the exhibitors would be enriched. The greater the exaggeration in such a series of pictures, so long as they were not libelous, the greater would be the profit of the picture-maker and exhibitor.

We decide that the name and picture of Binns were used by Vitagraph as a matter of business and profit and in violation of the New York Privacy Law. It is urged that there is danger of serious trouble in the practical enforcement of any rule which may be adopted in construing and enforcing the statute so far as it related to purposes of trade. If there is any basis for the suggestion of danger in enforcing a part of the statute under consideration it is the duty of the legislature to repeal such part thereof, or so modify it as to define with greater particularity what it intends should be prohibited, or perhaps permit the use of a person's name, portrait or picture for purposes of trade, if the oral assent of such person, or, if a minor, of his or her parent or guardian, is obtained therefor. ◀

So Binns won a unanimous judgment, and motion pictures, at least to a limited extent, were added to the scope of the privacy laws. It is important to note, however, that the judges in the Binns case left many questions open for future deliberations. Although "C.Q.D. or Saved by Wireless" was *based* on fact, it was essentially fiction. Binns himself was portrayed by an actor. Also, as the court indicates, Binns was not an incidental character in the story; the story really revolved around him. The court takes great pains to make it clear that it is not at all sure it would have decided the same way if it were dealing with *pure* nonfiction or with a mere *incidental* use of Binns's name or picture.

In 1915, however, a New York court elaborated on the scope of the privacy law and discussed specifically the question of only "incidental" use in a nonfiction movie. An early documentary film was released that year which dealt with white slavery. The scene was laid, it was averred, in an area of a city where white slavers maintained their marketplace. In shooting a certain street scene in the picture, one camera captured a factory building. The name of the company that used the building was easily readable. The owner of the factory sued the movie company for invasion of privacy. It was not comfortable to have his privacy invaded, even though there was no directly libelous implication that he had anything to do with the business of marketing human flesh. The opinion of the court is brief and to the point.

MERLE v. SOCIOLOGICAL RESEARCH FILM CORPORATION (1915)

▶ The use of Merle's name in this case is not for the purpose of obtaining trade or advertisement; apparently it merely appears in the picture because it was placed upon the building which is a part of the picture. Certainly where a man places his sign upon the outside of a building he cannot claim that a person who would otherwise have a right to photograph the building is precluded from using that picture because the sign also appears on the picture. To constitute a violation of the New York law I think it must appear that the use of Merle's picture or name is itself for the purpose of trade and not merely an incidental part of a photograph of an actual building, which cannot be presumed to add to the value of the photograph for trade or advertising, and even a use that may in a particular instance cause acute annoyance, cannot give rise to an action under the statute unless it fairly falls within the terms of the statute.

It is true that the complaint also states that the picture showed a factory "purporting" to be located in said building and to be plaintiff's establishment. If the Film Corporation actually used Merle's name in describing the interior of the factory, and did not merely photograph the exterior, then it might well be that such use would be within the purview of the statute, but I think that the complaint merely sets forth that in some manner from the nature of the pictures the inference arises that the factory belonged to the firm whose name was on the outside, and that the photograph of this sign constitutes the only use of Merle's name. Such a use is not a violation of Merle's right of privacy. ◀

Another question left open by the court in the Binns case was considered, also by a New York court, in 1919. In the Binns case the court decided that the word "trade," as used in the New York law, included fictionalized motion pictures. But what about newsreel films? Were they also made for the purpose of "trade"? Let us consider the case of Grace Humiston against Universal Film Company.

Miss Humiston was a lady lawyer, something of a rarity in 1919 and not a very common phenomenon even today. She sued Universal for using her name and picture in a motion picture without her consent, claiming that the use was one "for advertising purposes or for the purpose of trade" and therefore prohibited by the New York Privacy Law. The lower court in New York decided that she was right, even though, as we shall see, the film was a documentary. In reaching this result the lower court decided that the use of Miss Humiston's name and picture *in the movie* was a use "for purposes of trade" but not for advertising purposes. However, the court thought that the use of Miss Humiston's name and picture *on posters* advertising the motion picture was a use both for purposes of trade *and* advertising. Thus, according to the lower court at least, Universal had violated the New York Privacy Law on both counts.

According to the outline of the facts made by the lower court, it would seem that Miss Humiston was instrumental in solving a famous murder case of the day, the death of a girl named Ruth Cruger. The case was one of great public interest and was featured in the daily newspapers. The films she complained of were actual movies showing her seated in an automobile with a member of the New York Police Department and were taken while she was actually engaged in her work on the murder case. These shots were presented as one of ten subjects of current news interest, all of which were given equal prominence as part of a weekly film review made by Universal and known as "Universal Animated Weekly" or "Universal Current Events." The news films contained no advertising matter, and the frames containing Miss Humiston were, in the words of the lower court, "incidental to the presentation of a current event in motion picture form."

Universal appealed the decision of the lower court to a higher tribunal in New York and brought before that court for the first time the question of whether "incidental" use of a person's name and picture in a motion-picture newsreel without her consent violated her privacy. Here is the high court's decision:

GRACE HUMISTON v. UNIVERSAL FILM COMPANY (1919)

▶ Universal Film Manufacturing Company is one of five companies engaged in the business of producing motion picture films of current events and news items. The films produced by Universal containing such pictures of current events are entitled "Universal Animated Weekly" and "Universal Current Events." Each week Universal publishes and distributes one number or issue of the "Animated Weekly" and one number or issue of the "Current Events." Each number or issue is comprised in a reel of film approximately 1,000 feet in length presenting from ten to fifteen subjects, each a matter of current news. For the production of these newsreels Universal maintains a large organization devoted exclusively to the gathering and editing of news items in motion picture form. The photographs which are presented are taken by a corps of motion picture photographers or "reporters" stationed at various parts of the country. Each of these correspondents has a camera and when a news event occurs or is about to occur in the territory assigned to him, he photographs the event and forwards the negative to the main office of the defendant in New York. There are thus submitted each week to Universal, for inclusion in the two weekly reels of news films, many times more than the 2,000 feet of negative required, so that it is necessary to cull out of the great quantity of pictures submitted 2,000 feet of the most important material. From the negatives thus submitted the selection is made by men of newspaper experience who also compose the captions or explanatory reading matter which preface the presentation of the successive subjects portrayed.

Universal's news service is shown in motion picture theatres, schools, churches, cantonments, vessels of the Navy; in fact wherever there are motion picture machines. The newsreels are utilized by the government of the United States and by municipal governments for purposes of public good. They have been used for the promoting of the liberty loans, and by the Food Administrator, and by the Fuel Administrator, by the Secretary of War and the Secretary of the Navy for recruiting for the Army and Navy, and by the board of health of the city of New York to prevent the spread of Spanish influenza. These are all found as facts by the court below.

There is a clear distinction between a newsreel and a motion picture photoplay. A photoplay is inherently a work of fiction. A newsreel contains no fiction but shows only actual photographs of current events of public interest. The newsreel is taken on the spot, at the very moment of the occurrence depicted and is an actual photograph of the event itself. The photoplay, as the result of fiction, retains its interest, irrespective of the length of time which has elapsed since its first production, whereas, a newsreel, to be of any value in large cities must be published almost simultaneously with the occurrence of the events which it portrays. This news service, as far as it goes, is a truthful, accurate purveyor of news, quite as strictly so as a newspaper. While a newspaper account conveys the news almost entirely by words, the news service conveys the same by photographs with incidental verbal explanation.

This action is brought by Grace Humiston, who is a lawyer in the city of New York, to stop the publication of a film and for damages claimed to have been suffered by its publication. This film represented her as she was engaged in legal work connected with the solution of the mystery of the disappearance of Ruth Cruger. The body of this girl was, through the efforts of Miss Humiston, discovered buried under the floor in the back room of the shop of an Italian in the city of New York. The police had been searching diligently to unravel the mystery of the absence of Ruth Cruger, and it was not until Miss Humiston took charge of the matter and insisted upon excavating under the shop of this Italian that the body was discovered. The daily papers, all of them, displayed prominently the fact of this discovery, and the name and picture of Miss Humiston as the one through whose persistence and intelligence the discovery had been made. Facts in connection with this discovery were pictured by the reporters for Universal, and among other things was the picture of Miss Humiston in an automobile with a captain of police, while she was actually engaged in the matter. This picture was a truthful picture taken of a current event at the time that it happened. The lower court has decided that it was unlawfully published without the written consent of Miss Humiston, and this presents the first question for our consideration.

Now the New York Privacy Law was passed in 1903. It was passed after a decision by the Court of Appeals in 1902, in the case of *Roberson* v. *Rochester Folding Box Company* which decided that there was no right of privacy.

In view of the passage of this act at the next session of the Legislature after this decision was handed down by the Court of Appeals, it thus appears what was the primary object of the Legislature in passing this act. *At that time the moving picture industry had not been developed.* There was no such thing as the publication of current news items by moving picture films, so that it is clear that the Legislature did not have this class of publication in mind at the time of the passage of the law.

It cannot be contended that the publication of moving pictures is not a trade. But we think it is not such trade as was within the contemplation of the Legislature in the passage of the act. They are published for profit, as a newspaper is published for profit. Their profit depends upon their ability to present accurate and interesting news, as well as the photoplays of fiction. It is precisely the same with a newspaper. That the publication of moving pictures is a publication made in trade was decided by the case of *Binns* v. *Vitagraph Company.* It does not necessarily follow, however, that the statute was meant to apply to all publications, even for the purposes of trade. To determine whether the publication complained of was within the statute, the whole statute must be considered, both in its origin and in its effect. The presumable motive for its enactment has been indicated as shown in the *Roberson* case cited.

The effect of the statute is very far reaching and even

startling. Not only is the publication of a portrait or picture without the written consent of the party made a misdemeanor, but the publication of the name of a party without written permission is made a misdemeanor. The exhibition of a motion picture of a public parade would, under the trial court's interpretation, subject the defendant to prosecution for crime. The exhibition of a motion picture showing a game of baseball or a game of football would, under the trial court's interpretation of the statute, be a crime, unless with the written consent of every person either among the players or among the spectators shown upon the film whose likeness was distinguishable. The question is not whether any one, whose picture or name is represented, may feel aggrieved, but the commission of a misdemeanor is a matter of public concern, and the party guilty may be prosecuted upon the complaint of any person, whether aggrieved or not.

Waiving for the moment the question of constitutional right, every newspaper every day would be guilty of a crime, if the construction of the court below be right, in the description of any event wherein persons are named without their written consent. In the *Binns* case Judge Chase says that this act clearly would not apply in the case of a single publication in a single newspaper. Why not, if it applies to the case here presented? These motion picture films are distributed and shown to different audiences in different parts of the country, just as a newspaper is circulated in different parts of the country and reaches different readers. For this purpose a number of films are made just as a number of editions of a paper are printed and sent to different communities. When the matter is fresh the event is a matter of interest, but the public soon tires of it and wants fresh news. I am unable to see any practical difference between the presentation of these current events in a motion picture film and in a news-paper, and when it is considered that under Miss Humiston's interpretation of the statute the mention in any newspaper or motion picture film or any publication of any kind of a single name in connection with any private or public matter, without the written consent of the person named, is a misdemeanor. The court should be slow to so interpret the act.

If this statute had simply provided for the right of injunction to prevent the portrayal of the picture of any person without his written consent, a different question might be presented. Under such a statute the court in this case might hold the statute applicable. But where the statute goes further and includes either the name or the picture of a person and makes the publication of either without a written consent a misdemeanor, the reasonable and necessary inference is not only that the statute does not apply to the publication of a newspaper in a single issue, but also the statute does not apply to the publication of a picture or name in a single set of films of actual events issued at one time for distribution in different parts of the country before different audiences as a matter of current news. It matters not what may be the motive in the publishing of these films, whether instructive or whether to satisfy the morbid curiosity, any more than it matters what may be the motive in the publishing of actual news items in a newspaper. The rule of law as held by the lower court would make practically impossible the exhibition of films representing current events wherein the name or picture of a living person is given, whether of interesting, instructive or elevating events, or whether introduced for the purpose of courting publicity.

In the same issue of the "Animated Weekly" was published a picture of President Hibben of Princeton conferring a degree upon a distinguished foreigner. Under the rule of law announced by the lower court if such publication was without his written consent, Universal is guilty of a misdemeanor, not only in the publication of this picture, but in the mention of the name of President Hibben, in the descriptive words which appear as the picture is presented. Universal would be also guilty of a misdemeanor by exhibiting the picture of the diplomat upon whom the degree was bestowed, and also guilty of a misdemeanor in showing the portrait of some outsider who happened to be within the bounds of the picture. With this interpretation of the statute I cannot agree.

The authorities, so far as they discuss the question, seem to me to be in entire harmony with the conclusion which I have reached. In *Jeffries* v. *N.Y. Evening Journal Pub. Co.* Mr. Justice Whitney writes that the picture of a person is not used for trade purposes within the meaning of the section when used merely for the dissemination of information and not for commerce or traffic.

This decision has been approved in *Colyer* v. *Fox Publishing Co.* where it was decided that an actress whose portrait was published in a weekly periodical without her consent, but not for advertising purposes, could not recover damages under the act. In that case a professional diver had had her picture taken in costume which was produced in the Police Gazette without her consent, together with other vaudeville actresses in costume, under a heading "Five of a Kind on this Page. Most of Them Adorn the Burlesque Stage, All of Them Are Favorites with the Bald Headed Boys." It would seem that if under any such circumstances the statute could be held to apply it would have been held to have applied in that case, but it was there held that the publication of the photograph was not within the act, as for advertising or for trade purposes.

In the *Binns* case the presentation was not of pictures actually taken at the time of the occurrence of the events, but the film was taken in a studio with actors dressed for the occasion in order to present a representation of what might have occurred. It was held to be pure fiction and not fact, and as such it was held to be within the act and the exhibition of that film was enjoined. The representation of Lawyer Humiston was published in a single set of films to be distributed at the same time to different parts of the country as a news item. It was interesting when first exhibited. The fact that these films were widely distributed, so as to be seen by many people, cannot make the offense any greater than would be the offense in a newspaper with a large circulation publishing the same picture or the same names in a single issue. The fact that the picture may have been seen by the same person more than once would not condemn the publication, because a single issue of a newspaper is often seen several times by the same person.

The exhibitor of these films with the interest of the public in view is not going to exhibit any news item after the interest in the item has died out. The fact that this publication is so markedly different from the publication which is recognized as the inspiration of the passage of the law in question, in itself furnishes a strong probability that it is not within the prohibitive act, and when the right to an injunction and to damages is based upon an act made criminal by the same statute, the law should lead us to interpret the act in favor of the party charged with crime. ◀

The reader may recall that the New York Privacy Law embraces both civil and criminal provisions. The criminal provisions are hardly, if ever, enforced. Most people who feel that their privacy has been invaded are more interested in stopping the publication and in receiving money damages for the injury already done than they are in sending anyone to jail, even for a short period of time. It is therefore quite significant that the court here is emphasizing the criminal aspects of the New York law in supplying a rationale for not enforcing Miss Humiston's claim. One might even say that the court is stretching logic a bit in excepting Miss Humiston's situation from the decision in the *Binns* case. One gets the feeling that the court really doesn't approve of the *Binns* decision but can't do anything about it except limit its application. Such apparent evasiveness is common in the law. Since we traditionally give much weight to judicial precedents, they are more frequently distinguished on their facts than they are overruled.

Regardless of the logic used, however, it can certainly be argued that the result reached by this court is meritorious. The dissemination of news through films (and now through television) would certainly be hampered had Miss

Humiston prevailed. Indeed, in deciding against Miss Humiston in this case, the court recognized implicitly the right of the public to be informed about matters of current interest, which is a modern and vital interpretation of our guarantees of freedom of speech and press.

The court now turns to a discussion of the use of Miss Humiston's name and picture on posters which advertised the newsreel:

▶ A further question arises as to the use of the name and the picture of Miss Humiston upon posters used to advertise this exhibition. If it be held that they cannot be used under that statute for the purposes of advertising these motion pictures, then it is clear that they cannot advertise the motion pictures at all, because they cannot be fully advertised, at least, without giving the name of the parties represented. When King Albert landed in New York, one of these companies procured moving pictures of the landing. Those were exhibited the same night in the city of New York, and upon the billboard at the entrance of the theatre it was announced that pictures of the landing of King Albert were to appear that night. Were they guilty of a misdemeanor for this announcement? If the conclusion which which I have reached upon the other branch of the case be correct, the presentation of the film describing that landing would not be against the spirit of the act. If so, it is difficult to distinguish and say that the advertising of the film with the simple use of King Albert's name constituted a crime. If the use of his name alone in advertising the film did not constitute a crime, the use of his picture would be no more criminal. So, in this case, if the presentation of this film be not a crime, the use of Miss Humiston's name or picture in the approach to the theatre and upon the billboards in front as advertising what was to appear upon the screen is I think incidental to the exhibition of the film itself. The statute we think only prohibits advertising with respect to a trade falling within the scope of the statute. The act should not reasonably be construed to prohibit such use of a name or picture.

Decision for Universal Films. ◀

The reader will by now have noted that the purported consistency of the court is perhaps more beguiling than it is logical. In effect, the court is saying that if the use of Miss Humiston's picture in the newsreel was not a use for advertising or trade, then neither is the use of her name or picture to *advertise* the newsreel. Not only does this view do violence to the commonly accepted meaning of the word "advertise"; it also veers away from the salutary reasoning behind the major part of the court's opinion.

Although we may all agree that it is important for the public dissemination of knowledge that the more or less "incidental" use of a person's name or picture in a newsreel be protected, it is more difficult to see why one who goes out of his way to use the person's name or picture to advertise the product should not have to pay the piper. It certainly would seem that an advertising display of one's name or picture would represent, at least in the public eye, considerably more than "incidental use."

Just to show that the view expressed above is not without its supporters, we point out that two judges in the *Humiston* case, although agreeing with the majority opinion on the newsreel, thought that Miss Humiston should have a right to sue based upon the use of her picture on the posters.

The *Binns, Merle,* and *Humiston* cases, almost a half-century old, have set the pattern of the Right of Privacy in motion pictures, at least in New York. None of these cases, however, dealt squarely with the question of whether the use of a person's name or picture that was merely incidental to a *fictional* portrayal constituted a legal invasion of his privacy. It was not until 1928 that the New York court came to grips with this issue in the field of fiction.

Edna Ferber, an author of international distinction, wrote
Show Boat in 1926. In a book of about 400 pages there appears on page 109 the following paragraph—the only reference to one Wayne Damron in the book:

▶ A peaceful enough existence in its routine, yet a curiously
crowded one for a child. She saw town after town whose
waterfront street was a solid block of saloons, one next the
other, open day and night. Her childhood impressions were
formed of stories, happenings, accidents, events born of the
rivers. Towns and cities and people came to be associated in
her mind with this or that bizarre bit of river life. The junction of the Ohio and Big Sandy rivers always was remembered by Magnolia as the place where the Black Diamond
Saloon was opened on the day the "Cotton Blossom" played
Catlettsburg. Catlettsburg, typical waterfront town of the
times, was like a knot that drew together the two rivers.
Ohio, West Virginia, and Kentucky met just there. And at
the junction of the rivers there was opened with high and
appropriate ceremonies the Black Diamond Saloon, owned
by those picturesque two, Big Wayne Damron and Little
Wayne Damron. From the deck of the "Cotton Blossom"
Magnolia saw the crowd waiting for the opening of the Black
Diamond doors—free drinks, free lunch, river town hospital-
ity. And then Big Wayne opened the doors, and the crowd
surged back while their giant host, holding the key aloft in
his hand, walked down to the river bank, held the key high
for a moment, then hurled it far into the yellow waters of the
Big Sandy. The Black Diamond Saloon was open for business. ◀

A man who claimed that he was the Little Wayne Damron of Catlettsburg referred to, started a suit claiming that
Miss Ferber, her publisher, and the bookstore outlets that
sold the book all used his name for the "purpose of trade"
—the phrase used in the New York statute on privacy. He

did not claim that his name had been used for the purpose of advertising, either for the book itself or for any other manufactured product.

What does "purpose of trade" mean? Obviously not that it was used in connection with any item that happened to be sold. Little Wayne Damron did not claim that the mention of his name in any way affected the sale of *Show Boat.*

The opinion in the Damron case is succinct and, in this area of "not for advertising" incidental use of a person's name, seems to be what lawyers call a leading case. It was argued that many other great writers of that era such as H. G. Wells and George Moore were known to have introduced real characters into fictional or pseudofictional narratives.

The opinion:

WAYNE DAMRON v. DOUBLEDAY, DORAN & CO., INC. AND BOOK SHOPS CO. AND EDNA FERBER (1928)

▶ There are three actions, one against the author of a novel called "Show Boat," one against its publishers, and a third against a bookseller. In the story, which is spread over 398 pages, Damron's name is mentioned at one place, in a scene laid in Catlettsburg, Ky. He alleges that in this scene his name is used as that of one of the characters, and that he is made to appear as one of the characters. He argued that, on the use at a single place in the book, without his consent, of a name by which he has been known, the name "Little Wayne Damron," he can base an action under the New York Law. He is not seeking a decision that he has an action for libel. The law affords him a remedy if he has been libeled. His present claim is that he has a case, even if he has not been libeled.

In 1902 the Court of Appeals, in the case of *Roberson* v. *Rochester Folding Box Co.*, refused to restrain the unauthorized publication and distribution of prints and photo-

graphs of a young woman in advertising flour. At the next
session of the Legislature the statutory provisions on which
Damron relies were adopted in their first form. They provide
that "for advertising purposes," or "for the purposes of
trade," the name or picture of a living person may not be
used without his consent. Damron asserts that his name is used
in this book for the purposes of trade. The question is whether
the reference to him at a single place in the book is a use for
purposes of trade.

The Legislature, but not the courts, may widen the scope
of the statute. We have only to consider whether in its present form it applies here. The decisions of our courts show
that every unauthorized use of a name or picture in connection with trade or advertising does not imply a violation of
the statute. Were it otherwise, many lines of business would
have to be abandoned. The Legislature did not, for example,
intend to stop the dissemination of "news" as a business in
itself or as adjunct to the sale of advertising. The courts in
this instance, as in all others, must seek the true intent of
the legislation. The Roberson case indicates the mischief to
be suppressed, and the enactment leaves the extent to which
it is intended that the remedy shall be applied. The law was
not passed with the idea of interfering with the circulation
of newspapers or the publication of books within proper
limits, and the use of "local color" was not outlawed. It
goes without saying that the literary expediency may not
be advanced as an excuse for violating the statute.

In determining whether a name or likeness is used primarily for advertising or trade, we may have to weigh the
circumstances, the extent, degree or character of the use.
It is well established that every incidental mention of some
person's name in connection with advertising or trade does
not constitute a violation of the provisions under consideration. The single appearance of plaintiff's name in this book
is clearly not a use prohibited by the statute. Were we to
take any other view, it is apparent that consequences never
contemplated would follow from its enactment. It would
indeed impose uncalled-for burden and hazard were we to

hold that publishers and booksellers could not lawfully publish or deal in books without the production of genuine, written consents from every one mentioned even once, or that an author could not lawfully mention any one without the consent. ◀

Human beings are never really the complete masters of what they survey, and circumstance often manages to trap them. The law, being man-made, is a creature of the compromise man must make with perfection if he is to live with himself. As such it usually makes provision for man's characteristic imperfection. The cases you have just read are good examples of this. None of the judges who decided them would disagree that it would have been less troublesome if Merle's sign had not appeared in the picture or if Miss Ferber had used a name other than Little Wayne Damron. Of course it would. But since streets do contain buildings and there are people who rejoice in almost every name you can think of, concessions must be made in order to safeguard the communication of ideas and the dissemination of art.

The concessions made in these cases, although somewhat arbitrary from a logical standpoint, appeal to most of us because the risk of harm is slight, while the benefit to society, certainly in the case of *Show Boat,* is substantial. The art of balancing one against the other is not always such an easy business. The next chapter will demonstrate this by describing the pathetic case of William Sidis.

9

The Child
Prodigy,
the Maestro,
and the Pro

Have you ever been on a stage? Ever spoken before an audience? Did you, as a child, ever take part in a Christmas or Easter pageant? In other words, have you ever offered yourself, or been offered by your parents or teachers, for public display? If so, should you, do you think, demand the protection and privileges of anonymity in spite of your appearance or appearances in the public eye? In other words, does a public life have the same right to return to a private life as a private life has to turn public? This was the crux of the William Sidis case.

Before we discuss it, one point must be borne in mind. Ours is a nation of federal powers, as we have said. Each of our fifty states is a separate experimental laboratory of the law. In historic terms this experiment of federalism may be the most important contribution of our nation to the history of government. States' rights at times seem costly and confusing. However, whatever we lose by duplication and conflict we make up for by the opportunity of experimenting in each state rather than on a vast national level. In every field of law that has been severely influenced by changing folkways, the advantage of federalism is clearly exposed. In simplest terms the point is made by reference to the laws on divorce. Many people deride the lack of uniformity between states. But ask yourself only one question: If there were to be a single national law on divorce, which should it be? Adultery as the only ground, as in some states? Desertion, as in others? Or just incompatibility, as in others? It may well be one of the profound blessings of our Republic that our states can experiment until there is a common denominator of acceptance sufficient to impress the desires of the people as a whole into a national pattern, a national law. Now to our case.

William James Sidis lived in Massachusetts, and *The New Yorker* magazine was a New York City enterprise. Sidis sued in the Federal Court in New York, and in that court he asked for a ruling as to his rights of privacy in various states where the magazine was sold. This saved him the trouble of starting separate suits in each state. With this in mind, three federal, not state, judges discussed the rights of Sidis in California, Georgia, Kansas, Kentucky, and Missouri, and then separately turned their attention to New York.

The judges found these facts:

▶ William James Sidis was the unwilling subject of a brief biographical sketch and cartoon printed in The New Yorker weekly magazine for August 14, 1937. Further references were made to him in the issue of December 25, 1937, and in a newspaper advertisement announcing the August 14 issue.

He was a famous child prodigy in 1910. His name and prowess were well known to newspaper readers of the period. At the age of eleven, he lectured to distinguished mathemati-

cians on the subject of Four-Dimensional Bodies. When he
was sixteen, he was graduated from Harvard College, amid
considerable public attention. Since then, his name has appeared in the press only sporadically, and he has sought to
live as unobtrusively as possible. Until the articles objected
to appeared in The New Yorker, he had apparently suc-
ceeded in his endeavor to avoid the public gaze.

Among The New Yorker's features are brief biographical
sketches of current and past personalities. In the latter
department, which appears haphazardly under the title of
"Where Are They Now?" the article on Sidis was printed
with a subtitle "April Fool." The author describes Sidis'
early accomplishments in mathematics and the widespread
attention he received, then recounts his general breakdown
and the revulsion which Sidis thereafter felt for his former
life of fame and study. The unfortunate prodigy is traced
over the years that followed, through his attempts to conceal
his identity, through his chosen career as an insignificant
clerk who would not need to employ unusual mathematical
talents, and through the bizarre ways in which his genius
flowered (or withered) as in his enthusiasm for collecting
streetcar transfers and in his proficiency with an adding
machine. The article closes with an account of an interview
with Sidis at his present lodgings, "a hall bedroom of Boston's shabby South End." The untidiness of his room, his
curious laugh, his manner of speech, and other personal
habits are commented upon at length, as is his present interest in the lore of the Okamakammessett Indians. The subtitle
is explained by the closing sentence, quoting Sidis as saying
"with a grin" that it was strange, "but, you know, I was
born on April Fool's Day." Accompanying the biography is
a small cartoon showing the genius of eleven years lecturing
to a group of astounded professors.

It is not contended that any of the matter printed is untrue. Nor is the manner of the author unfriendly; Sidis today is described as having "a certain childlike charm." But
the article is merciless in its dissection of intimate details of
its subject's life, and this in company with elaborate accounts

of Sidis' passion for privacy and the pitiable lengths to which
he has gone in order to avoid public scrutiny. The work possesses great reader interest, for it is both amusing and instructive; but it may be fairly described as a ruthless exposure of a once public character, who has since sought and has
now been deprived of the seclusion of private life.

The article of December 25, 1937, was a biographical
sketch of another former child prodigy, in the course of
which William James Sidis and the recent account of him
were mentioned. The advertisement published in the New
York World-Telegram of August 13, 1937, read: "Out
Today. Harvard Prodigy. Biography of the man who aston-
ished Harvard at age 11. Where are they now? by J. L.
Manley. Page 22. The New Yorker."

THE OPINION OF THE COURT

We are asked to declare that this exposure transgresses
upon Mr. Sidis' right of privacy, as recognized in California,
Georgia, Kansas, Kentucky, and Missouri. Each of these
states except California grants to the individual a right to
be let alone to a certain extent. The decisions have been care-
fully analyzed by the court below, and we need not examine
them further. None of the cited rulings goes so far as to
prevent a newspaper or magazine from publishing the truth
about a person, however intimate, revealing, or harmful the
truth may be. Nor are there any decided cases that confer
such a privilege upon the press. We face the unenviable duty
of determining the law of five states on a broad and vital
public issue which the courts of those states have not even
discussed.

All comment upon the right of privacy must stem from
the famous article by Warren and Brandeis. Warren and
Brandeis realized that the interest of the individual in privacy must inevitably conflict with the interest of the public
in news. Certain public figures, they conceded, such as hold-
ers of public office, must sacrifice their privacy and expose
at least part of their lives to public scrutiny as the price

of the powers they attain. But even public figures were not to be stripped bare.

It must be conceded that under the strict standards suggested by these authors Sidis' right of privacy has been invaded. Sidis today is neither politician, public administrator, nor statesman. Even if he were, some of the personal details revealed were of the sort that Warren and Brandeis believed "all men alike are entitled to keep from popular curiosity."

But despite eminent opinion to the contrary, we are not yet disposed to afford to all of the intimate details of private life an absolute immunity from the prying of the press. Everyone will agree that at some point the public interest in obtaining information becomes dominant over the individual's desire for privacy. Warren and Brandeis were willing to lift the veil somewhat in the case of public officers. We would go further, though we are not yet prepared to say how far. At least we would permit limited scrutiny of the "private" life of any person who has achieved, or *has had thrust upon him*, the questionable and indefinable status of a "public figure."

William James Sidis was once a public figure. As a child prodigy, he excited both admiration and curiosity. Of him great deeds were expected. In 1910, he was a person about whom the newspapers might display a legitimate intellectual interest, in the sense meant by Warren and Brandeis, as distinguished from a trivial and unseemly curiosity. But the precise *motives* of the press we regard as unimportant. And even if Sidis had loathed public attention at that time, we think his uncommon achievements and personality would have made the attention permissible. Since then Sidis has cloaked himself in obscurity, but his subsequent history, containing as it did the answer to the question of whether or not he had fulfilled his early promise, was still a matter of public concern. The article in The New Yorker sketched the life of an unusual personality, and it possessed considerable popular news interest.

We express no comment on whether or not the news worthiness of the matter printed will always constitute a complete defense. Revelations may be so intimate and so unwarranted in view of the victim's position as to outrage the community's notions of decency. But when focused upon public characters, truthful comments upon dress, speech, habits, and the ordinary aspects of personality will usually not transgress this line. Regrettably or not, the misfortunes and frailties of neighbors and "public figures" are subjects of considerable interest and discussion to the rest of the population. And when such are the mores of the community, it would be unwise for a court to bar their expression in the newspapers, books, and magazines of the day.

Sidis charged actual malice in the publication. If his right of privacy was not invaded by the article, the existence of actual malice in its publication would not change that result. Personal ill-will is not an ingredient of the offense. Nor does malice give rise to an independent wrong based on an intentional invasion of Sidis' interest in mental and emotional tranquillity. This interest, however real, is one not yet protected by the law.

If the article appearing in the issue of August 14, 1937, does not furnish grounds for the suit, then it is clear that the brief and incidental reference to it contained in the article of December 25, 1937, is also not grounds for the suit.

Sidis also charged invasion of the rights conferred on him by the N.Y. Civil Rights Law. The New York statute forbids the use of a name or picture only when employed "for advertising purposes, or for the purposes of trade." In this context, it is clear that "for the purposes of trade" does not contemplate the publication of a newspaper, magazine, or book which imparts truthful news or other factual information to the public. Though a publisher sells a commodity, and expects to profit from the sale of his product, he is immune so long as he confines himself to the unembroidered dissemination of facts. Publishers and motion picture producers have occasionally been held to transgress the statute in New York, but in each case the factual presentation was embellished by some degree of fictionalization. The New

Yorker articles limit themselves to the unvarnished, unfictionalized truth.

The case as to the newspaper advertisements announcing the August 14 article is somewhat different, for it was undoubtedly inserted in the World-Telegram "for advertising purposes." But since it was to advertise the article on Sidis, and the article itself was unobjectionable, the advertisement shares the privilege enjoyed by the article. Besides, the advertisement, quoted above, did not use the "name, portrait or picture" of Sidis. ◀

This was a tough case. Human sympathy was all in Sidis' corner—that quiet harbor he loved—free from the public gaze. Once before and once too often he had been buffeted by parents and press into the limelight. He had not asked for it then and he deplored it now.

The biggest problem of the honest judge is the dual vision he has of the person standing at the bar. On the one hand, he must see the unique, individual human being; on the other, an instrument with which to fashion rules of law that may affect the lives of hundreds of thousands of other people. Judge Jerome Frank of our Federal Court system made his greatest contribution to jurisprudence in dealing with and reconciling this clash. A defendant charged in a criminal case should be treated as more than a statistic in the prosecutor's total of convictions obtained, he felt. At the same time, without defined though flexible rules of law, no one would know how to behave from day to day, and many would at times find they had bad-guessed themselves into jail.

So our court hurt Sidis . . . because of the need, as they saw it, of a greater and more general good.

This clash of viewpoints is typical of most privacy cases. It does not mean once-public-always-public, in all situations, for all persons, and to any extreme. But this decision was a pivotal one because it established the distinction between a "public" and a "private" person under the privacy law. Perhaps the Sidis case does not show this distinction to its best advantage. Let us therefore consider the case of a voluntary, professional public figure of great reputation, and his quarrel with a book publisher.

In 1947 Serge Koussevitzky, the great conductor of the Boston Symphony Orchestra, was busily writing his autobiography when he learned that Moses Smith, the well-known music critic, was preparing to publish a biography about him without his permission. His attorneys advised him that he had the legal right to prevent publication of Smith's book. If the court were to agree with Koussevitzky, historians would have to go hat in hand to a Hitler or a Stalin or a Castro to ask permission to write about their lives. One can imagine the kind of biographer men in public life would approve, were their approval mandatory. The distortions of history are already great enough without such an extra burden. Dr. Koussevitzky, however, felt otherwise. To start with, he asked for an order to prevent publication of the biography, at least until the court had rendered a decision. Such an injunction was granted, and Dr. Koussevitzky put up a bond so as to compensate the author and publisher should the court decide against him. The New York court then decided the substance of his case in an opinion that affords us an excellent, if brief, summary of the right of privacy in New York as of 1947:

SERGE KOUSSEVITZKY V. ALLEN, TOWNE & HEATH, INC. ET AL. (1947)

▶ Dr. Koussevitzky, an eminent conductor of a world-renowned symphony orchestra, and an outstanding international figure in the field of music, who earns substantial sums of money from his various musical activities, seeks to stop the publication of a book purporting to be his biography, for which he had refused authorization. The book contains pictures of him which he says are used without his permission, and it has the usual puffing or advertising cover jacket.

Dr. Koussevitzky charges that the book "falsely and wrongfully portrays his life and musical career" and that it contains much objectionable, untruthful, fictitious and defamatory matter which he more or less particularizes in his complaint. For his right to relief he relies mainly on what he claims to be a violation of the "Right of Privacy" afforded by sections 50 and 51 of the Civil Rights Law of New York. The precise question which he thus raises has never been decided in this State.

In 1890, the subject of the right of privacy was considered in a brilliant essay which has become a classic in the law (Warren and Brandeis on The Right to Privacy). In 1902, the question was presented to the Court of Appeals in *Roberson* v. *Rochester Folding Box Co.* By a divided bench of four to three, it was held that there was no common-law right of privacy in this State. Recovery was denied to a woman whose photograph was used by another without her authorization, in advertising its brand of flour.

The following year, the Legislature enacted sections 50 and 51 of the Civil Rights Law.

This statute sought to protect the sentiments, thoughts and feelings of an individual by embodying "a legal recognition—limited in scope to be sure, but a clearly expressed recognition nevertheless—of the right of a person to be let alone, a right directed 'against the commercial exploitation of one's personality.'" It made it a misdemeanor and a civil wrong to use the name, picture or portrait of any living person "for advertising purposes or for the purposes of trade" without first having obtained his written consent. The remedy thus afforded was threefold: compensatory, punitive and preventive. Prior restraint was specifically authorized.

It should be noted that Warren and Brandeis in their article realized that the courts would have to endeavor to reach the point of equilibrium between the opposing tendencies, on the one hand, to protect "the inviolate personality," and on the other, to keep the avenues of news and of the dissemination of information free and unimpeded. They drew a distinction between those persons in whose private affairs the community has no legitimate concern and those who have renounced to live their lives screened from public observation and who are the subject of legitimate interest to their fellow citizens.

From the outset, the courts, in interpreting the "Right of Privacy" statute, took the position that it had no application to items of current news and that those who were the subject of news, whether public figures or otherwise, were not embraced in its provisions. The statute likewise has been held not to apply to articles which, though not strictly news, are informative and educational and which make use of the names or pictures of living persons. In this class of publications, however, the picture or name must be sufficiently relevant to the subject matter to warrant its use and must have some legitimate public interest; in other words, the use must be of such a nature as would not outrage common ordinary decency. The courts have tended to be extremely liberal, particularly as to publications in newspapers and magazines, in their conception of the scope of "the dissemination of information." They have not, thus far at any rate, dogmatically applied the distinction laid down by Warren and Brandeis between a so-called private individual and a public figure, although they have frequently emphasized the existence of the latter and given him a rather broad and elastic definition.

Dr. Koussevitzky during the greater part of his life has been and continues to be an important public figure. His prominent achievements as a musician bring him constantly before the public eye and make his life of general interest. His stature as a conductor is amply attested by the numerous references to him in contemporary books, magazines and newspapers. He is well within the orbit of public interest and scrutiny.

Together with the removal of "current news" and matters of "public interest," from the operation of the right of privacy statute there appeared in court decisions a realistic definition of the words "for advertising purposes, or for the purposes of trade" as used in the statute. A literal construction of these words would have resulted in seriously hampering freedom of speech and of the press. All publications presumably are operated for profit and articles contained therein are used with a view to increasing circulation. Accordingly, emphasis was laid on the nature of the article, and of the use of the name or picture, and whether they were of public interest, rather than on the element of profit.

It is clear, therefore, that the right of privacy statute applies to the unauthorized use of a name or picture to sell a collateral commodity. That was the precise situation presented in the Roberson case and was what the statute was primarily intended to cover. The statute, it has been decided, also applies to the unauthorized fictional use of a name or photograph (see the Binns case).

The right of privacy statute does not apply to an unauthorized biography of a public figure unless the biography is fictional or novelized in character. An examination of the book complained of clearly shows that it is not fictional. That it may contain untrue statements does not transform it into the class of fiction. Truth or falsity does not, of itself, determine whether the publication comes within the ban of the Privacy Laws.

The book we are considering deals almost entirely with Dr. Koussevitzky's musical career. Very little is said about his private life. Indeed, the author suggests that Dr. Koussevitzky had room for nothing in his life but music and a devotion to his loyal wife and helpmate. Interspersed with the chronological narration of the facts are stories and comments in connection with Dr. Koussevitzky's musical career, some avowedly apocryphal, others of doubtful reliability. Curiously enough, although there are many depreciatory statements, they seem to be invariably followed by ameliorative observations of unreserved praise. The factual matter contained in the book testifies to Koussevitzky's triumphs as a conductor of the Boston Symphony and other great orchestras, to his courage and independence, and to his devotion to the education and training of young musicians. Most people know that a great conductor's work with his orchestra is not altogether carried on in an atmosphere of sweetness and light. The author evidently knows that too and loses no opportunity to inform his readers about it. In his final chapter, the author gives his personal estimate of Dr. Koussevitzky's place in musical history and in sentence after sentence we find out that depreciation and praise vie with each other for utterance.

There are statements in the book which Koussevitzky might naturally find to be highly objectionable, if he is at all sensitive about those things. He may be able to prove some of them to be untrue and even defamatory. There are however, no so-called revelations of any intimate details which would tend to outrage public tolerance. There is nothing repugnant to one's sense of decency or that takes the book out of the realm of the legitimate dissemination of information on a subject of general interest.

Since the biography does not fall within the law neither do the advertisements or announcements thereof. Such advertising, as is here complained of, has been held to be incidental to the publication itself.

As for the use of photographs of Dr. Koussevitzky, it has long been held that where one obtains a picture of a public person and there is no breach of contract or violation of confidence in the method by which it was obtained "he has the right to reproduce it, whether in a newspaper, magazine, or book. It would be extending this right of protection too far to say that the general public can be prohibited from knowing the public appearance of great public characters. Such characters may be said, of their own volition, to have dedicated to the public the right of any fair portraiture of themselves." ◀

Thus Dr. Koussevitzky lost his case, and the publisher and author collected, as they should have, on the bond. Since Dr. Koussevitzky also argued that the book should be suppressed because of alleged libel, the judge referred to the ancient theory of law which maintains that there is no right to prevent the publication of libelous material. (Once it is published, the victim may then take legal action.) So Dr. Koussevitzky lost on all counts.

Dr. Koussevitzky in his endeavor to suppress the Moses Smith biography pleaded the Right of Privacy. The reader may have wondered if this was truly what worried the great orchestra leader. Might he not have been disturbed by the idea that the autobiography on which he was working would not sell so well if the biography, soon to be marketed, met with public favor? The idea of unfair competition is at times akin to the Right of Privacy. The English trend in this new field of law has been more frank in recognizing that the right to prevent others from invading privacy is only one side of the coin. The other side may often mean the exclusive right to use one's own privacy, whether by picture or name, for one's own profit or benefit. The law has had some difficulty and will have more in preventing the fusion of these two approaches—in other words, to ascertain whether the Right to Be Let Alone is used as a bastion with which to protect the quietude of genuine privacy or as a device to enhance the value of one's own publicity.

The case of Ben Hogan in 1957 was troublesome to the judicial minds of Pennsylvania on this very score:

Hogan v. A. S. Barnes & Company, Incorporated

▶ This case presents a fact situation which, so far as our research discloses, is dissimilar from any which has ever come before an appellate court in the United States. However, the common law is not static but an ever-expanding body of law, and, therefore, the lack of direct precedent does not necessarily defeat plaintiff's right to recovery. As Chief

Judge Biggs stated in a recent decision which also involved a relatively new theory of law: "Concededly, the theory is a somewhat hazy one; but that is not unusual where the laboratories of the courts are working out the development of a new common law right."

In this case (which was tried without a jury before the writer of this opinion) the basic facts are not in dispute, but the parties, of course, are not in agreement as to the legal inferences and conclusions to be drawn from the facts. The material facts are as follows:

Ben Hogan, 44 years of age, has been a professional golfer for a period of 25 years and is recognized as one of the greatest golfers of all time. Since 1938 he has won many professional golf tournaments, including the most important in the country; he has received awards as "Golfer of the Year," "Sportsman of the Decade," and the Vardon Trophy; he has appeared in exhibitions; he has made personal appearances on radio and television; he has appeared in motion pictures; he was the author of the book "Power Golf," which Barnes published and which is the largest-selling book of golf instructions ever published, and he was the author of various magazine articles which appeared from time to time in Esquire, Reader's Digest, Saturday Evening Post, This Week, Look, Time, Life and Sports Illustrated.

A. S. Barnes & Company, Incorporated, is a New York corporation engaged primarily in publishing books on sports, and is the largest publisher of such books in the United States.

The origin of this litigation was the publication by Barnes on June 6, 1955, of a book entitled "Golf With the Masters." It was a book on golf written by one Dave Camerer, in which the names and photographs of a number of famous golfers, including plaintiff, are prominently displayed on the jacket and in the text. Most of the pictures of Hogan which appear in the book were taken while he was practicing on the putting green at Baltusrol Country Club, just prior to the 1954 United States Open Tournament, and he was not aware of the purpose for which the pictures were being taken.

On July 9, 1954, Camerer, the author of the book, wrote to Hogan stating that photographs of him had been taken at Baltusrol for illustrations in a book which Camerer was preparing for Barnes. The letter also contained a consent for Hogan to sign, for which Camerer promised to send Hogan $100 and two copies of the book when completed. The consent form provided for an assignment to Camerer by Hogan of all literary rights "in an article to be written under my (Hogan's) supervision"; that Camerer would have the right to use Hogan's name and signature as author, as well as any biographical data and pictures of him. Hogan's reply to this letter, dated July 21, 1954, contained only three words: "Are you kidding?"

On July 24, 1954, Hogan wrote to the President of Barnes Company informing him of the letter which he had received and asserting that the photographs at Baltusrol had been taken without his knowledge or consent to their use of publication. In this letter Hogan urged Barnes' president "not to accept for publication any material written about me, or my golf swing, either from this fellow Camerer or anyone else so far as that is concerned. This goes for photographs also."

Despite Hogan's express and forceful dissent as to the use of his photographs or name in connection with Camerer's proposed book, as published, it used his name and photographs. Hogan was never shown a manuscript of the book before publication, and he saw it for the first time when he was requested to autograph a copy while he was playing in the National Open Tournament in June of 1955.

The book "Golf With the Masters" was originally intended to be titled "Great Golfers," but about three or four months prior to its publication, Barnes decided to change the title to "Golf With the Masters," as it was the publishers' opinion that this latter title would sell more books than the original. The book was widely advertised and an excerpt appeared in the American Weekly of June 12, 1955. ◀

Hogan was greatly annoyed and, with the aid of his lawyer, "threw the book" at Barnes. In addition to allegations of libel and breach of fiduciary duty (neither of which is pertinent to this volume) Hogan claimed that the use of his name and picture in *Golf With the Masters* constituted an invasion of his Right of Privacy, constituted unfair competition in that it competed with his other books, and finally (and this one is new) constituted an *unauthorized* and uncompensated appropriation for commercial purposes of his "right of publicity." Read on:

▶ While there was once some doubt as to whether or not a right of privacy existed under the common law of Pennsylvania, there is now no question but that it does exist.

Right of privacy has frequently been employed as a generic term covering a great many diverse types of causes of action. The classic case in which the term "right of privacy" has been applied, however, is where the manufacturer or seller of a product has used a person's photograph without his consent in an advertisement of the product. Although all of the cases involving situations of this type have been classified as invasions of the right of privacy, we perceive a distinct difference between two basic types of situations.

On the one hand, where the person is previously unknown to the general public, that is one who has lived a life of relative obscurity insofar as publicity is concerned, the gist of his complaint is that, by reason of the publication of his picture in connection with the advertisement of a product, he has been unwillingly exposed to the glare of public scrutiny. In such a case, his right of privacy has truly been invaded.

On the other hand, where the person may be termed a "public figure," such as an actor or an athlete, the gist of his complaint is entirely different. He does not complain that, by reason of the publication of his picture in connection with the advertisement of a product, his name and face have become a matter of public comment, but rather that the commercial value which has attached to his name because of the fact that he is a public figure has been exploited without his having shared in the profits therefrom. It is common knowledge that many prominent persons (especially actors and ballplayers), far from having their feelings bruised through public exposure of their likenesses, would feel sorely deprived if they no longer received money for authorizing advertisements publicizing their countenances, displayed in newspers, magazines, buses, trains and subways.

It is, therefore, our conclusion that the true theory upon which Hogan seeks to base Barnes' liability to him is the very antithesis of the right of privacy. He does not complain that his name should have been withheld from public scrutiny; on the contrary, he asserts that his name has great commercial value in connection with the game of golf, and that Barnes' use of his name has resulted in damage to him. We therefore decide that Hogan's right of privacy has not been violated. ◀

Up to this point the Pennsylvania court is in agreement with the general rule, as enunciated in such New York cases as *Sidis* and *Koussevitzky,* that once in the public arena a person has pretty well forfeited his Right of Privacy. However, the decision doesn't stop there, but proceeds to take up what it has referred to as Hogan's "true theory" of the case.

Those who are intrigued by the kinship of the Right of Privacy and the collateral right to invade one's own privacy for purposes of publicity or profit should note well how the court states the issue:

▶ Therefore, in the instant case, if Hogan is to recover damages from Barnes on the theory of unfair competition, he must demonstrate: (1) That he has an enforceable property right in the commercial value of his name and photograph in connection with the game of golf; (2) That he did not authorize Barnes to make any commercial use of his name and photograph, and (3) That the publication, sale and advertisement by Barnes of the book "Golf With the Masters" constituted unfair competition as to Hogan. ◀

The court then decided that Hogan had an enforceable property right in the good will and commercial value of his name and photograph in connection with the game of golf.

The other requirement was fairly simple—that Hogan was unfairly competed against by the Barnes book.

▶ An examination of the jacket of Barnes' book reveals that the words which first attract attention are its title, "Golf With the Masters" and the names of 12 famous golfers, one of whom is Hogan. Under this appear the words, "The Secret to Better Golf by Dave Camerer. Photographs by Phil Mark."

Examining the contents of the book, a reader would be attracted by such bold-faced titles as "Hitting Your Tee Shots With Sam Snead", "Reaching For Your Spoon (3 Wood) With Cary Middlecoff", "4 and 5 Iron Sharpshooting With Jack Burke", "Playing the Punch Shot With the 5 Iron With Jimmie Demaret", "Attacking With Your 6 and 7 Iron Straight for the Pin—With Tommy Bolt", "The Pitching Wedge * * * Your Passport to Pars and Birdies—With Lew Worsham", " 'Don't Let Poor Recovery Shots Hobble Your Game,' Says John Revolta", and "Sand in Your Shoes * * * Trap Shots are Easy With Claude Harmon". ◀

The court concluded that a reader would receive the impression that these Masters, including Hogan, had had some part in the preparation of the volume. It's amusing to note that the court rested this conclusion on a "cursory" examination of the book.

The final blow was struck when the court wrote:

▶ There can be no doubt but that Ben Hogan has acquired
over many years a unique position and reputation in the
sport of golf. This position has been acquired by virtue of a
tremendous amount of work, ability and perseverance on his
part. As a result, his name and photograph in connection
with any aspect of the sport of golf have great commercial
value. Barnes, well realizing this fact, has unfairly attempted
to profit from it.

We find, therefore, that the circumstances under which
defendant published and advertised the book "Golf With
the Masters" constituted a misappropriation of the property
right which Hogan has in the commercial value of his name
and photograph.

We, therefore, hold that he has sustained his cause of
action against Barnes for unfair competition.   ◀

But this was not enough, for the worried judge dipped into
what he called the "right of publicity," and declared:

▶ We conclude, therefore, that defendant has misappropri-
ated plaintiff's "right of publicity," but that this is simply
an application of the doctrine of unfair competition to a
property right entitled "right of publicity." This, therefore,
is not a separate cause of action, but rather is unfair competition under another label.

Basically, the defense is that Hogan is a public figure, and
as such he may not complain of the publication of news or
information concerning him or of fair comment made about
him. We fully agree with this contention as an abstract statement of law; it does not, however, apply to the facts of this
case. As a public figure, Hogan could certainly not complain
of a news series written about him or a fair comment made
concerning him. There are undoubtedly many ways in which
his name may be and has been used in a publication without

giving rise to a cause of action on his part. The manner in which his name and photograph were used in this case, however, is not one of them. The very point of Hogan's case is that "Golf With the Masters" and the advertisement thereof did not indicate that it was a book about Hogan or his golf game, but rather that it indicated that it in some manner was a book in which the reader would be receiving some "tips" about Hogan's golf game, either directly or indirectly from Hogan. ◀

At this point the reader might well ask himself whether the court, in declaring this so-called "right of publicity," has created a boon or a burden. Even before this decision, courts were generally agreed that even public figures have certain rights of privacy left to them. For example, it was, and still is, clear that if the particular exposure of a public figure, as well as a private person, were indecent it could be stopped. Also courts do protect the likes of Marlon Brando from being made to appear as endorsing certain products. But the decision in the Hogan case goes further. By granting to a public figure a corollary to the Right of Privacy, namely a Right of Publicity, the court goes far to eradicate the public-figure exception in the law of privacy. Although Hogan's cause may seem just, if this doctrine becomes a precedent, future courts may find an amazing number of famous people who "just happen" to be writing their autobiographies (never to be finished) at the same time as other statements about them appear in print. What price privacy then?

Seemingly oblivious to such future reverberations, the court, having found Hogan to be injured, now attempts to assess the damage in terms of hard cash. We present this part of the court's opinion in order to give the reader a glimpse of the ineffable process of putting a price tag on injured psyches —one part calculation, one part rationalization, and a dash of intuition:

▶ Having found that Hogan has a cause of action for unfair competition by Barnes, resulting in injury to a property right of his, which may be called his "right of publicity," the final question for determination is the measure of damages. We start, of course, with the proposition that the extent to which Hogan's right of publicity has been damaged by defendant's book is not capable of exact measurement in dollars. However, as our Supreme Court recently stated:

"The law does not require that proof in support of claims for damages or in support of claims for compensation must conform to the standard of mathematical exactness. . . . Evidence in support of a claim for damages was sufficient if it affords a reasonably fair basis for calculating the plaintiff's loss. . . . If the facts afford a reasonably fair basis for calculating how much plaintiff is entitled to, such evidence cannot be regarded as legally insufficient to support a claim for compensation."

In the instant case we conclude that "a reasonably fair basis" for calculating the damage to Hogan has been provided by the evidence in his case. This evidence established these facts: (1) That Hogan has a unique position and reputation in the world of golf, in that he is universally recognized as one of the greatest golfers of all time; (2) that since the year 1937 he has earned approximately $1,000,000 from golf, and it is significant to note that of these earnings a little more than one-quarter represents winnings from golf tournaments, while almost three-quarters represents earnings from exhibitions, endorsements, royalties, personal appearances, motion pictures, magazine articles, etc.; (3) that from his writings on the subject of golf Hogan has received (a) $62,950 as royalties from the sale of his book "Power Golf," published by Barnes and (b) the following sums from magazine articles written by him: Reader's Digest, $1,500; London Sunday Express, $3,500; Cowles Magazine, $5,000; Saturday Evening Post, $2,500; This Week, $750; and Look, $5,000; and (4) that, in addition to the foregoing sums, Hogan received $20,000 from Life Magazine for the publica-

tion in Life Magazine and Sports Illustrated Magazine, of
an article purporting to reveal Hogan's so-called "secret,"
about which there had been considerable speculation in the
golfing world.

From this evidence there emerge the clear conclusions (a)
that, by reason of Hogan's unique position in the world of
golf, publications on the subject of his golfing style and
technique are a source of substantial income to him; and (b)
that a publisher who makes an unauthorized use of such
assets and appropriates them to his own commercial purposes,
subjects himself to the payment of damages.

In deciding that Hogan is entitled to recover compensatory
damages from Barnes, we also decide that in fixing the
amount of such damages we must take into consideration the
circumstances "a" that the publication of the book "Golf
With the Masters" and the supplementary publication of
excerpts from the book in magazines, etc., did not result in
profit to Barnes and "b" that Barnes' book did not deal or
purport to deal exclusively with Hogan and, on the contrary,
the evidence disclosed (1) that the jacket of the book listed
the name of Hogan with the names of 11 other golfers; (2)
in the book itself the names, styles and techniques of many
well known golfers in addition to Hogan were prominently
displayed by way of action photographs and comments by
the author, as demonstrated by the following analysis: (a)
The book contains 159 pages, of which only seven have reference to plaintiff, viz., on page 82, the opening paragraph
deals with the author's explanation of "Hogan's secret";
pages 101–05 contain nine action photographs of Hogan
with comments by the author as to Hogan's putting technique; and on page 117 there is a copy of a photograph
taken by Life Magazine, showing Hogan walking along the
fairway of the eighteenth hole at Baltusrol, the site of the
1954 National Open Championship; and (b) the book contains 171 photographs of numerous golfers other than Hogan
most of whom have attained National prominence, with comments by the author on their style and technique. ◀

So much for the calculation and rationalization. Now for the intuition:

▶ Under all the circumstances, we fix and assess Hogan's damages at the sum of $5,000. ◀

And who is to say that the intuition was bad? Intuition is the constant tool of lawyers and judges alike, perhaps because it provides an extra dimension in which to view the mass of relativities that is man. By making the publisher pay for its folly, the court might well be raising the business community to new standards of morality and conduct. Whether this value is strong enough to outweigh the dangers of the decision is not any man's guess; it is a thoughtful man's guess.

In discussing "misappropriation" and "unfair competition," the court in the Hogan case was giving labels to elements that are characteristics of the cases in our next chapter, which deal with invasion of privacy through advertising. The use of one's name or picture for advertising purposes usually presents a composite of violations among which are the two mentioned above, but all of which are subsumed under the broad heading of "invasion of privacy."

10

Advertising—
on Purpose
and by Accident

SINCE the publication in 1890 of the Warren-Brandeis article, and especially since the passage in 1903 of the New York statute, a raft of privacy cases have entered the courts. Our difficulty is not in finding significant conflicts but rather in selecting pertinent ones and excluding what lawyers or readers may consider equally important and entertaining.

That portion of the battle for privacy that deals with a name or picture for advertising of wares or services has fared comparatively well from our point of view and, we trust, yours. Even though some leaders in our society—Hollywood luminaries, publishers, or business tycoons—increasingly let their pictures be presented to our public for publicity or money, the unauthorized use of personal privacy to sell merchandise has been eliminated—unless the public personage consents in advance and in writing.

But there are still and always will be situations on the edges of the defined permissible uses that push judges beyond the periphery of established precedent into areas as yet uncharted. The four cases in this chapter are good examples of

such situations; and, because the judges involved were intelligent men well versed in the law of privacy, the cases are
also good examples of judicial solutions of subtle problems of
balance and degree.

We begin with a case that itself does not precisely involve
advertising but which, because of its thorough analysis of the
law to date and the philosophy beyond that law, has become
a landmark case in the field and has influenced the advertising cases that follow.

The case was brought by Sarat Lahiri under the New York
Privacy Law to stop the *Daily Mirror* from continuing to use
Lahiri's picture for trade purposes, and also for money damages for prior use. Here are the facts as stated by the learned
judge (Justice Shientag):

SARAT LAHIRI v. DAILY MIRROR, INC. (1937)

▶ The Daily Mirror, Inc. is the publisher of a newspaper
known as the *Sunday Mirror*. A feature of the paper is a
magazine section containing various illustrated articles of
more or less general interest. In the magazine section of the
issue of September 16, 1934, there appeared an article written by one Matthew entitled, "I Saw The Famous Rope
Trick—(But It Didn't Really Happen)." The article was
inspired by an offer of the "Magic Circle," a British society
of mystics, to pay a large sum of money to any one who
would cause a coil of rope to rise unaided until one end
would be suspended in mid-air, contrary to the force of
gravity, a feat known as the Hindu "Rope Trick."

The author attempted in the article to show that Hindu
mystics, by the exercise of hypnotic powers and the creation
of an illusion, firmly convinced bystanders that the rope was
actually rising into the atmosphere although in fact it remained coiled upon the ground at all times. He claimed that
the yogis were able to create the illusion by casting a spell
over onlookers, much as a snake fascinates a bird, rendering

them amenable to the suggestion that the rope in fact did rise of its own volition. The ability to create the illusion, contends the author, rests in an occult philosophy developed in the Far East through long cultivation.

The article in question was illustrated partly by specially posed colored photographs of a humorous nature indicating the rising of a rope and its ascension by a woman. Towards the end of the article, which was continued on another page, there appear three photographs. One is entitled, "India's Holy Men Studying"; the other is of a tower where the rope trick is alleged to have been performed; and the one complained of is a reproduction of a professional photograph of Lahiri, a well-known Hindu musician, playing a musical instrument as an accompaniment to an Indian female dancer. Beneath the photograph of Lahiri and the female dancer, the following explanatory words appear: "*MYSTIC*. Something of the Occult Philosophy Which Dominates the Far East May Be Seen, Even in the Gestures and Postures of Indian Dancers, Such as Those Portrayed Above." ◀

Justice Shientag then continues with a brief history of the Right of Privacy in New York, with which the reader is already familiar. In the course of this history, however, the judge takes time out to answer those other judges who, as we have seen, were reluctant to grant people relief under the privacy law because the law was in part penal (remember that in addition to civil remedies—for example, money damages—the statute also provides for the possibility of the invasion of privacy being held to be a misdemeanor—that is, a possible jail sentence or fine paid to the state):

▶ While "in part at least penal," in a larger sense the statute is remedial, having its root in dissatisfaction with what was felt to be an archaic rule of law. Interpretation should aid this purpose. "It would be a misfortune if a narrow or grudging process of construction were to exemplify and perpetuate the very evils to be remedied." A statute of this kind is not "to be obeyed grudgingly, by construing it narrowly and treating it as though it did not exist for any purpose other than that embraced within the strict construction of its words." It is "not an alien intruder in the house of the common law, but a guest to be welcomed and made at home there as a new and powerful aid in the accomplishment of its appointed task of accommodating the law to social needs." ◀

The judge then presents us with an able summary of previous attempts to define such elusive phrases as "advertising purposes" and "purposes of trade" (both of which the reader will recall appear in the New York law and elsewhere). We present this summary because it provides the reader with an intelligent perspective with which to view the development of the Right of Privacy in New York:

▶ The statutory terms, "advertising purposes" and "purposes of trade," have received numerous judicial definitions. The term "advertising purposes" means a solicitation for patronage. Unless the name, picture or portrait appears in, or as part of, an advertisement, no violation of the statute arises in this respect. The photograph in the instant case does not appear in any advertisement or in connection with any solicitation for patronage, and, therefore, no violation of this portion of the statute is indicated.

In defining the term "purposes of trade," however, the courts have drawn certain distinctions. In the following types of cases recovery was denied: The use of plaintiff's name and picture in a motion picture of current events; the use of a name once in a novel of almost 400 pages; the portrayal of plaintiff's factory on which his firm name clearly appeared, in a motion picture dealing with the white slave traffic; the use of the name and picture of an alleged strike breaker together with the names and likenesses of eight others on the frontispiece, and the mention of his name four times in 314 pages of a book dealing with strike-breaking; and the attributing of the authorship of an absurd adventure story purporting to be true, to a well-recognized and reputable writer.

The line of demarcation that has been drawn in defining "purposes of trade" in certain situations is not entirely clear. Whatever may be the rule under the state in the case of motion picture films (involving as they do repeated showings and sales or rentals to exhibitors), with respect to newspapers, recovery under the statute has for the most part been denied for the unauthorized publication in a single issue of photographs used in connection with the dissemination of current news and matters of information and general interest. The public policy involved in leaving unhampered the channels for the circulation of news and information is considered of primary importance, subject always, of course, to the common-law right of redress for libel. A free press is so intimately bound up with fundamental democratic institutions that if the right of privacy is to be extended to cover news items and articles of general public interest, educational and informative in character, it should be the result of a clear expression of legislative policy.

Some authorities have gone so far as to intimate that, apart from advertising, newspapers are altogether exempt from the present statute, so far as publication in a single issue is concerned. To so broad a rule, however, I do not subscribe. ◀

Justice Shientag then provides us with his own version of the applicable rules, and applies the facts in the *Lahiri* case to those rules:

▶ The rules applicable to unauthorized publication of photographs in a single issue of a newspaper may be summarized generally as follows:

1. Recovery may be had under the statute if the photograph is published in or as part of an advertisement, or for advertising purposes.

2. The statute is violated if the photograph is used in connection with an article of fiction in any part of the newspaper.

3. There may be no recovery under the statute for publication of a photograph in connection with an article of current news or immediate public interest.

4. Newspapers publish articles which are neither strictly news items nor strictly fictional in character. They are not the responses to an event of peculiarly immediate interest but, though based on fact, are used to satisfy an ever-present educational need. Such articles include, among others, travel stories, stories of distant places, tales of historic personages and events, the reproduction of items of past news, and surveys of social conditions. These are articles educational and informative in character. As a general rule, such cases are not within the purview of the statute.

The rules set forth apply regardless of the position of the article in the newspaper, whether it appears in the news columns, the educational section or the magazine section. It is the article itself rather than its location that is the determining factor. There may, however, be liability in a case coming under subdivisions 3 and 4 if the photograph used has so tenuous a connection with the news item or educational article that it can be said to have no legitimate relation to it and be used for the purpose of promoting the sale of the publication.

The instant article is not one of fiction. It is clearly one concerning a matter having a legitimate news interest. A British society offered a substantial prize to anyone able to perform the "famous rope trick."

The author of the article showed how the trick was allegedly performed in India and the possibility of the society being called upon to pay the prize. The use of professional actors to pose for some of the pictures illustrating the article did not change its character from one of news or general information to one of fiction. The only question is whether the picture complained of has so tenuous a connection with the article that it can be said to have no legitimate relationship to it. I think it has a relationship to the article. It is used to illustrate one of the points made by the author—the mystical quality of the East. There could have been no other motive for putting it in. It would be far-fetched to hold in this case that the picture was not used in an illustrative sense, but merely to promote the sale of the paper.

The evil sought to be remedied by the enactment of the New York Privacy Law was the unjustified use of one's photograph for advertising purposes or to promote trade. The picture here used was a professional photograph and it was published only once as part of the Sunday magazine section of the defendant's newspaper. There is nothing to warrant a finding that it was used to increase the commercial value of the newspaper. The history of the enactment of the "right of privacy" statute and the judicial interpretations thereof preclude a determination that a cause of action exists in this case. I find that the use of the photograph was not for trade purposes and that Lahiri has failed to bring himself within the provisions of the statute.   ▶

The *Lahiri* case points up the importance of "proximity" in these cases. Lahiri's picture was set next to the article on the Hindu Rope Trick and made a part of it. In this case the fact that the picture was directly related to the article helped the *Daily Mirror* because the judge decided that the article was one of public interest, and the picture of Lahiri partook of the protection afforded the article by this characterization. In the two cases that follow we shall see that proximity plays an important part in privacy cases involving advertising. Since it is characteristic of the cases that those who are sued must argue that they had no intention of linking their product with the name or picture of the person who sues them, the question often devolves upon the proximity of the one to the other. As we shall see, here as in all fields of law, judges may and do differ. Witness the plight of one Arsene Gautier, trainer of animals and unwitting television performer, who brought his plea for privacy to the New York Court of Appeals:

GAUTIER v. PRO-FOOTBALL, INC. (1952)

▶ Gautier is a well-known trainer of animals. On December 5, 1948, he performed before an audience of 35,000 persons in Griffith Stadium, Washington, D.C., between the halves of a professional football game, pursuant to a contract with Pro-Football, Inc., which owns the Washington Redskins football team. The contract provided that Gautier's act should not be televised without the written consent and approval of the American Guild of Variety Artists. It does not appear that such consent was ever sought or obtained, prior to the televising of the performance, although the performance in question was telecast in New York by the American Broadcasting Co., Inc., with the permission of the Washington television station, Pro-Football, Inc., and the commissioner of the National Football League. Gautier made formal objection to being televised.

The picture was sent by coaxial cable from Washington to New York and there transmitted to viewers from American's television station, WJZ-TV, while the audio portions were carried by direct wire, American's own announcer being employed. In the course of the program, paid commercial announcements were made in respect of Liggett & Myers Tobacco Co.'s product, Chesterfield cigarettes. The telecast was viewed via an estimated 17,000 of the 370,000 sets then in use in the New York area.

The manner in which Gautier's act was presented was as follows: After the first half of the game, and immediately before his act, a one-minute interim commercial announcement was made. Gautier's act was then presented for a period of seven or eight minutes, with a description by the announcer, but without any commercial reference; the announcer merely described to the audience the conduct of the act following a preliminary interview with Gautier before the start of the game.

There were other acts following Gautier's. Thereafter, and just before the start of the second half of the game, there was another interim commercial announcement.

Although the telecast was paid for by Liggett & Myers Tobacco Co., the entire program was not thereby constituted a solicitation for patronage. In return for such payment, that company secured the right to solicit patronage on that program by means of commercial announcements. Unless Gautier's name or picture were in some way connected with the "commercial," the mere fact of sponsorship of the telecast would not, in our opinion, suffice to violate the statute in this respect. Here no such connection was shown, for the commercial announcements were presented at usual and appropriate intervals; it was nothing more than coincidence that one such announcement, made at the close of the first half, occurred immediately prior to his act. He was not connected with the product either by visual, oral or other reference, nor was any issue of fact created by the physical juxtaposition of the single announcement prior to his performance. We conclude, therefore, that there was no use of Gautier's name or picture for advertising purposes, within the meaning of the New York Privacy Law. ◀

Gautier, therefore, loses, at least in the view of the majority, because his proximity to the advertisements was not misleading and was a matter of coincidence rather than intention. The court does not stop here, however. It realizes that it is dealing with a relatively new medium, television, and feels the need to say a few words about the application of the privacy law to this new potential invader of privacy, a menace that did not exist when the Warren-Brandeis article appeared in the *Harvard Law Review:*

▶ Like other media of communication, television may have either a trade aspect or an informative or news aspect. In the latter situation, it should be entitled to the same privilege accorded other such media where the statutory right to privacy is drawn in issue. It has long been recognized that the use of name or picture in a newspaper, magazine, or newsreel, in connection with an item of news or one that is newsworthy, is not a use for purposes of trade within the meaning of the New York Privacy Law. The connection must, of course, be a legitimate one; the individual may not be singled out and unduly featured merely because he is on the scene.

While one who is a public figure or is presently newsworthy may be the proper subject of news or informative presentation, the privilege does not extend to commercialization of his personality through a form of treatment distinct from the dissemination of news or information. Thus, in two other cases persons had been photographed for newsreel purposes, to which no objection was made. The films were later sold and used as part of short feature pictures dealing in a humorous manner with the sports involved, which were distributed for profit in numerous moving picture theatres. This, we said, was a use for purposes of trade. Similarly, in the *Binns* case, we held that one acclaimed as a hero for his feats in connection with a rescue at sea was entitled to protection against fictionalization of his exploit, and the use of his name and personality for mere commercial, as distinguished from news, purposes.

One traveling upon the public highway may expect to be televised, but only as an incidental part of the general scene. So, one attending a public event such as a professional football game may expect to be televised in the status in which he attends. If a mere spectator, he may be taken as part of the general audience, but may not be picked out of a crowd alone, thrust upon the screen and unduly featured for public view. Where, however, one is a public personage, an actual participant in a public event, or where some newsworthy incident affecting him is taking place, the right of privacy is not absolute, but limited. Here Gautier consented to perform before 35,000 spectators in a professional football game that had wide and legitimate public interest. While not a part of the game proper, he did become a part of the spectacle as a whole by appearing between the halves, and voluntarily occupying the very center of attraction for several minutes. Under these circumstances, it can hardly be said that his right of privacy was invaded. ◀

So decided the majority. However, as we have said, judges don't always agree, and even if they agree they sometimes agree for different reasons. If a judge disagrees with a decision of a majority of his colleagues he is said to "dissent." You have read a number of dissents in this volume. But if a judge agrees in the result, but for reasons other than those stated by the majority opinion, he is said to "concur" in the decision. In this case, one judge filed a separate "concurring" opinion. The reader will note that he has an entirely different reason for denying Gautier the relief he had asked for, a reason that might at first seem farfetched, but, on reflection, is very much in line with the Pennsylvania court's decision in the Ben Hogan case:

DESMOND, Judge (concurring)

▶ It seems to me that the televising of Gautier's act was, in indisputable fact, a use thereof "for advertising purposes," without plaintiff's consent. The performance of his trained animals became part of a long televised show sponsored by, and advertising the product of, a manufacturer of cigarettes. But that does not end this case. My difficulty is that there was no invasion of any "right of privacy." Gautier, a professional entertainer, gave his show before a vast audience in an athletic stadium. His grievance here is not the invasion of his "privacy"—privacy is the one thing he did not want, or need, in his occupation. His real complaint, and perhaps a justified one, but one we cannot redress in this suit brought under the New York "Right of Privacy" statutes, is that he was not paid for the telecasting of his show. The decisions all show that the intent of the "Privacy" statutes was to forbid and punish the exploitation, for gain, of a man's individual personality, that is, invasions of his right to be let alone. Enacted to fill a gap in existing law, they should not be held to apply to a violation of a contract right to be compensated for public or semi-public theatrical, or similar, exhibitions. In no real sense was Gautier's "privacy" infringed upon. ◄

Just as in the *Hogan* case, the judge here is talking about a Right of Publicity instead of a Right of Privacy. However, while this concept was used to Hogan's advantage, it helped to defeat Gautier. There is a veiled suggestion in Judge Desmond's opinion that Gautier should perhaps have brought an action similar to the one that carried Hogan to victory in Pennsylvania five years later. But Gautier didn't take this hint, or perhaps he was too worn out to go on, and we are as yet unable to predict just how long the New York courts, or any other courts, will allow this budding concept to flourish. Because publicity is becoming more and more of a product in our society, it is difficult to imagine where such a right might begin or end. Should it be limited only to public personalities of the most obvious sort, a Marilyn Monroe or a Ben Hogan? Or should it also attach to people who are only partially in the public arena, a Binns, perhaps, or even a Humiston? One thing seems clear, however: to the extent that the Right of Publicity is developed, people will tend more and more to shun actions in "privacy" in favor of trying to capitalize on the monetary value of whatever Right of Publicity they might have. And whatever value there may or may not be in this, it is a far different concept from the right of "inviolate personality" and the protection of the "sentiments, thoughts and feelings of the individuals" with which Warren and Brandeis were so vitally concerned.

The *Gautier* case involved what was presumably an unintentional use of a person's name and picture. We now turn to a recent case in which the use was intentional but, claimed the user, not really connected with the product advertised. As you read this case, note the attempt by the defendant (the company sued) to shield itself with the decisions in the *Lahiri* and *Gautier* cases and note how it failed, at least in the eyes of the majority of the New York Court of Appeals, for whom Chief Judge Conway speaks:

Joseph C. Flores v. Mosler Safe Company (1959)

▶ The complaint alleges that Mosler Safe Company is engaged in the business of manufacturing and selling safes and vaults in New York and elsewhere; and that it knowingly used Flores' name for advertising purposes without having obtained his prior consent in that it printed, produced and widely distributed, by the mails and otherwise, throughout New York State a certain advertisement for its products in which his name was illegally used.

The advertisement consists of a reprint of a news photo and the accompanying captions and news account as they originally appeared in the New York Times and appended thereto, below the original photo, captions and news account, is Mosler's advertising copy. The photograph is a rather spectacular and eye-catching picture of a burning building. The news report of the fire, which consists of a total of 47 lines spread over three columns below the picture and its caption, sets forth an account of two men. One of these men was Flores, a business guest of the second man, who was a tenant of the property. Flores was returning merchandise to the tenant at the time the fire broke out. The tenant dropped his keys and, there being no illumination, both men started lighting matches to aid them in the search for the keys. The account further sets forth that one of the matches ignited nylon netting and thus started the fire which spread rapidly through four floors of the building. Mr. Flores' name is mentioned three times, his address in up-State New York once, and his occupation (motel keeper) once in the course of the 47-line news account of the fire and its origin. The appended advertising copy, which urges readers to protect their business records from destruction by fire by the use of one of Mosler's safes, consists of 11 lines of different face type extending across the width of the three columns and occupies approximately one quarter of the face of the circular. Nowhere in the circular is there any indication that Flores in any way endorses the Mosler safes nor is it alleged that he is a person whose name would attract greater attention to the advertising copy.

There can be no doubt but that the circular, taken in its entirety, was distributed as a solicitation for patronage. The question before us, then, is whether the manner in which Flores' name was used therein comes within the prohibition of the statute as a use for advertising purposes. Mosler Co. bases its defense on the theory that the use of Flores' name was merely an incidental mentioning of his name in a news report, that it was completely unrelated to the advertiser's products although in physical juxtaposition to the advertising matter, and that such a use of an individual's name does not constitute a violation of the statutory prohibition.

In this State, the right of privacy or the right of a person to live his life quietly and to be left alone rests solely in the individual and is limited by statute. In construing the statute it should be noted that although it is in part penal, the purpose of the statute is remedial and rooted in popular resentment at the refusal of the courts to grant recognition to the newly expounded right of an individual to be immune from commercial exploitation. Justice Shientag, in his opinion in the Lahiri case, in establishing a guide in the construction of these sections has said that "A statute of this kind is not 'to be obeyed grudgingly, by construing it narrowly and treating it as though it did not exist for any purpose other than that embraced within the strict construction of its words.' It is 'not an alien intruder in the house of the common law, but a guest to be welcomed * * * as a new and powerful aid in the accomplishment of its appointed task of accommodating the law to social needs.' "

In the Gautier case a well-known trainer of animals presented his act, pursuant to contract, as part of the half-time activities at a professional football game. This act was televised in violation of the contract and was shown in New York. A one minute paid spot commercial had immediately preceded the televising of the act. However, there were no commercials during or immediately after the presentation. We rejected Gautier's contention that this constituted a violation of his statutory right of privacy, holding that it was a mere coincidence that the commercial, which was one of many presented at appropriate intervals, occurred immediately prior to the presentation of his act and that he was not connected with the product by either visual or other reference. In addition, we placed great stress upon the fact that the plaintiff was a public figure who voluntarily became involved in a special and public event in which the public clearly had a legitimate interest and applied the well-established exception that a public personage or an active participant in a public event cannot invoke the protection afforded by these sections when his name, picture or portrait is used in connection with a truthful recounting or portrayal of an actual current event as is commonly done in a single issue of a regular newspaper.

In the case at hand, however, we are presented not with a simultaneous reporting by a public media of communication of the actions of a person who has voluntarily entered the public eye, but rather with a deliberate later publication of a no longer current news item in an individual firm's advertising literature.

Further, in *Lahiri* v. *Daily Mirror* we had a use of a photo in connection with an item of general public interest and information in a newspaper and not a republication in a circular designed solely for the purpose of selling its author's products.

Mosler Safe Company also looks for support in the case of *Damron* v. *Doubleday, Doran & Co.* It urges that this case points up its proposition that recovery is not justified since this was merely an incidental mentioning of Flores' name in a manner unrelated to the product advertised.

Mosler Safe Company contends that there is no violation since there is no implication in the circular that Flores indorses the product and since Flores' name is mentioned only in the original news account of the fire as reprinted in the circular and not in the advertising material that defendant appended to the original photo, captions and news account. No authorities are cited for the proposition that the use of the name or photograph must at least imply an indorsement of the product in order for a use in an advertisement to constitute a violation of the statute, and our research has failed to disclose any such authorities.

As to the contention that there is no violation of the statute since Mosler did not use Flores' name in the appended advertising copy, the fact remains that Mosler freely and deliberately chose to adopt and reprint the entire original photograph, captions and the news account which contained his name in its circular. Mosler gives us no reason for so doing, but rather says only that the use was an incidental one, unrelated to the product. Flores, on the other hand, contends that Mosler selected the material of which the advertisement consisted, that it could have cut out all or part of the original newspaper coverage and that it deliberately chose to include the entire coverage in its circular in order to put more realism in the circular and to attract attention thereto. He also points out that the use of the picture and captions alone without the news account which contained his name could have conveyed the idea which it was apparently trying to put across to its prospective customers, viz., that fires occur frequently, that they are often started by small acts of carelessness and that they could be disastrous to a businessman. We can hardly hold, as a matter of law, that such contention is unsound.

Mosler further argues that this use is not prohibited by the statute since the use of Flores' name would not in any way draw trade to its firm. Such contention might be valid if only the prohibited use was one for "purposes of trade." However, the statute makes a use for "advertising purposes" a separate and distinct violation. A use for advertising purposes has been defined as a use in, or as part of, an advertisement or solicitation for patronage.

In view of the fact that Mosler chose to reprint the entire original news coverage of the fire, including the entire news account which mentioned Flores' name several times and described how either he or the other person present started the fire by their carelessness or negligence, in a circular designed for the sole purpose of soliciting purchasers for their products, and since every fair intendment and inference must be given to Flores, we do not believe that it can be said that this complaint fails to set forth a use of Flores' name which is a violation of his right of privacy as a matter of law. ◀

Thus, the majority decides that Mosler may not use Flores' name and picture to advertise its product without his consent even though the event used in the advertisements was a newsworthy one. The reader should note that the intention of Mosler to use the material for advertising purposes was clear and that the court seems to place much weight on this point, as it does on the proximity of the use to the advertisement. A minority of the Court of Appeals of New York, however, disagreed with the result:

VAN VOORHIS, J. (dissenting)

▶ The important question to be decided in this case is whether a news event can be utilized in conjunction with advertising—or in novels or short stories, on the stage or

on the screen—if to do so involves mention of persons whose
names have already been published as having participated in
the event. Here Mosler manufactures and sells fireproof safes.
It wished to bring home to prospective purchasers the danger
of destruction of valuable papers by fire. In order to do so,
it published a photograph of a well-known Broadway fire,
beneath which was reprinted the newspaper article describing
the event at the time when the fire occurred. Flores was mentioned in this newspaper article for the reason that merchandise caught fire while he was returning it to the building
which burned. All of these facts were in the public domain.
The newspaper violated no rights of privacy infringed by
republishing the same facts at a later date. The law is clear
that the use of Flores' name and picture in connection with
the publication of newsworthy events is not prohibited by
sections 50 or 51 of the New York Privacy Law. Under this
account of the Broadway fire, reproduced in the form in
which it had previously appeared in the newspaper, was
written in the advertisement: "The disastrous fire shown
above didn't happen to you. . . . But suppose the next one
does?" The question here is whether the use of this public event, in the public domain, is forbidden for this purpose.

In our judgment these circumstances do not amount to
any violation of the law. Mosler was not limited in its advertising to warning against the general nature of fire. It was
entitled to point up its appeals to the public by calling attention to particular fires in public memory in order to illustrate
the danger resulting from fire. People think in terms of
specific situations. It was legitimate for Mosler to refer to
specific fires and to describe how they occurred, provided that
these facts were already in the public domain. Flores became
a public character as a participant in this event, by the same
token whereby an actor, musician or other personage becomes
a public character in his special context.

A different construction would produce awkward results.
The words "for advertising purposes or for the purposes
of trade" are held to include the use of names in fiction. Would
the author of a war novel, for example, be prohibited from

mentioning the names of Generals Eisenhower or MacArthur
in connection with military campaigns or battles that actually
occurred, merely for the reason that those public events
had a story woven around them? If the Privacy Law had then
been in force, would it have prevented Thackeray from publishing *Vanity Fair* in New York State because the novel
dealt with the Battle of Waterloo, if Napoleon or the Duke
of Wellington had been alive? Such a legal theory would
render any historical novel an impossibility if it concerned
recent events. The courts have drawn no distinction between
fictionalizing a character and using the name for other purposes of trade or for advertising. If it is prohibited to use an
actual public event and the names of persons involved in it
to advertise fireproof safes, it is equally prohibited in books,
movies, radio or television to mention the names of real persons in fiction even if they are referred to only in connection
with what they actually did. It is one thing to introduce real
people into fictional episodes. That is prohibited. It is something else to introduce actual historical events into a story,
or to build the story around such events. That is not prohibited unless the real people are made to take part in imaginary events. If a prominent banker is held up and robbed,
and the incident gets into the news, I perceive no infringement of any right of privacy for a detective agency or a
burglar alarm company to advertise that if their services or
equipment had been employed the robbery would not have
occurred. Many other illustrations can readily be imagined.
This kind of advertising seems to me to be particularly legitimate in that (if truthful) it directs attention to the purpose
of the goods offered for sale by designating their application
to particular situations which are already in the public domain. There is no essential distinction, it seems to me, between doing this and an ordinary newscast sponsored by
some advertiser. People whose names are in the news have no
right to object. This is not a situation where particular
individuals are advertised as sponsoring the product or where
their names or pictures are merely published in connection
with an advertisement rather than as participants in some
public event to which the advertisement relates. ◀

Judges Desmond, Fuld, Froessel, and Burke agree with Chief Judge Conway; Judge Van Voorhis dissents in an opinion in which Judge Dye concurs. The vote was therefore five to two.

Who is right? Whose philosophy should prevail in the future? Of course, there is no clear answer. Your own decision will depend largely on your own prejudice in favor of privacy and on the extent to which you are convinced by the minority's dire prophecies. For our part, we favor the majority opinion. The growth of advertising, even granted all the good it has done, undeniably has increasingly jeopardized the right of a person to the privacy of his face and name. We believe that courts should be hesitant to permit incursions on this right, especially where, as here, no overriding public purpose seems likely to be served by encouraging the advertiser to continue his practices. Nor do we feel that the minority is completely accurate in stating that "the courts have drawn no distinction between fictionalizing a character and using the name for other purposes of trade or for advertising." In cases such as *Lahiri, Gautier,* and *Damron,* the courts do indeed seem to have made an implicit distinction between fiction and advertising. And it is well to remember that the *Flores* case involves *advertising* and does not involve a "trade purpose," as do the cases involving fiction.

Although we have, until now, tried to avoid presenting the reader with a clear impression of our own opinion in each case, we have tipped our hand in this case because we allow ourselves the hope that at this stage the reader is sufficiently well informed to make up his own mind and is, to some degree at least, safe from the pressures and prejudices of those of us, lawyers and judges alike, who have made that area of human endeavor called "law" our particular stamping ground.

Of course, an expression of confidence should be accompanied by a reward. So here is our last "advertising" case. The reader will note that it is not, perhaps, in the mainstream of privacy law. Nor can one suggest with any persuasiveness that it was foreseen by even the likes of Warren and Brandeis; yet who can doubt that the emotional injury sustained was as severe as any we have read about thus far?

Whether they know it or not, dogs, too, have a right of privacy. This is the story of a dog whose privacy was assaulted. Unfortunately, we do not know the name of the dog. The phrase "owner and mistress," however, fails to convey the extent of the attachment of the lady for her dog, for she was also its defender. In fact, so strongly engaged were her emotions that, on behalf of her pet, she sued the *New York Times*, the New York *Daily News*, the National Biscuit Company, the McCann-Erickson Advertising Agency, a photographer's agency named Rapho-Guillumette Pictures, and a photographer named Koffler. And this—we'll tell you in advance, in case the suspense may be too great—was one dog that had his day. In court.

Few cases involve a conflict between two persons only. There were many forces and factions behind David and Goliath or Romeo and Juliet. So it was with Ruth Lawrence and her beloved dog; they symbolized a call to arms, and many people hastened to do battle.

Ruth Lawrence, in June, 1942, took her dog to a professional photographer named Koffler. The only agreement reached was on the price of the pictures. Koffler shot three dozen pictures and sent the prints to Miss Lawrence for her selection. She chose two and paid for them and later ordered and paid for two additional prints.

Then a man named Guillumette, acting as an agent for the photo studio, submitted to the McCann-Erickson agency a number of dog pictures taken by Koffler, among them the portrait of Miss Lawrence's dog. McCann-Erickson bought the positive print of a Lawrence dog for $25, not for themselves but as agents for the National Biscuit Company. In February, 1943, the National Biscuit Company used this dog's picture as an advertisement in five separate newspapers, including the *New York Times* and the *Daily News*.

Whom does Ruth Lawrence sue for what she thought was her Right of Privacy in her dog—or in the dog's own Right of Privacy? She sues everyone involved, even though there was nothing on the photos bought for advertising to show Ruth Lawrence's relation to the photographer or for that matter to the dog.

The court at the outset absolved the National Biscuit Company and the newspapers from any blame or legal liability. They had had no contractual relationship with Miss Lawrence. They had never heard of the dog. But should they have been more careful? More important, should they be made to curtail their promotional activities after they learned about the true ownership of the dog's pictures? The court then put the grips of the law on Koffler, the photographer, and his agent Guillumette:

▶ Lawrence's claim to damages may be asserted solely against the photographer Koffler and the agent Guillumette. It is well settled that the relationship between a photographer and his customer is that of employee and employer; a contract exists between them which grants to the customer all proprietary rights in the negative and in the photographs purchased by the customer. The ordinary contract between a photographer and his customers is a contract of employment. The conception as well as the production of the photograph is work done for the customers and they, not their employee, are the exclusive owners of all proprietary rights.

Lawrence's property right stemmed directly and exclusively from her contract with the photographer by which the photographer's agent is bound, but the other defendants who were not parties to the contract are not liable for damages unless it is proved that they acted in collusion with the photographer or the agent.

The decision of the court in the *Roberson* case made it clear that a person does not have a property right in an image independent of the statutory right of privacy. That statutory right of privacy concededly does not cover the case of a dog or a photograph of a dog. Whatever rights a person may have in a photograph of his dog are dependent upon the existence of a contractual relationship between that person and the photographer. If, for example, a photograph of a dog happens to be taken by a photographer on his own initiative without any arrangement with the owner of the dog, the owner making no payment therefor, all proprietary interest in that photograph, including the right to copyright the same lies solely with the photographer. On the other hand, as in this case, if the photograph is taken at the request of the owner of the animal who pays the photographer for taking it, all proprietary interest in that photograph, including the right to copyright it, lies with the owner.

In *Murray* v. *Gast Lithographic, Etc. Co.* (1894, New York) it was held that a parent could not maintain an action to prevent the unauthorized publication of a portrait of an infant child and could not obtain damages for injuries to his sensibilities caused by the invasion of his child's privacy, because "the law takes no recognizance of sentimental injury independent of a wrong to person or property." ◄

Had the decision stopped here, we might just chalk it up as another defeat for human sentimentality at the impersonal hands of the law. But it doesn't. The judge seems to be against dogs but he really isn't. Instead he is indulging in a bit of judicial creativity. By pooh-poohing the notion of privacy in this case, he avoids being kidded at his club, but by introducing the doctrine of a contractual relationship between Ruth Lawrence and the photographer, he permits himself to take a hop, skip and jump over the prior judicial and statutory refusal to protect what really amounts to the privacy of a pet. If the verdict that follows seems inconsistent with the rest of the judges' opinion, bear in mind that the judge was himself probably a sentimentalist at heart—might even have had a dog of his own. Listen:

▶ Since those cases were decided the law has given recognition to the right of privacy so far as the use of photographs or names of human beings for advertising purposes is concerned.

It follows, therefore, that Ruth Lawrence is entitled to a permanent prohibition against all of the defendants restraining any further use of the dog's photograph but that so far as money damages are concerned she is entitled to relief only against photographer Koffler and the agent Guillumette. ◀

Judgment for Ruth Lawrence—and dog lovers everywhere.

11
Final
Remarks—
Vintage 1962

You have now read many of the leading cases on the Right of Privacy. There are, of course, others, and we hasten to point out that our selections have been subjective. The kaleidoscope of law presents constantly shifting and changing patterns of light and dark through which to view society. We have chosen the patterns we thought most revealing. Whether other lawyers may differ with our choice is unimportant so long as the cases we have here presented have given the reader a flavor of this modern invention of man called the Right of Privacy.

What form will this young Right of Privacy have in its maturity? The answer is difficult to predict. It does seem probable, however, that individuals will rely on the right more heavily as time goes on in order to keep their own individual outlines from being merged indistinguishably into the commonweal. As long ago as 1902—as a *New York Times* edition reported—President Theodore Roosevelt was beset and bothered by the importunate photographers of the press. Not surprisingly, in 1905 the Federal government provided

227

protection for the portrait, as a *trademark*, of a dead President during the life of his widow. And now, again, the First Citizen of the Land is forced to draw a "privacy line." In 1961 the newspapers carried a story to the effect that President Kennedy extracted commitments from his household staff not to disclose publicly what went on within the domestic wing of the White House. Others before him had been less cautious and had paid the price. Today, at least, we may safely say that a man's home is, in law, his castle—even if it is the White House.

No doubt we all will be drawing lines and digging in as the nets of public snoops are thrown around us in ever-widening arcs. But lest we feel too sorry for ourselves, we should remember that as a nation we have far outdistanced other countries in the recognition of the Right of Privacy. England, for example, from whom we took the seed of this right, has never developed it. There simply is *no* Right of Privacy in England, and kindly judges who want to find some reason for compensating an injured party have to stretch the law of unfair competition or breach of copyright pretty far. In the recent case of *Williams* v. *Settle,* for example (referred to early in this volume), the English Court of Appeal awarded $2,800 to a man whose wedding pictures were printed in newspapers without his consent. Apparently the pictures were commissioned for the wedding and contained some shots of the man's father-in-law, who was later murdered. Prints of the pictures were then sold to newspapers by the photographer. Although under our law the irate bridegroom might have had an action in privacy, he had no such action in England. He won his case only because the judges decided that he, in essence, had a copyright in the photographs and that this copyright was breached by their subsequent publication without his consent. Whether or not this case portends the recognition of a Right of Privacy in England it is too early to say. The contortions of the court, however, are reminiscent of the early cases discussed in this volume, and there is some reason to believe that a parallel right will eventually develop in England.

What will finally come to pass in France is also uncertain. Certain it is, however, that the proponents of privacy are trying hard. On March 9, 1961, the *New York Times* reported that a case was begun in Paris by five prostitutes against the French national television system for something "equivalent to invasion of privacy." It seems that these ladies were photographed without their consent as part of a documentary film concerning prostitution as a social problem. The film was shown on television, and they were unhappily surprised to recognize themselves in it. Who says that privacy is not on the move? Indeed it is encouraging to note that, although most of the people on our planet are still illiterate, the United Nations has included a declaration on privacy in its recent draft convention of civil rights.

Law is a process infected with eternal youth. There is always the hope of progress—except among a people whose lives are bound in a rigid, unchanging culture. But even among such people—usually ruled exclusively by ancient taboos and the directives of tribal chiefs—the introduction of a written language produces the need of change in the tribal rules. And, of course, for people living under a dictatorship, there is little room for give and take, for those variables that are the tonics of growth.

In ancient times, law—as indicated in Leviticus—concerned itself mostly with animals, the prime property of man. Much law dealt with domestic animals, and it needs only a passing backward glance to recall that if "an ox gore a man to death the owner of the beast shall suffer by his ox being stoned and his flesh not eaten." Plutarch tells of a dog that bit a man. The decree of law was clean and simple: the dog shall be bound to a log four cubits long. A slave killing a freeman is given over to the relatives of the deceased. Malignity of an animal evoked revenge—the least efficient weapon of the law. From such issues and such punishments most of mankind has traveled only a short distance. Not so with our Republic, which became heir to Anglo-Saxon jurisprudence.

The secret root of the law is the consideration of what is expedient for the community concerned, although judges rarely admit that fact. Since Freud, however, much is being written about the fact that judges are human beings who find it quite difficult and at times impossible to get outside their own frames of reference.

Law does always try for consistency, but it appreciates that the comfort of orthodoxy can never be fully reached. New principles, as Judge Oliver Wendell Holmes pointed out so many times, are adopted from life at one end while we retain old ones from history at the other end. In a society of law and justice we cannot afford to slough off old rules in too abrupt a fashion.

A sound body of law should correspond to the actual demands of the people—whether right or wrong. For then the people have the privilege of being wrong and learning, as man does so often, from his own mistakes.

For centuries there was no recognizable demand of people for privacy. However, in the past hundred years we have been commanded to refrain from certain invasions of privacy —of course not all. But the difficulty for laymen and lawyers is to determine the scope of the commands so as to reform or correct those that no longer fit snugly and comfortably into the interstices of our society.

The basic command was articulated by the Warren-Brandeis article, but that article could not have been written at the time of Prince Albert's case. It anticipated the era of unlisted telephone numbers, an extra charge levied by the telephone company for the Right to Be Let Alone by telephone.

After study of this article by courts in various states, a

pattern of general external acceptance developed. The general rules of law had values, but the development and consequent difficulties arose as always in the law because the law must always be ready to sacrifice an individual in order to accomplish external comfort for the general welfare.

In the field of privacy the problem seldom deals with attempts to violate another's rights. Rather, we find our difficult path between the marketplace of thought for the benefit of all and the desire of many to be let alone. Whose comfort shall be sacrificed for the good of you or me? The intent of the mass media to make a profit at the expense of our privacy is a growing pressure. Today one can only smile ironically at the words of Dr. Johnson, written in the eighteenth century: "The trade of advertising is now so near to perfection that it is not easy to propose any improvement." No such luck!

As to advertising and privacy, the issues are different and have been substantially resolved along broad general lines. The nexus between the picture and the product is usually fairly evident, and the sponsor has the opportunity to search with dollars for those who actually *want* their faces displayed in public.

In general terms, leaving aside a variance within a state or between states as to the money sanctions imposed on violators, there is no profound difference in the development of privacy in the states like Georgia, which proceeded without legislation, and those like New York, which passed new laws on the subject. In about half of our states there is as yet no determination of the basic problem or creation of the Right of Privacy. But this is not too disturbing since questions of privacy tend to be concentrated in only two states—New York and California—which together (regrettably enough) control the pipelines of communications and entertainment. And only in four states has the right expressly been rejected.

The law of privacy of letters may soon get a complete

reappraisal, and this time the court will also have to address itself to the growing practice of tape-recording telephone conversations—often without knowledge or approval of the speaker on the other end. For those readers who wish to browse further into privacy and the law, a request addressed to the publishers—The Macmillan Company, 60 Fifth Avenue, New York 11, N.Y.—will be answered by references to monographs, books, and miscellaneous writings on the subject.

The nonlawyer often labors under the mistaken impression that the law is writ somewhere on a secret tablet—readable only to members of the bar. It ain't necessarily so, as a gentleman named Sportin' Life once remarked. Hence readers should add a morsel of humility to any excitement they have garnered about law and privacy. They can no more know all the answers than does any lawyer. But a wide public knowledge in this and other fields of law may not only afford pleasure for the musing mind but may also give aid and comfort to judges and lawyers. The gap in communication between men of discipline in any field and the rest of the public is an essential deterrent to the wise working of a full democratic process. Lawyers are specialists—but so also are archeologists, social scientists, and all the other experts who try to fathom the mysteries of nature and, above all, the mysteries of the behavior of man himself. Courts function most wisely not by popular plebiscites but by reacting to an interested and informed public.

As with all of life, whenever many men talk as if they know all the answers to any given question, we can be quite certain that at such times the questions are more important than the answers. So we hope you will have an open and questioning mind, to the point where you will allow your friends to enjoy the Right to Be Let Alone—except from your unanswered questions about the desires of the people of our Republic for privacy.

Index

Abernethy v. *Hutchinson* (1825), 59–60, 115
Adams, John Q., 130, 131
Adams, John Quincy, 25
Advertising, 222; and privacy, 231; purposes, 206–207; versus ideas, 146–147
Albert, Prince, 12–22 *passim*, 114, 230
American Bible Union, 29, 30
American Law Review, 143
Anatomy of a Murder, xii
Animated Weekly, 171
Anthony, Susan B., 80, 85, 90, 91
Atkinson, John, 100–103
Atkinson v. *John E. Doherty & Co.* (Michigan, 1899), 100–103
Atlanta Constitution, 130
Artistic rights, 144–145

Barnes, A. S., Co., 192–202 *passim*
Bathurst, Henry, 2nd Earl, 36
Bayard, Mabel (Mrs. Samuel Warren), 46
Bayard, Senator Thomas Francis, Sr., 46
Biggs, Judge, quoted, 193
Binns, John R., 159–164 *passim*
Blackstone, Sir William, 110, 133
Boston Symphony Orchestra, 187
Bottling Act, 155
Brandeis, Louis D., viii, 45–47, 71, 96, 111, 120–121, 122, 130, 137, 142–143, 183–184, 188, 223; arti-
cle on Right of Privacy quoted, 47–49
Brandeis (Mason), quoted, 46
Bruce, Vice-Chancellor Knight, 56
Burke, Judge Adrian P., 222

Camerer, Dave, 193–202 *passim*
Chesterfield, Lord (Philip Stanhope), 35–37
Chronicle, New York, 29, 30
Churchill, Sir Winston, 12, 22, 78, 79
Clarendon, Earl of, 115
Clarendon, Lord, 27, 115
Columbia Law Review, 125–126
Columbian Exposition of 1893, 80
Colyer v. *Fox Publishing Co.*, 172
Congregation of the Children of Israel, 98
Constitution, federal, 149–151; First Amendment to, viii–ix
Convenience, private justice, morality and, 61–62
Conway, Chief Judge Albert, 222; opinion in *Flores* case, 215–219
Cooley, Thomas M., 48, 49, 74
Cooper Institute, 82
Copyright, breach of, 228
Corliss, George H., 74–77 *passim*
Corliss, Mrs. George H., 74–77 *passim*
Corliss v. *E. W. Walker Co.* (Massachusetts, 1894), 74–77, 116, 117

Correspondence and letters, ownership of, 25; personal, 23–43
Cottenham, Lord, 56–57, 93
Crowell, William, 29
Cruger, Ruth, 166, 168
Curl, bookseller, 6–8, 10, 27

Daily Mail, London, 23
Daily Mirror, New York, 204–209 *passim*
Daily News, New York, 223, 224
Damages, calculation of, 200–202
Damron, Wayne, 176–179
Defamation, 4, 51–52, 67
Desmond, Judge Charles S., 222; concurring opinion in *Gautier* case, 213–214
Dockrell v. *Dougall* (1898), 115–116
Doubleday, Doran & Co., Inc., 177–179
Duke of Queensberry v. *Shebbeare* (1758), 115
Dye, Judge Marvin R., 222

Eisenhower, Dwight David, 12, 22
Eldon, Lord (John Scott), 34, 39, 56, 59, 62
The Elements of Torts (Cooley), 49
England, as source of law, vii–viii
Evening Post, New York, 49
Express, London, 23

Fair trial, right to, xii
Federalism, 180–181
Ferber, Edna, 176–179
Fiction, and privacy, 175–179
Field, Judge Stanley M., 222
Flores, Joseph C., 215–219 *passim*
France, invasion of privacy in, 229
Frank, Judge Jerome, 186
Franklin, Benjamin, 25
Franklin Mills Company, 108–126 *passim*
Free speech, and privacy, 107; versus Right to Be Let Alone, 140–142
Freud, Sigmund, 230
Froessel, Judge Charles William, 222

Gautier v. *Pro-Football, Inc.* (1952), 210–215 *passim*, 217, 222

Gee v. *Pritchard* (1818), 34, 39–40, 115
George III, 56–57
Gobbledygook, legalistic, xi
Godkin, E. L., 49
Golf With the Masters, 193–202 *passim*
Grace Humiston v. *Universal Film Company* (1919), 165–175 *passim*
Graves, privacy, perpetuity and, 97–103
Gray, Justice, dissenting opinion in *Philip Schuyler* v. *Ernest Curtis, etc.*, 92–96
Gwinnett, Button, 25

Hamilton, Alexander, 80
Hardwicke, Lord Chancellor (Philip Yorke), 35, 36; opinion in *Pope* v. *Curl*, 6–9
Harper's Weekly, 76, 77
Harvard Law Review, viii, 45, 46, 111, 120–121, 142
Harvard Law School, 46
Hibben, John G., 171
Hofstadter, Judge Samuel H., 22
Hogan, Ben, 192–202 *passim*
Hogan v. *A. S. Barnes & Company, Incorporated* (1957), 192–202, 214
Holmes, Judge Oliver Wendell, 230
Hoyt v. *Mackenzie and Others* (1848), 26–29, 33, 34, 40
Humiston, Grace, 165–175 *passim*

Ideas, versus advertising, 146–147
Injury, personal, 4

Jacobus, Harold, 98
Jacobus, Irene, 98
Jacobus, Jacob, 98–99
Jacobus, Manahn, 98
Jacobus v. *Children of Israel* (1899), 97–100
James Woolsey v. *Owen B. Judd* (1855), 29–34
Jefferson, Thomas, 25, 41
Jeffries v. *N.Y. Evening Journal Publishing Co.*, 172

John R. Binns v. *The Vitagraph Company of America* (1913), 159–164, 169, 170, 172, 173, 175, 190, 212

Johnson, Samuel, on advertising, 231

Joseph C. Flores v. *Mosler Safe Company* (1959), 215–219, 222

Justice, private, 61–62

Kennedy, John F., President, 228

Kent, James, 110

Khrushchev, Nikita, 12

Koffler, photographer, 223, 224

Koussevitzky, Serge, 187–192 *passim*

Lahiri, Sarat, 204–209 *passim*

Lancet, The, 59

de La Place, Pierre Simon, 37

Law, American, viii; ancient, 229–230; Anglo-Saxon, 230; common, 137, 150; constitutional, 149–151; English, vii–viii; and instantaneous photography, 121–122; and literature, 38–40; natural, 135–136; Roman, 133, 136–137; statutory, 150. *See also* Privacy; Right to Be Let Alone; Right of Privacy

Lawrence, Ruth, case of, 223–226

Legal precedent, versus public good, 132

Legal rights, beyond the grave, 86–88, 97–103

Letters, and correspondence, 24–43; privacy of, 231–232; Right of Property in, viii, 96

Leviticus, 229

Libel, 51–52, 67, 95, 105, 106, 118

Liberty, meaning of, 134–135; personal, 134

Literature, and the law, 38–40

Lord and Lady Percival v. *Phipps,* 36

Lumpkin, Thomas B., 130–147 *passim*

MacArthur, Douglas, 78

McCann-Erickson Advertising Agency, 223–224

Madison, James, 25, 41

Man, versus society, 132–134

Manley, J. L., 183

Marion Manala v. *Stevens & Meyers* (1890), 50

Mark, Phil, 197

Marks-"Mogulesko" case, 72–74

Marshall, John, vii, 113

Mason, Alpheus Thomas, 46

Merle v. *Sociological Research Film Corporation* (1915), 164–165 173

Milton, John, 37

Misappropriation, of property, 198–202 *passim*

Moore, George, 177

Morality, private justice, convenience and, 61–62

Morgan J. Pierpont, 124

Mosley Safe Co., 215–219 *passim*

Mount Vernon Association, 82, 90

Murray v. *Gast Lithographic, Etc. Co.* (1894), New York, 103–107, 116, 225

National Biscuit Company, 223, 224

New England Life Insurance Company, 130–147 *passim*

New York City Police Department, 166

New York Penal Code, Section 245, 118

New York State Civil Rights Law, 127–129, 152, 154, 156, 160, 162, 163, 169, 173, 176, 178, 185, 188, 203, 204, 211, 220

New York State Court of Appeals, 124, 125; dissenting opinions in *Flores* case, 219–221; and *Gautier* v. *Pro-Football, Inc.,* 210–215; on letters, 26–28; opinions of in *James Woolsey* case, 30–41; and *Philip Schuyler* case, 79–96, 102; on privacy, 3–4; and *Rhodes* v. *Sperry and Hutchinson,* 152–156 *passim;* and *Roberson* case, 108–126 *passim,* 129, 143

New York State Supreme Court, 22, 128; on claims for damages, 200

New York Times, 126, 223, 224, 226; on invasion of privacy in France, 229; quoted on *Roberson* case, 123–124

New York World-Telegram, 183, 186

The New Yorker, and *Sidis* case, 181–187 *passim*

Newton, Isaac, 37

North, Justice, 60

O'Brien, Judge, article in *Columbia Law Review,* 125–126

Obscenity, censorship of, xii

Parker, Judge, 124, 125, 153

Pavesich v. *New England Life Insurance Co.,* 130–147, 150

Perpetuity, graves, privacy and, 97–103

Person, protection in, 73–74; public and private, 186–187

Personal immunity, Cooley on, 49

Philip Schuyler v. *Ernest Curtis, Alice Donlevy and Others* (1895), 79–96, 102

Photographs, unauthorized publication of, 207–208

Photography, amendments to New York Civil Rights Law, 128–129; instantaneous, and the law, 121–122; and privacy, 49

Plagiarism, 12

Plumer, Sir Thomas, Vice-Chancellor, 36

Plutarch, on law, 229

Police Gazette, 172

Pollard v. *Photographic Co.* (1888), 60

Pope, Alexander, 6–9, 27, 36, 37

Pope v. *Curl* (1741), 6–10, 12, 29, 35, 36, 37, 40

Possessions, private, defining of, 11–12

Pound, Dean Roscoe, 45–46

Press, freedom of, viii–ix; and privacy, 50–51, 107

Prince Albert v. *Strange and Others* (1849), 12–22, 55, 56, 60, 93, 103, 114, 230

Privacy, 12; and advertising, 231; ancestry of, 4; connotations of, 1–3; and free speech and free press, 107; graves, perpetuity and, 97–103; invasion of, 23, 202, 229; laws of, and motion pictures, 159–179; as legal principle, 4–5; in letters, 26, 231–232; liberty of, 138–140; as minority concept, 1; and photography, 49; presidential, 227–228; and the press, 50–51; and property rights, 17, 22, 26, 28, 33–34, 96, 119–120, 121–123; and publication, 64–68; and publicity, 135, 192–202; rule of, viii. *See also* Privacy Act; Right to Be Let Alone; Right of Privacy; Privacy Act of New York Civil Rights Law, and amendments to, 127–129, 152, 154, 156, 160, 162, 163, 169, 173, 176, 178, 185, 188, 203, 204, 211, 220

Property, common-law right to artistic and intellectual, 52–54; kinds of, 54–57; in letters, 96; misappropriation of, 198–202 *passim;* and privacy, 17, 22, 26, 28, 33–34, 119–120, 121–123, 196; protection in person and, 73–74; sanctity of, 5–6. *See also* Right of Property

Proximity, 209

Publication, and privacy, 64–68

Publicity, and privacy, 192–202; Right of, 199

Rapho-Guillumette Pictures, 223–226

Reid, J. A. and R. A., 76

Rhodes, Aida T., 152–156 *passim*

Rhodes v. *Sperry and Hutchinson* (1904), 152–156

Right to Be Let Alone, vii, xii–xiii, 5, 73–74, 147; development of areas of, 158–179; free speech versus, 140–142; graves and, 97–103; publicity, privacy and, 192–202; by telephone, 231

Right of Privacy, vii, xii–xiii, 28, 43, 70–73, 89, 119–120, 214; development of, in New York, 206–207; development of, in United States, 41–69 *passim;* in England, 227–228; evolution of, 5–6; extent of, 63–68; and fiction, 175–179; in motion pictures, 175; in New York Civil Rights Law, 127–129, 152, 154, 156, 160, 162, 163, 169, 173,

176, 178, 185, 188, 203, 204, 211, 220; newness of, 3–4; and property rights, 22, 23; of public institutions, 147; remedies for invasion of, 68; and Right of Property, 121–123; in Utah, 147; waiver of, 138. See also Privacy; Privacy Act; Right to Be Let Alone

"The Right to Privacy," article by Warren and Brandeis, 74, 96, 102–103, 111, 120–121, 130, 142–143, 183–184, 188, 203, 230; quoted, 47–69 passim

Right of Property, viii, 4, 9, 26, 43, 198–202; and Right of Privacy, 121–123

Right of Publicity, 214

Rights, for artist, 144–145; as political person, 145; of public institutions, 147; as public person, 145

"The Rights of the Citizen" (Godkin), 49

Roberson, Abigail, 108–126 passim

Roberson v. Rochester Folding Box (1902), 108–126 passim, 129, 137, 143, 146, 152, 153, 160, 169, 177, 178, 188, 190, 225

Romilly, Sir Samuel, 34

Roosevelt, Franklin D., 78

Roosevelt, Theodore, 227

Sarat Lahiri v. Daily Mirror, Inc. (1937), 204–209, 215, 216, 217–218, 222

Saturday Evening Gazette Boston, 46

School of Design for Women, New York City, 82

Scientific American, 76, 77

Schuyler, George L., 80

Schuyler, Mary M. Hamilton, 79–96 passim

Schuyler, Philip, 79–96 passim

Scribner's Magazine, article on rights in, 49

Serge Koussevitzky v. Allen, Towne, & Heath, Inc. et al. (1947), 187–192, 196

Shakespeare, William, 37

Shientag, Bernard L., 219; opinion in Sarat Lahiri case, 204–209

Show Boat, 176–179

Sidis, William, case of, 179, 180–187, 196

Slander, 51, 67, 105, 106

Smith, Moses, 187–192 passim

Society, man versus, 132–134

Speech, freedom of, viii–ix. See also Press

Sperry and Hutchinson Company, 152–156 passim

States' rights, 180–181

Statute of Queen Anne (8 [1710], c. 19), 8

Story, Justice Joseph, 30, 31

Strange, William, 12–22 passim

Sue, Right to, 98–99

Swift, Jonathan, 6–9, 27

Thompson v. Stanhope, 35–37

Trade, purposes of, 165, 176–177, 185, 206–207, 222; secrets, 62–63

Trespass, 4

Truman, Harry, 78

Tuck v. Priester (1887), 60

Unfair competition, 12, 197–202 passim, 228

United Nations, declaration on privacy in civil-rights convention, 229

United States Sanitary Commission, 82

United States Supreme Court, 151

Universal Film Company, 165–175 passim

Van Voorhis, Judge, 222

Victoria, Queen, 12–22 passim, 55, 114

Victoria and Albert Gallery of Etchings Catalogue, quoted, 13

The Vitagraph Company, 159–164 passim

Der Wächter, 70–71

Walker Company, E. W., 74–77 passim

Warren, Samuel D., viii, 45–47, 71, 96, 111, 120–121, 122, 130, 137, 142–143, 183–184, 188, 223; article on Right of Privacy quoted, 47–69

Wayne Damron v. *Doubleday, Doran & Co., Inc., and Book Shops Co. and Edna Ferber* (1928), 176–179, 218, 222
Wells, H. G., 177
Whitney, Justice, 172
Williams v. *Settle*, 23, 228

Winyard, 10–11
Woman's Memorial Fund, 79–96 *passim*
Wyatt v. *Wilson* (1820), 56–57

Yovatt v. *Winyard*, 10–12, 62